WOMEN POLICE

PATTERSON SMITH REPRINT SERIES IN
CRIMINOLOGY, LAW ENFORCEMENT, AND SOCIAL PROBLEMS

PUBLICATION NO. 28: PATTERSON SMITH REPRINT SERIES IN
CRIMINOLOGY, LAW ENFORCEMENT, AND SOCIAL PROBLEMS

WOMEN POLICE

A Study of the Development and Status of the Women Police Movement

BY

CHLOE OWINGS

*Docteur de L'Université de Paris (Lettres); Laureate de
l'Institut de France, Académie des Sciences, Morales
et Politiques; Author of " Le Tribunal pour
Enfants, Étude sur le Traitement de
l'Enfance Délinquante en France"*

WITH A PREFACE BY

LIEUTENANT MINA C. VAN WINKLE

*Director of the Woman's Bureau, Metropolitan Police
Department, Washington, D. C.; President of the
International Association of Policewomen*

Written for the International Association of Policewomen

Montclair, New Jersey

PATTERSON SMITH

1969

Originally published 1925
Reprinted 1969
Patterson Smith Publishing Corporation
Montclair, New Jersey

SBN 87585-028-6

Library of Congress Catalog Card Number: 69-14941

CONTENTS

v

Contents

Chapter V

Other Countries

Chapter VI

The United States Before 1917

Chapter VII

The United States From 1917 to 1922

Chapter VIII

The United States Since 1922

Chapter IX

The United States Since 1922 (*Continued*)

Chapter X

Chapter XI

Community Problems and the Police

Chapter XII

Program of Work

Chapter XIII

Form of Organization—Type of Women— Method of Selection

Chapter XIV

Training and Training Schools

PREFACE

This history is an authentic record of the police-woman's service since its inception in this and foreign countries. It is a book of value to those seeking actual facts on this service, and is uncolored by personalities and their individual opinions. It should help to formulate a uniform program for policewomen in all police departments—uniform so far as technique and principles are concerned; the details of organization must be always in harmony with local needs and with the police departments in which policewomen find themselves.

Many police departments now have Women's Bureaus, or are contemplating their establishment. They employ policewomen singly or in groups varying in number. Where Bureaus exist and function properly they are acting as a socializing agency to the whole police force, resulting in a better and more intelligent attitude on the part of policemen toward men, women and children requiring their attention.

This social influence which penetrates the police service in general also affects the attitudes of judges and prosecutors trained in the individualistic, un-social theory of a legal system which seldom takes

ix

into account the conservation and protection of social interests. Policewomen by use of the social method and modern clinical facilities for study and treatment of individual cases can suggest to the courts means for guidance and proper care of those who come to their attention. By insisting upon the social protection of women, children and the community, rather than upon the vindication of "rights" which are presumed to inhere in the individual and the state, they are introducing into the administration of criminal justice a social viewpoint which should influence a change of attitude on the part of the courts and the public toward those accused of delinquency and crime.

It has been my privilege to visit most of the large and many of the small cities where women are employed in police departments in this and foreign countries. I have interviewed mayors, police commissioners, police chiefs and hundreds of men in the ranks as to their views on the service of policewomen. Where good qualified women are employed no opposition to the service exists and there is endorsement of and pride in their work as well as enthusiasm in recommending the service to other communities. Opposition is unavoidable where women of easy familiar habits find their way into departments either through political or other influence, and who, unable to do the work required, try to cover up their ignorance by maudlin sentimentality in dealing with persons coming under their control. Vulgar, uneducated, untrained police-

women degrade the service in the eyes of both the
public and the policemen. They are a bad influence
with clients in the community and a menace to police
service in general.

The police problem is at best seriously complicated. In many communities it is burdened by
politicians who subvert the power of this agency to
their own uses and cause corruption and the break-
down of morale in police ranks. There are those
police departments that are a law unto themselves,
where it is believed that the policies and practices
are none of the public's business. In some departments the executive heads are most susceptible to
public opinion as reflected in the press and to
general criticism because of which their policies and
functions are subjected to many changes, not always
for the good of the service nor the achievement of
law enforcement and justice, but always reflecting
the power of public opinion whichever way expressed. In addition it must be remembered that
the police are a part of the whole system of criminal
justice steeped in false tradition which obliges them
to consider crime instead of criminals. It is therefore not strange that they have lagged behind other
public services and that improvements have been
made only after long and bitter experience. But the
police are now gradually assuming a broader responsibility in the prevention of delinquency and
crime.

There are fortunately many police departments
where the administrators are courageous, upright

men who would render intelligent service tending to
prevent and control modern problems if the public
were sincerely interested in their aims and in the
welfare of the community. These officials are looking to the people for support and in this the public
has a grave responsibility. As Colonel Arthur
Woods, former Police Commissioner of New York
City, states: "The duty of the public toward its
police force is to provide it with sound leadership;
to keep informed as to how the work is being done;
to insist that the policeman's welfare, physical, mental, and moral, is well looked after; to demand from
the force a high grade of duty; to despise and con-
demn dishonesty or any unworthy conduct in a policeman, or one who tempts him; to be quick, cordial
and generous in perceiving good police work and in
giving it whole-hearted approbation. With this sort
of public attitude our police forces would be regene-
rated; the service rendered to the community would
rise higher and higher and the policemen, besides
doing their work better in the old, tried conventional
paths, would reach out to new methods, would find
and carry into operation means of preventing crime
and to save those who are attempting to commit
crime so that besides apprehending criminals they
would go a step farther and prevent crime and then,
again, another long splendid step forward and prevent people from becoming criminals."

Where there is progressive leadership it is a
simple matter to secure the appointment of policewomen. In order to achieve this, no new machinery

need be erected. Very little new equipment is essential. Telephone, telegraph, stationery, record forms, and postage appropriation are all at hand. The employment of one or more policewomen in many cases entails no extra appropriation because these cities have found it difficult to maintain a full corps of policemen, and there are no obstacles in their law preventing the appointment of women to existing vacancies. Often the groups which make the demand for policewomen do not realize the necessity for selecting trained, educated women and of fixing standards for their functions, until too late and they find that incapable women have been appointed. It is the duty of both the police department and of the public to see that policewomen are not only well trained and educated, and especially where they are to serve singly or in small groups that they be thoroughly experienced in social service. They should realize too that while the personnel of Bureaus in urban centers may have various kinds of training, the administrators must be women of broad education and experience in social work. When trained women are not available, the department must select good, well-educated women and provide them with training in social work and police procedure, which will give them a background for their important duties. Such training could be given either in schools organized for this purpose in the Police Departments or in Universities having facilities for giving courses similar to the one outlined in this volume.

The same ideals underlie the establishment of the service of policewomen everywhere. How strongly this standard affects the proper functioning of policewomen is evidenced by the successes and failures in the work. Where women of the right type have been employed the ideal of preventive-protective work by the police has prevailed. Their functions both here and abroad have, in general, been similar. In cold print the differences in police-women's standards and functions seem more strongly emphasized and greater than they are in practice. Having seen numerous policewomen at work in their own communities, I am convinced that the work is more alike than it is different. Every-where, excepting in those cities where women have been denied the power of arrest or where police officials under orders from others deliberately ob-struct the service of women by diverting it from proper channels and fixing handicaps that cannot be overcome by subordinates, I find policewomen are doing preventive-protective work whether prescribed for them or not. Their attitude results from neces-sity in their day's work. Observation of the work of London policewomen indicates that they serve as do good policewomen in the United States. On paper you find rules and regulations and in personal contact with superiors instructions that seem to be in conflict with their practice. In England there is an unwritten law in police departments which is perhaps the strongest tradition in their police work, namely, to do everything possible in order to prevent the necessity of arrest although yet they do not acknowledge as preventive work their service of warning and their provisions for proper attention to and care of persons not chargeable with breaking the law. We possess sufficient proof that preventive-protective work as a natural outgrowth of community needs is carried on in degrees of effectiveness according to the ability and worthwhileness of the policewomen.

In one of the largest American cities it is claimed that a preventive-protective program is in operation. Here it means merely that every circuitous route is tried to prevent the necessity of going to Court with a case even when this amounts to compounding the offense. In still another large American center, the policewomen frankly state that they are not permitted to do preventive-protective work, but inquiry reveals that they are doing it unofficially and at their own expense. In the near future, there will be general official responsibility for this work, the police are merely the machinery through which this necessary public service is rendered and the official agency, established with legal authority for such purpose. While private organizations with quasi-police power volunteering to perform public functions cannot be held responsible for their acts nor for the acts of their members, the police are individually liable to the community, through civil procedure in the courts or by means of official discipline, suspension, fine or dismissal. The fact that the private agency seeks police power in order to do preventive-protective work is in itself the best argument that this is primarily a public function. Policewomen in general stand firmly in the belief that private social workers must cease to think of the police as a thing apart in the community and must, instead, become their strongest allies.

Women's organizations and policewomen are striving for the establishment of Women's Bureaus in police departments whether formed of one or more women with a woman directing each bureau, who shall be immediately responsible to the department head and shall have rank equal to that of male officers immediately subordinate to him. Unless this practice obtains, the work will be absorbed by men's units of the force, its meaning will be entirely lost to the community while the police and other government officials will remain uninformed of results and unable to estimate the value of the service.

Experience has emphasized the necessity of such a bureau being an integral unit having as close co-ordination with the central department plan of the police as that of the traffic and detective bureaus. Wherever separation for the good of the service seems advisable, it is an indictment of the local community whose responsibility lies in making possible the free development of clean, effective police service by both policemen and policewomen under the same administration.

The almost impassable gap which past prejudices have permitted to exist between the work of the police and all other preventive agencies must be

bridged if we sincerely desire in the future to make
headway in the struggle against delinquency and
crime. The trained policewoman can and is furnish-
ing this connecting link. Through her speaking, as
she does, both the social worker's language and that
of the police, we can join the forces of the community
and create through mutual understanding that
close cooperation so necessary to the preservation of
the social body. In this service the police are "the
first line of defense."[1]   Of all the agencies
interested, they have the freest contacts with and
easiest access to the people in the neighborhoods to
which they are detailed, while this new inclination
on their part towards social, preventive practice
corresponds to that of the schools as expressed by
the work of the visiting teacher.

To enumerate the value of socialized police service
and its contribution to public welfare would require
a review of modern preventive-protective social
measures and their value to the community. No
other social agency, nor all of them together, can
make such a program generally effective without
this most important group.

Every community will some day have accessible
to all of us a "Clearing House," with experts for
diagnosis and prognosis of individual cases and
problems, where treatment will be prescribed and
carried out for the purpose of adjusting the individual to normal society. Those professionally
interested in such service will have the same basic

[1] Commissioner Richard Enright.

training and the same definite aim,—the welfare of society through all necessary agencies including the police.

MINA C. VAN WINKLE,
President, International Association of Policewomen.
Director, Woman's Bureau, Metropolitan Police Dept.

WASHINGTON, D. C.
June, 1925.

INTRODUCTION

The preparation and publication of this volume was undertaken by the Bureau of Social Hygiene in response to a request made by persons interested in the women police movement, and more particularly in the training of suitable women for responsible positions in cities where women might be employed on the police force in numbers sufficient to warrant a Woman's Bureau.

The School of Social Work in New York City and George Washington University in Washington, D. C., were among the educational institutions offering courses for such training. Other institutions were considering introducing them.

All over the country, women's clubs and social service organizations, interested in preventive work, were asking where information could be had concerning the history and working methods of women police, preparatory possibly to the advocacy of women police in their own communities. Nowhere was there gathered together in one book the material they needed. It was necessary to direct students and inquirers to scattered articles in many papers and magazines.

The Bureau of Social Hygiene was aware that

the employment of women on the police force of our cities is still in the experimental stage, despite the two decades that have elapsed since the birth of the movement. It knew that all the questions involved were still largely matters of controversy. It decided, however, that it could perform a real service in getting together what material was in existence concerning the history of the movement and presenting in an impartial way a picture of the working of women police in the more important cities where they are now employed.

To this was added a discussion of the functions of police with special reference to the possible contribution of women.

The Bureau had a precedent for this undertaking in Raymond B. Fosdick's two volumes, "European Police Systems" and "American Police Systems." The historical portion of the book here presented should be of permanent value. Other portions will need rewriting in the next five or ten years.

KATHARINE BEMENT DAVIS,
General Secretary, Bureau of Social Hygiene.

AUTHOR'S NOTE

Many persons consider the appointment of women to police departments as an important part of an effective program for the protection of young people and the prevention of delinquency. Interesting experiments in this field, with varying programs, are being carried on in different parts of the world. As is true in all vital social movements, new factors may arise which will tend to alter the channels of activity. It therefore seems important that the influences governing the present development should be recorded. Particularly is this true because, as a social question, "Women Police" is as yet distinctly a movement with all the characteristics of a thing in motion and whose final direction and goal are not yet clearly conceived nor definitely formulated.

In no country, unless in England, have the various parts of this movement been correlated into a standardized formula. Within each country there are not only differences of opinion as to the basic utility or contribution of women officers of governmental departments and of private social agencies, but among these persons who advocate the appointment of women as police officers there are differences of opinion as to their functions, conditions of service, and the form of organization under which they should operate.

Further, not infrequently, two persons of the same country, both equally well informed, employ different terms in speaking of the same thing. It is difficult in the present phase of development of the movement to determine the exact meaning of terms used not only by persons of different countries but of the same country. It is reported, for instance, that the women officers in one city in the United States thought they were applying the "preventive and protective functions" as advocated by public service workers, when they "protected" the girl from arrest and then "prevented" her appearance in court, or her contact with other agencies, public and private, which exist to help her.[1]

This lack of standard definitions of terms with the exact equivalents in each of several languages handicaps discussion. The task of presenting a true picture of the movement is rendered more difficult when the only available information from most countries must be gleaned from the printed word, and particularly so, when statements by different persons concerning an identical subject are dissimilar. A correct interpretation of documents, letters, articles, and books written from various points of view and not based on a common acceptance of terms is very nearly impossible.

This study attempts only to bring together between the two covers of a book the available information on the subject as a basis for study and reflection for those interested in the question.

[1] For discussion of preventive and protective work see Chapter XI.

WOMEN POLICE

Chapter I

THE BRITISH ISLES

*Early efforts to secure women for protective work—
Reports and acts affecting the general movement—The
Women Police Volunteers—The Women Police Service—
The Women Patrols—Women Patrols in London—Their
present status.*

England is the only country wherein the subject
of employment of women on police duties has been
the object of a special, thorough, serious inquiry by
a governmental committee. The fact that, although
having practically complete local autonomy, the
police bodies of the various counties and boroughs
receive their authority from general laws and are
subject to inspection by the Home Office, tends
toward more uniformity in the development of any
given police function.

An important factor in the growth of the women
police, or indeed of any special movement, is the
compactness of the territory to be covered and the
resulting facility in the exchange of ideas and experiences with the inevitable checking up of the

respective efficiency of different methods of work. For these reasons, together with the fact that more documentation on this subject is available in England than in other countries, it is both possible and useful to record somewhat at length the development of the movement for women police in Great Britain.

EARLY EFFORTS TO SECURE WOMEN FOR PREVENTIVE WORK

In England as early as the Eighteenth Century, during the hearing on a case in court—*R. vs. Briggs*—there was a discussion of the legality of women to serve in a certain compulsory office. One of the judges remarked: (9) * "I do not know why a woman should not be appointed to be a constable." However a century passed before women were employed in police departments. In 1883 the Metropolitan Police in London appointed two women to supervise women convicts. Later it was considered that one woman could quite easily manage the amount of this work which existed. More recently the entire responsibility of such supervision has been assumed by the Central Association for Supervising Conviction on License. (1)

In 1905 a woman, Miss McDougall, was attached to the Metropolitan Police Force to conduct in-

---

* Numbers in parentheses refer to paragraph numbers in the Minutes of Evidence of the Committee on the Employment of Women on Police Duties. H. M. Stationery Office, 28 Abingdon St., London, S. W. 1. 1921. (Cmd 1133) 2s net.

quiries in cases of outrage on women and especially in cases of children.[1] "The children get very frightened and it was found necessary . . . for a woman to get hold of them and soothe them and to become expert in getting them to give evidence in court." (179) For many years in England the care of women and children, while in custody and before the magistrates, as well as their escort, have been entrusted to women, principally the wives of resident police or women called in as the occasion required. (94) Each year it has been found desirable to make this a whole time employment in an increasingly larger number of places and the term "police matron" imported from America and adopted by the Home Office in 1908 is now used to designate the women employed on these duties.

Before the World War and culminating in the first half of the year 1914, there was considerable agitation in many sections of England for the employment of women police as a part of the organization for the prevention and detection of crime. In England spasmodic efforts to secure the official appointment of women police had for some time existed, but had met with scant sympathy from the authorities concerned.[2] Private organizations such as vigilance committees and councils for pro-

[1] Report of the Commissioner of the Metropolitan Police, London, 1918-1919.
[2] Women Police in Great Britain. M. G. Garden. Sept., 1924. Published by the International Bureau for the Suppression of Traffic in Women and Children. 2 Grosvenor Mansions, 76 Victoria St., London, S. W. 1, England. Sept., 1924 (11514-K).

moting public morality, employed agents—women and men—to observe and to refer to the police, conditions needing attention.[3]

In June, 1914, a deputation from the National Council of Women and other organizations, called on the Home Secretary urging the appointment of women police.[4] In this same month the Criminal Law Amendment Committee summoned a conference on women police in Caxton Hall, Westminster. When the Criminal Justice Administration Bill was under consideration by Parliament in that same year, Lord Henry Bentick proposed an amendment, providing for the appointment[5] "in every county borough and in every metropolitan borough of the county of London and by order of the Secretary of State in any other local authority, two or more women constables . . . duly sworn, and given such duties as the chief constable in county borough or the Chief Commissioner of Police in London may direct." This amendment was withdrawn and Lord Henry proposed to make his clause permissive instead of obligatory, but the whole amendment was dropped in order not to impede the early passage of the bill which was considered urgent by everyone interested.

The Penal Reform League, wishing to keep the

[3] See Files of the Vigilance Record.

[4] The History of the Official Policewomen (to July, 1924). National Council of Women—Parliament Mansions, Victoria St., Westminster, London, S. W. 1. Price 6d—postage extra.

[5] Quarterly Record Penal Reform League, 1914. Vol. VI., No. 3, 68A, Park Hill Road, N. W. London. Price 6d.

movement for women police in the open, became
particularly active in this field after the withdrawal
of Lord Henry's amendment. They desired to prevent the mere perfunctory appointment of women
police officers by authorities who were not convinced
of their need and yet being obliged by law to appoint
them might follow age-old police traditions and
select women not necessarily fitted for the work
and further would curtail their usefulness by unwise
regulations. The League therefore called a meeting on July 13, 1914. In response to their invitation
there convened a joint committee composed of representatives from the following societies: The Committee of Social Investigation and Reform,
The Criminal Law Amendment Committee, Girls'
Friendly Society, Ladies' National Association, Local
Government Advancement Committee, National
Union of Women Workers, Society for Promoting
the Employment of Women, State Children's Association, Women's Industrial Council, Women's
Local Government Society, the Young Women's
Christian Association, Women's Imperial Health
Association, the Women's Cooperative Guild and
the Women's Sanitary Inspection Association.

At this meeting a resolution was passed urging
the appointment of "women police constables with
powers equal to those of men constables in all county
boroughs and the metropolitan boroughs of the
County of London." It was further urged "that
the women appointed should be of high reputation,
character and experience."

Following closely upon this the Criminal Law Amendment Committee and the National Vigilance Association sent delegates to interview the under secretary of state on the subject. Concurrently a group composed of delegates appointed by the Women's Industrial Council had asked the Parks Committee of the London Council and the first commissioner of works to appoint women park keepers —functionaries who are charged with the maintaining of order and decency in public parks and have power of arrest to enforce the laws relating to this subject.

For a long time before the War, publications in England concerned with public morals and decency carried, in nearly every edition, discussions of the fact that children, particularly little girls, were too often victims of men of degenerate sex tendencies. Running through all such reports can be traced the firm thread of thought that in order to cope with this social menace which causes such individual catastrophes, women police were needed. Almost coincident with the declaration of war, the movement for women police received a strong impetus and since that time its development has been continuous.

REPORTS AND ACTS

The important Home Office and Scottish Reports and Circulars, Committee Reports and Legislative Acts affecting the general women police movement in the British Isles were as follows:

August, 1916. Police Factories (Miscellaneous Provisions) Act, which enabled the pay of wholetime women police in England to become chargeable to the Police Fund.

August, 1919. Scottish Office Circular 1485—Pay and clothing for full time women police allowed to rank in claims on Police Grants.

Police Act, 1919.[6] Constituted the Police Federation and empowered the Secretary of State and the Secretary for Scotland to make regulations as to government, mutual aid, pay, allowances, pensions, clothing expenses, and conditions of service of all public forces within England, Wales and Scotland. Every police authority was ordered to comply with the regulations so made.

December, 1919. Sex Disqualification (Removal) Act (Parliamentary) established the legality of women as members of police forces.

February 12, 1920. Scottish Office Statement to police authorities in Scotland interpretating the Sex Disqualification (Removal) Act.

August, 1920. Report of Committee on the Employment of Women on Police Duties.

September 7, 1920. Home Office circulated the Report to Police Authorities in England and Wales, with a covering letter which advised that new women police should not be attested and to defer standardization of pay on the basis of the report.

March 17, 1921. Home Office Circular recom-

---

[6] Women Police. After the Report. *The Women's Leader*, August 29, 1924. Dean's Yard, Westminster, S. W. 1, London. Price 1d net.

mended to police authorities to standardize the pay of women police on the basis of the Report of August, 1920.

May 23, 1921. Scottish Office Circular sanctioned pay and allowances of women employed on full time police duties, in uniform or plain clothes, in the prevention and detection of crime.

June, 1921. Police Pension Act made women police pensionable and established their position.

February 12, 1922. The Report of the Committee on National Expenditure (Geddes Committee) that "We have considered the question of the employment of Women Patrols—their powers are very limited and their utility from a police point of view is, on the evidence submitted to us, negligible."

March 1, 1922. The Home Secretary met the Joint Central Committee of the Police Federation who adopted the recommendation for the removal of all women police.

July, 1924. Report of the Departmental Committee on the employment of women police.

The intervening actions and reactions can be traced to one or the other of these "high spots" in the development of the movement.

WOMEN ORGANIZE FOR POLICE DUTY

Early in the War two separate movements for Women Police sprang into being: the Women Police Volunteers from which later developed the Women Police Service, which in 1920 became the Women's

Auxiliary Service, and the Women Patrols of the National Union of Women Workers of Great Britain and Ireland. Because of the fact that the present day women police movement in the British Empire owes its origin primarily to these two groups of women workers, the history of their work constitutes the early beginnings of the actual movement, and as such, deserves a rather careful study. The present official women police are largely a direct continuation of the women patrols. For this reason, its early history is placed last in order to conserve continuity.

THE WOMEN POLICE VOLUNTEERS

The Women Police Volunteers had in its beginning two sponsors, Miss Nina Boyle, Secretary of the Women's Freedom League and Miss Margaret Damer-Dawson, a member of the Criminal Law Amendment Committee who was familiar with police systems and the work in the suppression of the traffic in women and children. In August, 1914, Miss Damer-Dawson (905) organized a small group of women with motor cars to meet trains bringing refugees from Belgium. In the beginning there were 10 cars in use. A Committee of "Chelsea People" whose object it was to provide lodging for the vast number of Belgian refugees was organized by Lady Lytleton, Miss St. John Partridge and Miss Dawson. The latter remained head of the transport department and the work in the stations.

At first the workers wore neither uniform nor insignia.

The need for a body of trained women grew naturally out of conditions which were constantly encountered. For instance, Miss Dawson because of her experience in work dealing with traffic in women and children, recognized certain symptoms which indicated its existence in the London railway stations. One woman changed the color of her hair and her dress three times in the same evening and was intercepted in the act of taking away two refugee girls who were being convoyed by Miss Dawson herself. This was late in August or early in September.

Miss Dawson discussed these facts with the committee and pointed out the apparent need of trained, uniformed women. She then received a visit (907) from Miss Constance Maude, a writer, who told her that the same idea was held by Miss Boyle whom Miss Dawson immediately consulted. They found that together they could raise about 40 women. Miss Dawson secured the approval of Sir Edward Henry, the Police Commissioner, for the formation of a corps of women and for the proposed uniform, designed by herself, and the hat, chosen by Miss St. John Partridge.

The avowed object of the Association was to train and supply a force of efficient women police "which shall prove by its work and reliability that there is a permanent sphere for policewomen in every county, city and borough throughout the United

Kingdom.'' From the very beginning they "eschewed voluntary service and have demanded the recognition of the truth that 'the labourer is worthy of his hire.' '' [7]

Until the latter part of November, 1914, the Women Police Volunteers worked in the London railway stations. The Commissioner of Police, Sir Edward Henry, suggested the names of several text books for use in their training and they attended various police and children's courts. The recruits were trained by a police drill sergeant who also gave them instruction in police duties. The plan of procedure in the installation of the women police was as follows:. In the County of London, wherever a society agreed to raise money to pay two women police for any Metropolitan borough, Commandant Dawson notified the Commissioner of Police who then gave a letter to the superintendent who was visited by Miss Dawson and a working schedule was arranged.

Captain Kensington, brother-in-law of Miss Dawson, who was then stationed at Grantham as staff captain of the 11th Division, informed Miss Dawson of the conditions in that small city of 20,000 people, unaccustomed to military occupation, and with 25,000 men in uniform stationed just outside the city limits. Through Captain Kensington the authorities invited Miss Dawson to a conference which resulted in the formation of a committee by the Hon. Lady Thorold. Enough funds were raised

[7] Women Police Service Report, 1918-1919.

to start the work of women police who were attached to the Provost Marshal under the chief constable.[7] On November 27, 1914, Miss Dawson and two women police, Miss Mary S. Allen and Miss Harburn, went to work in Grantham. From the beginning they faced especially difficult situations. The General in command had issued an order prohibiting all women from going on the streets from 8 P.M. to 7 A.M., an order which had raised a strong protest on the part of some women's organizations who criticized the Women Police Volunteers for working in a town where such restrictions existed. Miss Dawson's attitude was that, if the restriction was a mistake, the Women Police Volunteers could easily point it out and secure its repeal. As a matter of fact they did this within a month.

By virtue of an old military order which the General resurrected the women police volunteers were authorized to enter houses within a given radius from a central point. They found that women, prohibited from going on the streets in search of men were procuring liquor in large quantities and entertaining men inside their houses. They literally turned out hundreds of girls and soldiers from these houses and reported the fact to the Chief Constable. The restriction was removed.

The women police then turned their attention to clearing lanes and dealing with drunken crowds. By day they visited the families of girls whom they had encountered on the streets at night. When, in December, 1915, the private funds were exhausted the

Town Council continued the two women who were paid from the regular police appropriation. They retained the uniforms of the Women Police Volunteers but exchanged the cap badge for the arms of Grantham. The formal swearing in by the magistrate marked the introduction of women police into the trained uniformed police forces of England. This incident raised a legal question as to whether the swearing in was of any value and the Home Office at that time decided that it could not be considered legal, for women, under the Act of 1890, were not "persons" for the purposes of the police. (908)

WOMEN POLICE SERVICE

In February, 1915, Miss Boyle, Deputy Chief of the corps of Women Police Volunteers and a strong feminist, considering that Miss Dawson had endangered women's interests in permitting women police to enforce a restrictive order affecting only women, asked her to resign her position. Miss Dawson called a meeting of the entire corps, about 50 in number, and laid the matter before them— with the exception of Miss Boyle and one other all approved her action. Nevertheless Miss Dawson resigned from the Women Police Volunteers leaving the name and legal papers to Miss Boyle.[8] She then

[8] Little more is heard of the Women Police Volunteers except that "they were regarded with disfavor (A-29) ** by the Police

** Numbers in parentheses preceded by A refer to paragraphs or

formed a new corps which she called the Women
Police Service.

In May, 1915, placing two new women in Grantham, Miss Dawson together with the two pioneer women police and a fourth one, moved on
to Hull. Two of these women police were paid out
of police funds. Their first duties in Hull were to
care for women and children and get them safely
home during the Zeppelin raids. They were also
given the task of organizing and directing the 40
volunteer women patrols in Hull, who worked but two
hours a week.[9]

After Hull the women police were sent to Reading
and from there to several training centers. In April,
1916, the Women Police Service entered upon activities which were to form one of the cornerstones in
the foundation of the woman police movement in
England. At this time they undertook to train
women police for the government munition factories. The Minister of Munitions asked Sir
Edward Henry, Commissioner of the Metropolitan
Police of London, for a force of trained uni-

Authorities owing to the unconstitutional views and methods of its
moving spirits.''

[9] In March, 1920, in this city, 13 volunteer patrols were still
enrolled, while the workers of the Women Police Service numbered
5, 4 women police and an inspector, all paid from the regular
police appropriations. On June 24, 1924, The Watch Committee
decided not to employ women police, and declined to receive a deputation of the National Council of Women. (The *Times*, London,
June 25, 1924.)

page number in ''The Minutes of Evidence of the Committee on
the Employment of Policewomen.'' (1924) 28 Abingdon St., London,
S. W. 1. Price, 5s net.

formed women police to place in the factory areas where a large number of women were employed. Sir Henry replied that he had no such force but that he would gladly recommend the Women Police Service. Negotiations progressed rapidly and an agreement was reached whereby the Women Police Service undertook to train women for the ministry. During the years 1916, 1917, 1918, (964) 2085 women applied for training.[10] From this number 1044 were accepted. Thus the government munition factories were supplied with 985 trained women who did splendid service which was generously and publicly acknowledged by the government officials.[11]

In the beginning funds for this training were provided by private contributors and particularly by one donor who had lost her two sons in the war and was using the fortune that would have gone to them to further the women police movement. In January, 1917, the Ministry of Munitions gave a grant to the organization of £850 which in January, 1918, was not only increased to £1700 per annum but an additional grant of 25s per week per recruit was given during the training period. As soon as the women were actually trained and employed by the government they were paid directly by it.

The women recruits were given training in drill, evidence, police court procedure, police law as distinct from statutory law relating to women and chil-

---

[10] For Report on Training Schools see Training Schools, Chapter XIV.
[11] Women Police Service Report, 1918-1919.

dren, first-aid, jiu-jitsu, factory law, and how to
search (957-958). This period of training at the
central school, which lasted a month, eliminated the
unfit. Those who were selected as capable of discharging duties were sent on to finish their preparation under the officers of the Association at the different places where they were stationed.

The duties of these women police in government
factories were anything but monotonous. In addition to her "ordinary duties" for instance, one
officer told her inspector that she was a fireman, fur-
nace-stoker, inspector of boiler leaks, telephone and
telegraph operator, nurse to children, gardener, and
gate-opener.[12] A constable who overheard her, remarked: "Well, I have done all that and one thing
more—fed the pigs."

From 1914 to December 31, 1921, in addition to
the 985 women who applied to the Ministry of Munitions, the Women Police Service trained and placed
246 other women in various cities. Of this number
150 were employed by official police forces; 5 were

[12] In Gretna where 167 women were stationed as of June 6, 1918,
their work consisted of the following duties:

a. *Factory.* 1. Searching women operatives. 2. Patrolling danger
area. 3. Examining passes at main gate and examining passes at
search gate. 4. Controlling canteen. 5. Controlling pay-office queues.
6. Receiving reports re losses of factory and private property and
searching for same. 7. Reporting any contravention of factory
rules.

b. *Township.* 1. Patrolling township and outlying districts. 2.
Receiving complaints, etc., in charge room. 3. Meeting and seeing off
of all factory trains. 4. Attending to sick girls on arrival from factory. 5. Making investigations and reports in police cases concerning
women and children. 6. Attending court when necessary. 7. Taking
care of women prisoners in cells and escorting them.

employed by other governmental departments, 25 by large private manufacturing companies and 66 by various war Social Service and Law Enforcement groups. On December 31, 1921, 110 of those serving under police authority and 19 of those otherwise employed were still working.[13]

The work of the Women Police Service outside of the munition factories is illustrated by a summary of a year's work in Marylebone.[13] This work consisted of day patrolling of streets with particular attention to street gambling of children, rough play, street fires, employment of children, night patrolling of streets with the object of preventing undue loitering, soliciting by men or women for purposes of prostitution, inspection of films shown in moving picture houses, together with the general sanitary and lighting arrangements and the behavior of crowds; inspection of cheap shows; observation of brothels and public houses. In addition to this general work, many individuals were assisted by friendly advice, counsel in court procedure; procuring needed help from the private social agencies. Special attention was given to incorrigible or homeless girls and women found intoxicated on the streets were seen safely home and visited the following day. In many towns in England and Scotland the chief constables employed women trained by the Women Police Service.

During all this period the Women Police Service was among the groups actively engaged in trying

[13] Women Police Service Report, 1918-1919.

to create an intelligent public opinion which would demand the appointment of women police with an official status. A notable meeting was held at the Mansion House, London, organized by the Women Police Service and the Criminal Law Amendment Committee and presided over by the Lord Mayor himself.[14] The list of those in attendance bore witness that the meeting was "influentially supported."

A resolution, moved by the Bishop of Kensington, and carried unanimously was "that this meeting urges the inclusion of properly qualified women in the Police Force with full official recognition and status, and that suitable provision be made by the proper authorities for the necessary training of these women."

Chief Damer-Dawson and Miss Mary S. Allen in 1916 addressed a number of meetings in Scotland.[15] They were accorded interviews with the Chief Constables of Edinburgh and other authorities and were themselves sworn in as constables for Scotland. In June, 1920, the Scottish Headquarters of the Women Police Service were opened in Edinburgh and in October of that year their first training course was offered and several trained women were supplied to various towns and to one of the railway companies for duty in their stations. During 1916, the organi-

[14] The Police Review and Trade Gossip, Organ of the British Constabulary, March 17, 1916. The remarks reported as made by Miss Dawson are particularly brilliant and effective. 8 Red Lion Square, London, W. C. Price 6s per annum.

[15] Women's Auxiliary Service. Its Work and Ideals. Undated four-page Pamphlet, Women's Auxiliary Service, 7 Rochester Row, London, S. W. 1.

zation was interested in establishing women police in Ireland.[16]

When Sir Nevil Macready organized the Metropolitan Police Women in 1918, the Women Police Service offered its trained women. The Commissioner while recognizing the value of their work in munitions factories did not appoint them to the police force. Some of them were known as militant suffragettes and had been before the courts for assaulting the police (179). Given the conservatism of the average police constable and the fact that they were not enthusiastic over the advent of women police, it was advisable to appoint only women with clear court and police records. A further obstacle was their declaration that they "were there to show how the police work should be done and how to purify the male police."

In February, 1920, the Commissioner of the Metropolitan Police summoned to court 5 members of the Women Police Service on the complaint that the uniform worn by them "appears so closely to resemble that it can reasonably be taken for that of the Metropolitan Police Women," which was in contravention to section 10 of the police act of 1919 (180). As a result of the case, slight changes were made in the uniform and cap and the name changed to "Women's Auxiliary Service."

During the years 1920-21, the staff addressed over 150 meetings in England and Scotland which were sponsored by some 70 different associations (12).

[16] See Northern Ireland, Chapter II.

By public addresses and by the written word the
Women's Auxiliary Service has continued its work
for the appointment of women police. Of the 85
women serving under provincial chief constables in
May, 1924, 35 are said to have received their
initial training with the organization (A-P 75).

In response to a request of the War Department
(2) they instituted a uniformed women police service
in Cologne in the occupied area in 1923.[17]

At the Imperial Exposition at Wembly, May-June,
1924, the London Council for the Promotion of Public Morality employed a number of the Women's
Auxiliary Service in plain clothes to "observe as
the general public would, but when necessary to observe a little more closely and then report to the
Council. If necessary the Council reports to the
police and steps are taken" (A-1435).

The present Commissioner of the Metropolitan
Police of London (A-118 to 140) objects to their
wearing a uniform resembling so closely that of the
women police. He considers that their actions are
liable to be attributed to the official police, a fact
which does not promote good feeling between the
police and the public (A-1529).

The officers of the Women's Auxiliary Service
consider that the unofficial character of the organization permits of a greater freedom in their efforts
to mold the development of the general movement
for women police. They point out that confusion
in the minds of the public occurs nowhere except in

[17] See Germany, Chapter IV.

London which has been their principal training
ground for recruits. At present there are no women
in training. Several are serving in Cologne. The
officers are engaged in speaking and writing on the
subject of women police.

WOMEN PATROLS

Very soon after the outbreak of the war in
August, 1914, the danger arising from the uncon-
trolled excitement which possessed much of the
girlhood and womanhood of the country was realized
by many women's organizations.[18] The National
Council of Women of Great Britain and Ireland was
among those who took steps to grapple with the
danger.[19] They appointed an *ad hoc* committee upon
which a very large number of related societies were
represented.[20] This Committee met almost daily and
after anxious deliberation, decided to organize a
body of voluntary Women Patrol's who were to be
neither detectives nor "rescue workers," but more

[18] "It was the same story in England as in all countries which
were parties to the War. Conditions were conducive to much that
was socially undesirable and individually harmful to young girls who
were excited and thrown off their balance by the unaccustomed presence of so many soldiers and recruits in uniform." *England's Girls
and the Women Police* by Priscilla Moulder. Life and Labor, May,
1919, vol. IX. Published by Women's Trade Union League of
America, 311 S. Ashland Blvd., Chicago, Ill.

[19] Women Police, M. G. Garden, Sept., 1924.

[20] The late Mr. Alexander Coote, a great authority on this question
and enjoying the full confidence of the Home Office and Scotland
Yard, represented the Vigilance Association. Miss Nora Hall, another expert, was sent by the Church Army. The Committee was
presided over by Mrs. Creighton of the National Council of Women.

like experimental women police. The Home Secretary gave his full official recognition to the Women Patrols and the Commissioner of the Metropolitan Police of London promised to give them his cordial support.

The Committee in September, 1914, engaged 26 organizers to train the recruits. However, although they were social workers, the organizers themselves needed special training for this pioneer work.[19] Qualified members of the committee gave them a series of lectures designed to present "a clear and comprehensive view of the objects and scope of the proposed patrol work—a sound conception of the ideals to be aimed at, the perils to be avoided and the best methods of dealing with the problems of the streets and open places."

Work was started by the first organizer on the 27th of October, 1914, and from first to last between 4,000 and 5,000 women patrols were enrolled and instructed in the duties they were called upon to perform.

Bodies of patrols were created both in London and the provinces. Each patrol wore an arm-band, and carried an identity card and a small book of regulations, all three bearing the same number. As evidence of his official recognition of the patrols, Sir Edward Henry, then the Commissioner of the Metropolitan Police, signed each card which read as follows: (259)

"*Notice to Police*, the bearer, Mrs..............No....
is a worker authorized by the National Union of Women

Workers of Great Britain and Ireland, and the police are
desired to render her any necessary assistance.

(Signed) E. R. HENRY,

Commissioner of Police.''

The same result was obtained in the provinces by
the circularization of the chief constables in the
name of the Home Secretary. Similar steps were also
taken in Scotland and Ireland.

WOMEN PATROLS IN LONDON

The Committee organized by the National Council
of Women was carrying on its work by voluntary
funds. In 1916 (A-29) the Home Office approved
the payment to it of a subsidy of £400 a year subject
to discontinuance on three months' notice. This
money was used for training women for service in
London.

Sir Edward Henry in 1916 directed that most
careful and minute observation be made of the
methods of work of these women. As a result of the
reports which he received, in June, 1916, he employed
and paid from police funds 8 of the patrols to
investigate and report on the conduct at cinemas in
the Metropolitan District.

Following on the success of this work, 30 ''Special
Women Patrols'' were officially employed to patrol
Hyde Park and other open spaces in London. They
worked under a supervisor appointed on March 10,
1917, by the National Council of Women but paid

out of the police fund.[21] To distinguish them, when on duty, from the purely voluntary patrols they wore the official police armlet. On April 10, 1917, two whole-time Women Patrols were appointed for work in Leicester Square with the Metropolitan Police and, in June following, all of the work done by 40 women patrols with the Metropolitan Police was made whole time and an unlimited number of patrols were employed for part time, on miscellaneous duties and paid by the day.

About this time, in October, 1917, the Admiralty employed 4 women patrols and a leader at Holton Heath Cordite Factory, and the War Office, beginning November, 1917, employed at Woolwich Arsenal under the direction of the Metropolitan Police, 9 patrols and a leader.

These women patrols although paid from the police funds had no power of arrest and were not incorporated into the Metropolitan Police Force, but were simply working in conjunction with them. In London their chief duty was the patrol of open parks. As a rule, each woman patrol was accompanied by a man constable because she had no power of arrest. Their work received much favorable comment.[22]

When Sir Edward Henry retired in August, 1918,

[21] Under authority of the Police Factories (miscellaneous) Oct., 1916.

[22] One of the H. M. Inspectors of Constabulary in England and Wales for 1917 says in effect that the work of the patrols in the provinces had been of great value and that its success provided a strong argument for the employment of women in the regular police force. *England's Girls and the Women Police.* Priscilla Moulder.

he was succeeded as Police Commissioner by Sir
Nevil Macready who approved the work of the
women patrols. During the three months which
followed his appointment the Committee of the
National Council of Women, who still directed this
work, carried on negotiations with the Commissioner
and the Home Secretary, looking toward the formation of an official body of women patrols for London.
A very comprehensive scheme of recruiting, selection
and training of the Metropolitan Police Women
Patrols was drawn up at Scotland Yard and
approved at the Home Office. On November 21,
1918, the order constituting a Division of Women
Police Patrols, came into operation (22). Several
Chief Constables in the provinces had already employed women police, but this order created the first
definite official body of women police in Great
Britain.

Mrs. Stanley, Supervisor of the women patrols,
on November 21, 1918, was made Superintendent of
the Metropolitan Police Women Patrols—a body
with an authorized strength of 1 Superintendent, 1
Assistant Superintendent, 10 Sergeants and 100
Women Patrols.

At the same time a Selection Board was appointed
consisting of the newly appointed woman superintendent, a police inspector, who had had wide experience in dealing with women, and of Mrs. M. G.
Garden—Hon. Secretary of Women Patrols of the
National Council of Women who was President of
the Board.

Some 2000 applicants presented themselves (A-1534). Out of this number 50 were considered capable of performing the work. Some of the most desirable would not accept when they learned of the uncertainty of the future and pay. The period of contract was for twelve months from date of appointment—renewable—but their service could be terminated at any time by the Commissioners giving either one month's notice in writing or by payment of one month's salary in lieu of notice (A-29). Among those women appointed there were several teachers and trained nurses. The majority were former munitions workers and bus conductresses. There were a goodly number of the W.A.A.C's. and three or four policemen's wives. The patrols were not sworn in. They were given warrant cards identical with cards issued to men constables except that the word "appointment" was substituted for "warrant" number.

By December 23, 1918, the selection of the women had been completed and the Commissioner issued an order inaugurating the Metropolitan Police Women Patrols. These new members of the Force were not placed on duty *en masse* nor were they all trained at the same time. They were sent in groups of 25 to Peel House,[23] and it was not until February 25, 1919, that the first squad completed their training and were put on police duty.

Their primary duty was in effect to deal with cases of wayward girls, women and children who

[23] The Training School of the Metropolitan Police Department.

were ill, injured, destitute, homeless or involved in
sex offenses. (32) In addition to this duty they
were to observe and make inquiries or detect
offenses, in plain clothes, if necessary, where women
or children were involved in such offenses as those
connected with: The White Slave Traffic and other
offenses under the Criminal Law Amendment Act,
Disorderly Houses, Prostitution, Betting and
Gambling Houses, Licensed Premises, Night Clubs
frequented by both sexes, Vagrancy Act, such as
fortune telling, etc., and Pickpockets. Further they
were: to assist officers of the Criminal Investigation Department in suitable cases, and in taking
statements in alleged criminal assault on females,
to assist Constables in taking particulars of
ordinary occurrences in the streets, to convey or
assist in conveying women and children to or from
hospitals, workhouses, police stations, remand
houses, industrial and reformatory schools, in-
firmaries, also female inebriates to inebriate homes,
to watch female prisoners, detained in hospital, or
females who had attempted suicide.

The orders which were given to women police
with regard to such routine details of their work
as entering particulars of cases in pocket books,
time cards, saluting, etc., were similar to those given
to male constables. Women police were also to be
given access to police orders, and other official
publications.

In fact, except that they were not attested and
had not the power of arrest and were not eligible

for pensions, the members of the Women Police Division were on much the same footing as the male force. The various superintendents reported where, in their opinion, women patrols could most usefully be employed, and their superintendent then issued orders to the women to proceed to that district.

The Superintendent of the Training School reported that, in every case, the women patrols have proved good pupils and as students were in no way inferior to their men colleagues.[24]

The following table gives a slight indication of the work performed by the Metropolitan Police Women Patrols: [24]

WOMEN PATROLS

RETURN OF WORK, 2ND JUNE TO 30TH NOVEMBER, 1919

Persons Cautioned		*Police Court Charges*		*Persons Assisted*	
Violation of public decency	3952	Women prostitutes	49	Lost children	57
Women soliciting	1030	Women, insulting behavior	34	First aid rendered	118
Girls loitering	152	Man, insulting behavior	1	Accidents (minor)	16
Men annoying females	40	Men, drunk and disorderly	5	Respectable lodgings found	427
Persons begging	184	Women, drunk and disorderly	21	Helped at dangerous crossings	314
Damaging property	1964	Larceny	8	Children	314
Lighting fires (on heath)	30	Indecency (man and woman)	1	Cripples	10
Trespassing	308	Indecent exposure (men)	3	Blind	649
Riotous behavior	1695	Gross indecency (man and boy)	1	Aged	199
Breach of bathing regulations (Hyde Park)	24	Begging	7	Drunk	27
Using obscene language	5	Deserter	1	Miscellaneous inquiries	30,952
Lads gambling	15	Assault	3	Girls passed to homes infirmaries, etc	221
Children riding behind vehicles	49	Found wandering (boys)	2		
		Lunatics	2		
		Fortune telling	1		
		Affiliation orders	2		
		Summons	5		
		Commitment warrant	1		
Total	9448	Total	147	Total	31,173

[24] Report of the Commissioner of Police of the Metropolis for the year 1922 (Cmd. 1904) H. M. Stationery Office, 28 Abingdon Street, London, S. W. 1. Prise 1s. net.

The establishment reached its sanctioned strength of 10 Sergeants and 100 women patrols in September, 1919, but during the month of November only about 40 women patrols could be employed as winter overcoats were not available. Work had to be entirely suspended in a number of places and this seriously affected the returns.

After the first year's experience, the Commissioner considered that the work of the Woman's Division had so far developed that it was necessary to formulate their duties and conditions of service. For this purpose he appointed a committee, of which the superintendent of police, Mr. Billings, and the head superintendent of the women patrols, Mrs. Stanley, were members. The result of the deliberations of this committee were embodied in the Police Order of February 4, 1920.

The original establishment continued (A-29) until December, 1921, the appointments being renewed year by year. A variation was then made. Two inspectors were appointed (with pay of their rank) and the number of sergeants was reduced by two.

The institution of a Women's Division in the Metropolitan Police Department was widely discussed among police authorities and social agencies in the British Isles. The interest was such that in 1920 the Home Secretary appointed a committee to inquire into and report on "the employment of women on police duties."

The Committee, composed of five men, four of whom were members of Parliament, and two women, one a member of Parliament, took up its work in February, 1920. Forty-eight witnesses were called and examined before the Committee, including high police and government officials, women and police officers, and representatives of organizations interested in the movement.[25]

In August, 1920, the report of the Committee was issued.[26] It carried the conclusion that "After careful consideration of all the evidence we are of the opinion that in thickly populated areas, where offenses against the law relating to women and children are not infrequent, there is not only scope, but urgent need for the employment of policewomen. In particular we feel strongly that in the investigation of cases of indecent assault upon women and children the services of policewomen may be of great assistance in taking statements from the victim. We also desire to express our agreement with the view which was put before us by one witness, that, as information regarding the facilities provided for treatment of venereal diseases can now be obtained from the police, it is important that policewomen should be available to give this information to women."

Almost immediately the Home Office circulated the Report to the Police Authorities in England and Wales, with a covering letter which advised "that the women police should not be attested and that

[25] Listed in alphabetical order in the Minutes of Evidence.
[26] Report Cmd. 877. H. M. Stationery Office, 28 Abingdon St., London S. W. 1. 3d.

action concerning them on the basis of the report should be deferred."[27] The covering letter aroused the women's organizations to action and on February 25th, a deputation called on the Home Secretary and so forcibly represented the matter that on March 17th he issued a circular advising that women officers should receive pay in accordance with the recommendation of the Report. The pay of the Metropolitan women police was made retroactive to January 1st, 1921, on this basis. The pay of women police was thus standardized throughout the British Isles. The Police Pension Act of 1921 established the position of women police on a firm basis and allowed them pension benefits.

Perhaps nothing since the war has aroused the English women's organizations so generally to action as the Report of the Committee on National Expenditures (Geddes Report) appearing on February 12th, 1922.[28] In a voluminous report, women police were dismissed with the following short paragraph. "We have considered the question of the employment of women patrols—their powers are very limited and their utility from a police point of view is, on the evidence submitted to us, negligible."[29]

[27] The History of the Official Women Police (to July, 1924). National Council of Women.

[28] Minutes of Evidence—Committee on the Police Service. Cmd. 874, 6s.

[29] The Home Secretary on March 7th in the House of Commons said, in answer to a question, that the only witnesses consulted on this question by the Geddes Committee were himself and the Commissioner of the Metropolitan Police. Requests from the National

Immediately the National Council of Women organized a public Protest Meeting where 47 women's societies were represented. The year 1922 was mainly spent in efforts to prevent the abolition of *all* women police. Debates in Parliament were numerous. On March 1st, Lady Astor, during a debate on national expenditures asked in the House of Commons if the government had definitely decided to abolish all women police. The reply was "I believe that is so." That same day the Home Secretary met the joint Central Committee of the Police Federation, who recommended the removal of all women police.

Following instructions from the Home Secretary (A-29) to discontinue the renewal of contracts for women police, the Commissioner of the Metropolitan Police Force took the necessary measures to execute that order. This action was vigorously opposed. In Parliament there were many debates, conferences, and discussions, while outside of Parliament, women's societies organized public protest meetings and delegations to visit government officials.

In the course of a warm discussion on June 29th, 1922, in the House of Commons, the Home Secretary referred to "the disloyalty of the women's division of police." This statement although later challenged and disproved, could not immediately be proved false, and it influenced the vote which followed and

Council of Women and other groups to be heard, were refused by the Committee. (See footnote 27.)

which authorized the retention of only 20 out of the
114 Metropolitan Women Police.[27]

Two sections were created in the Metropolitan
Police District in each of which a "welfare worker"
was stationed for special work in cases of sex
offenses, particularly incest involving children. (A-
75) One of these was in charge of Miss McDougall
and in the second district one of the twenty women
police was responsible for this special work. Three
patrolled Hyde Park (A-216) two patrolled Hamp-
stead Heath Paths, and others were sent where most
needed and where they worked under men officers.

On February 1, 1923, The Home Secretary gave
the power of arrest to the women police who are now
called "women constables" (A-30) and who have
the same standing as men constables. The senior
woman police was given the rank of inspector. Her
duties are concerned solely with conditions of service—clothing, lodging, recruiting, promotion, etc.,
and not with the supervision of the work of the
women police (A-40).

Four extra women were recruited in the spring of
1924 for special service with the Metropolitan Police
at the Imperial Exposition at Wembly, but were paid
from exposition funds. In July, 1924, there were
seventeen official women police available for any
given day's duty (A-1489).

The need seems so urgent to some private organi-
zations that they maintain agents in the field.
Among them are various Church Organizations, the
Vigilance Committee and the London Council for the

Promotion of Public Morality. This latter employs 16 agents—men and women—"particularly in regard (A-64) to cafés or restaurants, contraceptive shops, licensed houses in the East End and observation in open spaces."[30] They have no power of arrest and can only "observe" and procure "evidence" which is submitted to the police. The following figures indicate the type of conditions observed and, in most cases, checked with the aid of the police.

Summary of reports of the Council's Agents—conditions observed in places named between 7 P.M. and 11:15 P.M. (A-p. 65):

Dates in 1922 between	Place	Number of Nights	Total Cases of Sexual Intercourse	Total Cases of Indecency or Exposure	Improprieties[31]
May 16–June 11	Clapham Common	10	19	12	465
17– 7	Hyde Park.......	10	28	40	678
20– 16	Hilly Fields......	10	8	9	310
16– 29	Hackney Downs..	10	22	42	387
20– 9	Hampstead Heath.	10	63	84	726
19– 22	Primrose Hill.....	10	33	58	377
Total........	....	60	173	245	3243

It appears difficult for private organizations in England to find suitable persons of sufficient train-

[30] With the exception of Hyde Park, the Metropolitan Police patrol only the paths of Public Parks in London.

[31] Rule 25 of the London Council prohibits as an offense "impropriety" which is defined as "lying on the ground in an indecent position." These figures are limited to couples lying—"in such an attitude as to indicate physical excitement" and which is considered inimical to the "interests of women and children."

ing to undertake street patrol, nevertheless, these agencies have undertaken to cope with the problem, which they recognize as of prime importance.[32] Patrols are maintained in the West End, in the vicinity of the largest railway stations and in other crowded sections of London. The organizations maintaining homes for girls affirm that the number of girls whom they reach in time to prevent delinquency has greatly decreased since virtual suspension of patrol work by police women.[32]

The Annual Conference of the National Council of Women, of the National Union of Societies for Equal Citizenship and of various other groups passed resolutions looking toward the effective application of the recommendations of the 1920 Committee on the Employment of Women on Police Duties.[33] These resolutions and recommendations were presented to the Home Secretary and the Secretary for Scotland.

The National Council of Women prepared, in 1923, a questionnaire based on the recommendations of the Committee of 1920 which they sent to the Chief Constables of the 37 police forces reported employing women police.[34] Their replies showed that 13

[32] Report of the Work of the Voluntary Rescue and Preventive Homes in the Metropolitan Area—Central Council for Rescue and Preventive Work—Carnegie House—117 Picadilly, London, W. 1923.

[33] The National Union of Societies for Equal Citizenship, Annual Report 1923-1924—15 Dean's Yard, Westminster, S. W. 1. 3d. net, and Reports of the National Council of Women of Great Britain and Ireland. Parliament Mansions, Victoria Street, S. W. 1, London, 2s. 6d. net.

[34] Women Police—A Questionnaire—National Council of Women, Oct., 1923.

towns, and 2 county forces, had discontinued their women police, and that 5 towns and 1 county had reduced the number originally employed.

In October, 1923, the National Council of Women called a conference in London on women police when the results of the questionnaire were discussed and resolutions were passed urging the Home Secretary to institute women police according to the recommendations of the Baird Committee of 1920 and asking that deputations be received. It was not, however, until March 25th and 26th, 1924, that the Home Secretary and the Secretary for Scotland consented to receive deputations organized by the National Council of Women and composed of representatives of 52 national societies.[35] On the latter date, the Home Secretary announced his intention of setting up a new committee "to review the experience available in regard to the employment of women police and to make recommendations as to their future organization and duties." This committee, composed of 4 men and 2 women, was regularly appointed on April 12th following. The Committee held 7 meetings and examined 25 witnesses. Their Report, submitted to the Home Secretary, July 25th, 1924, agreed in substance with that of the 1920 Committee. It showed (par. 2) that women police were employed in the metropolitan police district, in 6 counties and in 27 city and borough forces, the total strength of women police in England and Wales being 110. Some forces

35 London Times, March 27, 1924.

had discontinued the employment of women police,
or had reduced their numbers partly for reasons of
economy and partly due to change in local conditions. In some cases employment of women had
been discontinued because police authorities were
not satisfied that their employment had been a
success.

Pronounced organized opposition to women on
police forces has come mostly from the police
organizations themselves. Following the earlier ex-
amples set by the Police Federation of England and
Wales in June, 1921, and by the joint Central
Council of the Scotland Police Federation in 1920,
the Police Committee of the Association of Municipal Corporations [36] at a meeting June 5th, 1924
(A-p.80) moved that "there was no general public
demand for the appointment of women police and
that such appointments by police authorities should
be optional and not compulsory." The representatives of this committee accepted (A-1761) the necessity of preventive work, but questioned that it should
be done by women as members of the police forces.

The Police Federation of England and Wales at
a bi-monthly meeting attended by 18 members
from various parts of the country prepared a statement to be presented to the 1924 Home Office Committee. This Joint Central Committee considered
(A-p. 70) that "the employment of women police is

---

[36] This Committee is composed of eight members elected from the
eight police areas of England and Wales and two ex officio members
from the five largest towns—a total of fifty-eight.

not justified" and their very definite antagonism to
women police was admittedly based on the fear (A-
1269) that women might be substituted for men.
They objected emphatically to women working under
any other than men officers, and to women ranking
higher than constable. The representatives of this
Central Committee agreed that warning young girls
was police work in its best sense—that is, preventive
work—but declared that the men officers did not do
it (A-1640). In spite of the opposition from these
groups and certain individuals, and with the help
of other groups within the ranks of the police,
women's organizations gained ground. On December 11th, 1924, the Home Secretary replying to a
question in Parliament said "the present strength
of the Metropolitan women police is 24. We
have decided to increase the establishment to
50, and steps are being taken to recruit up to this
figure.[37]

THEIR PRESENT STATUS

The establishment is at present limited to 50, including a proportion of higher ranks.[38] The women
patrols are now sworn in as constables, with the
same power of arrest as the male members of the
Force, but it is understood that they are not expected to undertake any duty which they may be

[37] The Women's Local Government News, 19 Totthill Street, Westminster, London. Price 3d. net.
[38] Communication from the Home Office, 457, 470/65. Feb. 5,
1925.

physically unfitted to carry out. They are assigned to those Police Stations in which their services seem most usefully employed, and form part of the ordinary establishment of the Division, working under the direction of the Superintendent and his officers.

Their duties are mainly connected with giving advice to girls and young persons whom they find frequenting the streets, with a view to preventing delinquency. They have also been employed on duties in connection with the detection of indecency or criminal conduct by males, particularly in relation to children and young persons, when the chances of detection by a male officer might probably have been less; and certain of them have been selected to assist in the delicate work of taking statements in respect of these offenses. They have occasionally been employed on certain other duties in connection with cases in which females are concerned, but the Home Secretary considers that sufficient experience is not yet available on which to decide whether this sphere of their general employment can be usefully extended.

CHAPTER II

THE BRITISH ISLES (*Continued*)

Provincial Women Police—Northern Ireland—Scotland.

PROVINCIAL WOMEN POLICE

The women police movement in England and Wales outside of the Metropolis while influenced greatly by the work in London was nevertheless an independent effort. Each Chief Constable could take the measures which he deemed advisable. An important factor, and perhaps the most important in the situation, was the National Council of Women working through the Committees on Women Patrols of its 89 branches and the 150 affiliated organizations.[1]

From the early days of the war, the volunteer women patrols worked under the same conditions as those in London. The movement grew less rapidly in the counties and the smaller boroughs than in the

[1] "The National Council of Women adequately represents the conservatively minded women of Great Britain. It is not far wide of the mark to say that what the National Council of Women decides today England will decide tomorrow, since the resolutions stand little chance of being carried at the Annual Conferences of this body until they are so generally accepted by moderate women all over the country as to be ripe for legislation." (*Time and Tide*, October 3, 1924. Vol. 5, No. 40. Price 4d. 88 Fleet St., London, F. C. 4.)

Metropolis and larger towns where social conditions were more acute and required immediate action.

The first appointments of women police were in Grantham and Hull in 1914 and 1915 respectively. The numbers of women employed in the County and Borough police forces of England and Wales varied as follows from 1917 to 1924.[2]

Year	Women Police	Police Matrons	Office Clerks and Telephonists	Total
1917	43	31	89	163
1918	86	40	148	274
1919	144	105	108	357
1920	126	105		
1921	105	108		
1923	85			
1924	88			

There were 3 distinct centers of activity—Bristol, Liverpool and Glasgow, in all of which cities, committees of the National Council of Women established training schools for women patrols and women police. Later these became the "Federated Training Schools of Bristol, Scotland and Liverpool" and as such cooperated closely in general propaganda for the appointment of women police in Great Britain.

By 1919 the movement had become sufficiently

[2] 1. The History of the Official Policewomen—National Council of Women of Great Britain and Ireland—Parliament Mansions, S. W. 1. London, 1924. Price 6d. net. (1923) 2. Report of H. M. Inspectors of Constabulary, H. M. Stationery Office, 28 Abingdon Street, London, S. W. 1. (19—) 1924. Price 9d. net. (1924) 3. A Handy Guide to the Police Forces of the British Empire, March, 1924, the *Police Review* Publishing Co., 8 Red Lion Square, London, S. C. 1. Price 7d. net.

crystallized to have developed three separate categories or types of appointments and appointees.[3]

(1) *Paid Patrols.* (Sometimes called semi-official policewomen) are not appointed by the police authority, though they work with its recognition. Their pay is drawn through the medium of a voluntary committee; they hold no rank under the police, and they have no expectation of a pension. Their duties are mainly street and park patrol, with preventive cases arising therefrom.

(2) *Policewomen* are employed by the police authority, but are not sworn in. They draw their pay through the usual police channels, but often at a very low rate. They usually hold no rank under the police, and their expectations of a pension are vague. Their duties are mainly street and park patrol, with preventive cases arising therefrom, and occasionally court, escort, or investigation duty.

(3) *Women Constables* are employed by the police authority and have police powers. They draw their pay through the usual police channels, and though it often falls below that of the men, it is usually at a rate holding some relation to that of men. They hold rank as constables, sergeants, etc., under the Chief Constables, and have a definite expectation of a pension. Their duties are all or any duties of a constable, especially those relating to women and juveniles.

The number of women employed (in the prov-

[3] Policewomen's Conditions of Service by D. O. G. Peto, *The Englishwoman*, December, 1919.

inces) in 1919 under each of these headings was
20 to 30 Paid Patrols, 100 Policewomen and 20 to
30 Women Constables.

BRISTOL

In 1914 the National Council of Women
organized a group of voluntary women patrols in
Bristol (558) and in 1915 opened a school there for
their training. The work developed through much
the same vicissitudes as in other parts of England.
In February, 1916, came the first official recognition
(A-p. 45) where as an experiment 5 women were
employed in the department of criminal investigation. At the end of a year a Women's Police Department was created on a permanent basis with a
woman superintendent in charge.

Three years later, when she resigned to take a
higher salaried position in social work, the uniformed patrols were placed under the central division superintendent and the plain clothes women
under the criminal investigation department. In
June, 1924, they were so supervised. At this date
there were 3 uniformed patrols, 3 plain clothes
women and 2 matrons, working under the
same conditions as the men on the force. The
allowed strength of the women is 24 but 13 is the
highest number ever employed at one time (A-1007).

LIVERPOOL

In Liverpool the situation has developed somewhat differently. During the war the staff

of the training school directed the work of some 80 uniformed volunteer patrols who carried the regular worker's card, and who wore armlets and special constables' badges in their hats. After the war these volunteer patrols gradually withdrew. The Training School received from the Watch Committee in 1917 a grant of £100 which was increased to £600 in 1919 and which is now £2000. The school in June, 1924 (A-1717-1733) had a separate department called the *Women Police Service* where 8 patrols do expert work following a program based on nine years' experience.

As early as 1916 the chief constable gave the Patrols special facilities for dealing with children found begging on the streets. In 1922 they were made inspectors of common Lodging Houses for the purpose of securing compliance with the By-Law which forbids girls under 17 to reside in any but specially licensed Lodging Houses. They assist the police in special investigations and inquiries.[4]

All home visiting and investigation is done in plain clothes but on street patrol and in police court a uniform is worn. One night a week the patrols don plain clothes and speak to the girls whom they have watched while in uniform. The Director and the Patrols are convinced that they could do better work as regularly appointed women police.[4]

The chief constable calls this "Social Rescue Work" which (A-1237) he believes to be of great

---

[4] History of the Liverpool Women Police Patrols and Training School for Women Police. H. M. Cowlin. January 6, 1925.

importance but does not consider it work for the police.

The Police Department as such in June, 1924 (A-p. 45), employed 18 women—8 matrons, chiefly widows of policemen, for the custody and escort of women prisoners; 7 clerks and typists; 1 woman inspector in plain clothes who takes the statements of women and girls and investigates cases of sex offenses: 1 woman in the Reformatory and Industrial School Department who investigates children's cases and 1 woman for investigation in cases of violation of the Licensing Laws and Betting Acts.

LANCASHIRE

Lancashire is one of the counties which has employed women police. In June, 1924 (A-p. 40), there were 19 ununiformed women officers all selected personally by the chief constable. The first appointments (1205) were made from the women on the clerical staff whom the chief constable considered as having aptitude for detective work. The ages on appointment ranged from twenty years up and the present average age is thirty-five years. Seventeen of the number are unmarried women and 2 are widows. They are attached to the Detective Division, rank as inspectors, sergeants and policewomen, and have the same conditions of service and pay as men officers of similar rank.

During the first year of service they are trained in the theoretical side of criminal work—records, reports, convictions, card indexes, typing. The chief constable gives them special instruction before they are sent on their first assignment.

The women police are detectives (A-900) and are employed exactly the same as men; but women and girls never come before the women police unless some offense has actually been committed or some definite complaint has been made. They do no preventive work whatever (A-90), in fact (A-903), they "make it a point to keep perfectly clear from any sort of welfare work." The women police handle any kind of crime as it is reported (A-941) whether murder, housebreaking, burglary, or other charges.

GLOUCESTERSHIRE

In Gloucestershire public sentiment in the beginning was unfavorable to the appointment of women police (A-p. 27). As an experiment, 2 were appointed in June, 1918. The number was gradually increased until in April, 1919, there were 8—3 in Gloucester, 3 in Cheltenham and 2 in Stroud. The next year the number was reduced by 1 and a redistribution effected. When in 1922 there arose a discussion of economizing in police expenditure and it was proposed to discontinue 2 of the women officers, the local authorities would not consent under any circumstances to cancel their employment. The Gloucestershire women police have police powers, wear uniform and work under the direction of men officers.

BIRMINGHAM

The City of Birmingham has a chief constable who proceeded in about the same manner as the chief constable of Gloucestershire. On June 4, 1917, 2 of the police matrons in Birmingham were appointed to police duty as an experiment. They were sent out to patrol the streets, coffee houses, lodging houses,[5] railway stations and other places where the public congregates or passes, and told to observe and report conditions (A-p. 49). The chief constable found that the work of women police "filled up a gap in dealing with matters on the streets that the police (men) themselves could not touch, and which could not be dealt with by philanthropic workers."

In that same year of 1917, 2 more women police were added and their number was increased in 1918 by 2 and in 1919 by 4. Owing to measures of economy, vacancies occurring have not been filled. In June, 1924, there were 5 constables and 1 sergeant—and their number is now soon to be increased. Those constables assigned to the Central District work under the woman sergeant. The work of those detailed to other districts is directed by the officer in command. Besides this number a special woman investigator was appointed on November 24, 1924 to the criminal investigation department.

The duties of the Birmingham women constables now include patrol, search for missing girls, in-

[5] In England girls under 17 years of age cannot legally reside in any but specially licensed lodging houses.

vestigation, and treatment in cases of neglected, abandoned or delinquent children and girls, women and girls in need of employment, lodging and treatment of venereal diseases.

BRIGHTON

In Brighton the women police were instructed to adopt the attitude of the chief constable, to wit— wait until a person had actually committed an offense against the law, which required court trial, before taking any action whatever (A-17). The women appointed to police service in this city resigned after short periods of service and were not replaced.

NORTHERN IRELAND

Documentary evidence of efforts by the National Council of Women of Great Britain and Ireland for the appointment of women police in Northern Ireland is not at hand. The only reference to the historical development of the work in Ireland available has reference largely to the connection of the Women's Auxiliary Service with that country.

Early in the war the Inspector General of the Royal Irish Constabulary recommended that police-women should be appointed in one of the north of Ireland cities.[7] The women were selected and sent

[7] The Women's Auxiliary Service, "Its Service and Ideals." 7 Rochester Row, London, S. W. 1. (4-page undated pamphlet, but published prior to 1923).

to the Women Police Service for training. In due
time they were returned to the city whence they
came and today they are still employed by the
chief constable and are proving themselves valuable
public servants. In June, 1920, members of the
Service were supplied to the authorities to work
under the Royal Irish Constabulary. After the
English Treaty with Ireland the members of the
service on duty were returned to their headquarters,
and for some months the link with Ireland seemed
broken. But in June, 1922, it was renewed, when by
the request of the Secretary of Home Affairs in
Northern Ireland, Sir Dawson Bates, Commandant
Allen went to Belfast to discuss the advisability of
the appointment of members of her service for duty
with the Royal Ulster Constabulary. The conditions
in Ulster called for women to deal with political
offenders and, early in July, 16 members of the
Women's Auxiliary Service were on duty in various
places in the north, where they are still serving.[8] Commandant Allen visited Belfast in January, 1923, to
address meetings there and in Londonderry on the
need for the permanent employment of women, with
full police powers on police duties. These meetings
were largely attended and the audiences were most
enthusiastic. Owing to the fine work of the Women
Citizens' Association and other organizations, these
meetings were being followed up by further propa-

8 ''These women became the nucleus of the present Women Police
Service in Ulster.'' *Time and Tide*, 88 Fleet Street, London, E.
C. 4, June 20, 1924, p. 591. Price 4d.

ganda. Deputations composed of representative
Ulster men and women arranged by the Belfast
Women Citizens' Association waited on the Secretary of Home Affairs. The policewomen in Northern Ireland were sworn in as constables.

SCOTLAND

Volunteer Women Patrols were organized in Scotland in 1914 by the Scottish Branch of the National
Council of Women. The first move for the appointment of an official woman police was made by the
Scottish Vigilance Association. At the request of
this organization, the Glasgow Corporation, in
August, 1915, asked the opinion of the Scottish Office
on the appointment of a woman police officer in
Glasgow. The Scottish Secretary sanctioned (52)
this appointment but cited a previous "Opinion"
of the Lord Advocate that women could not act as
constables in Scotland.

The Police Factories Act made it possible to pay
women police officers in Great Britain from police
funds. This Act, however, had little effect in Scotland inasmuch as the police pay and clothing grant
was stereotyped and since there was no possibility
of securing a larger police grant, the employment
of women police in Scotland was for a long time
blocked.

In September, 1918, a deputation from Glasgow,
Dundee and Aberdeen requesting that the appointment of women police be legalized was received in
Edinburgh by the Scottish Secretary who agreed, in

principle, that such appointments could be made, but could offer no solution as to the payment of their salaries from police funds.

The National Council of Women, in June, 1918, opened the Scottish Training School for Police-women and Patrols.[9] The object of the school —which was financed by private funds—was to foster the appointment in Scotland of trained full-time official women police to take over and develop the work being carried on by voluntary patrols. The Glasgow Town Council cooperated by giving all possible facilities for the training of students. During the autumn months 3 women were trained in the school, 2 of whom worked for a year in Edinburgh employed by the National Vigilance Association. In 1920 one of them became Edinburgh's first official woman police (1923). Twelve women patrols were trained for the Royal Air Force in 1919.

There was little demand for trained women police and the Training School Committee soon realized that it was useless to train women for posts that did not exist.[10] They therefore turned their efforts toward the education of public opinion in Scotland.[11] In the eighteen months preceding April, 1920, over

[9] See Chapter XIV, Training Schools.

[10] One of the vexing questions in Great Britain as well as in the United States is to regulate or coordinate demand and supply. The Chief Constable in Glasgow said ''when I told the Training School . . . I would be glad for recommendations from them, they had no women to recommend.'' (2200).

[11] Mr. David Buchan Morris, representing the Convention of the Royal Burghs, agreed with this need for education. ''I have formed (2528) the opinion that the police authorities in the Scottish Burghs, especially the smaller ones, have not given the matter very full con-

30 meetings were addressed in Glasgow and two-thirds of the Ward Committees sent to the Town Council resolutions favoring women police. In Edinburgh over 20 meetings had been held. At the invitation of societies similar to the Women Citizens' Association and the Cooperative Women's Guild, 22 meetings were held in other towns in ĩn Scotland.

On April 2, 1919, the subject of women police appeared on the agenda of the Annual Convention of Burghers, and it was moved "that the views be ascertained of the municipalities administering their own police affairs in Scotland regarding the expediency of employing women police and that it be referred to the Annual Committee to take steps to make effective the views of the municipalities who have favored the proposal" (2519). A circular to this effect was immediately sent to 29 Burghs, handling their own police affairs, all of whom responded. The summary of replies reported to the Annual Committee of the Convention on July 9, 1919, and forwarded to the Scottish Office showed that 7 of the large towns favored the appointment of women police—Edinburgh, Glasgow, Dundee, Aberdeen, Ayre, Dumfermline, and Rothay. These 7 towns represented more than half of the town population of Scotland [12] (1923).

sideration. This largely arises from the fact that such experience as has been gained has not been generally available, and that there is not a sufficient body of information to go upon.''

[12] In March, 1920, with three exceptions, these opinions remained practically without change.

Two Burghs, while favorable to the general idea, considered that conditions in their particular Burgh did not warrant the appointment of women officers, and the remaining 20 were indifferent or unfavorable to the principle. Glasgow replied that the Watching and Lighting Committee had agreed to recommend that a number of women be appointed to the city police force. The Town Council of Glasgow having been approached by some women's societies (2171), asked the chief constable to report on the matter.[13]

The excllent work of the only woman police [14] in Glasgow influenced both the Town Council and the chief constable in their decision to appoint 10 women police, a decision not immediately executed.

The Scottish Office on August 1, 1919, issued Circular No. 1485 which while stating that women officers could not have police powers, allowed the pay and clothing for full-time women police to rank in claims on the police grant. The Police Act of this same month and the Sex Disqualification (Removal) Act advanced the movement materially in Scotland. In February, 1920, the Scottish Office circularized the chief constables in Scotland as to the effect of this last named bill.

Beside the several women attached to the police in 1920, but without power of arrest, there was a number of women called "women police" or "women patrols" working in various cities in conjunction

---

[13] Evidently as a result of the public meetings referred to above.
[14] Appointed about 1916 (2647).

witfi the police under private organizations such as the National Vigilance Association (400). Glasgow had appointed but 3 of the 10 women officers sanctioned by the Town Council.

While such societies as the Central Council of the Scottish Cooperative Women's Guild, representing nearly 18,000 members, the Scottish Council for Women's Trades, the Women Citizens, the National Union of Societies for Equal Citizenship were in 1920 thoroughly backing the movement of women police in Scotland, the Joint Central Committee of the Scottish Police Federation considered "the employment of women on police work as unnecessary" (2642).

A Scottish Office circular of May 25, 1921, sanctioned pay and allowances on the Report basis for women who are employed on whole time police duties.

From this point the movement in Scotland was subjected to the same events which influenced the movement in Great Britain as a whole.

As of December 31, 1924, there were 13 women police employed in Scotland—2 in Edinburgh and 11 in Glasgow.[15] In the latter city "the women are now sworn in and have the same powers as the male members of the force.[16] The chief constable divides the work of women police into four classes as follows:

---

[15] Communication from the Scottish Office, Whitehall, S. W. 1, London.
[16] Communicated by the chief constable, Glasgow, October 22, 1924.

Class 1—Work which can obviously be more suitably undertaken by women than men, i.e.:—sexual offenses
against, and all cases involving women and children.

Class 2—Work suitable for a woman because of her sex,
and because in these particular cases she would be less
noticeable than a man. Such work includes:

    (a) handling cases of delinquent children.

    (b) observation in cases of pocket-picking, shop-
lifting, stealing, brothel-keeping, etc.

    (c) patrol of amusement places.

    (d) inquiry work for Government Departments
and Police Departments.

    (e) investigation of fortune tellers.

Class 3—Work usually undertaken by men—but equally
suitable for women, and which relieves the men and
fills in the spare time of the women. This class includes patrol of the usual public places allotted to
women patrols and inquiries regarding lost property,
pensions, and aliens.

Class 4—Special work such as court attendance, search for
missing women and girls, work with children who are
abandoned, neglected, infected with venereal diseases,
or molested by men.

These instructions have been given here because the
chief constable has classified these duties rather uniquely—
and adds that they are instituted as a six months experiment.[17]

[17] "Policewomen have proved highly satisfactory . . . and are a
necessary part of the Force." March 17, 1925.

CHAPTER III

THE BRITISH DOMINIONS

Australia—Canada—Irish Free State—New Zealand—
Union of South Africa.

AUSTRALIA

Official information is available from six cities in
Australia. Brisbane-Greensland has "no women
police, and it is not proposed to appoint any at the
present time."[1] There are 5 cities, however, in
Australia which have women police. Placed according to date of appointment they are: Sydney,
Adelaide, Melbourne, Perth and Hobart.

Sydney, New South Wales, was the first city in
Australia to appoint women police.[2] Two special
constables were officially appointed on July 1, 1915.
There are now 4. The senior member is paid at the
rate of 18/1d. per day and the others received 15/1d.
daily.

The duties of these special constables as approved
by the Chief Secretary are as follows: "1. To keep
young children from the streets, and especially at

[1] Communication from the Under Secretary, September 23, 1924.
[2] Communication from the Under Secretary, September 3, 1924.

night. 2. To assist in the prevention of truancy from school. 3. To watch the newspapers and to put detectives on the track of those who are apparently endeavouring to decoy young girls by advertisements or by any other means. 4. To patrol the railway stations and wharves when long distance trains and steamers come in, in order to guard and advise women, girls and children who are strangers and have no friends waiting for them. 5. To patrol congested neighborhoods, and to look after drunken women and to obtain assistance for their neglected children. 6. To keep an eye on houses of prostitution, and on the wine shops and hotels frequented by women of the town, in order to prevent young girls being decoyed and drugged with liquor or entrapped. 7. To protect women and girls in public parks and when leaving work in the evening. 8. To assist, when practicable, in enforcing the regulations concerning pedestrian traffic.

In addition to these duties, all inquiries in connection with relief matters, where it is desirable that the inquiry should be made by police in plain clothes, are handled by special women constables.

Adelaide, South Wales. In Adelaide women police were appointed in December, 1915.[3] In addition to the women who perform the duties of matron and general searcher, there is one Principal Woman Police Constable, who controls and supervises the work of the 10 women police. The women police do not wear uniform. They receive the same pay and

[3] Communication from the Under Secretary, August 26, 1924.

allowances as ordinary members of the Police Force. They are entitled to the same pension benefits as men.

The women police function in a separate department and are directly responsible˙ to the Commissioner of Police. In his report for the year ended June 30, 1923, the Commissioner says: "The women police carry out a most important and valuable duty to the public of this State. Most of the work is preventive and passes unnoticed by the public, but will have a lasting effect on the lives of those with whom the women police come in contact." [4] He reports in great detail the work accomplished during the year which is similar to that in other cities and concludes: "They have performed their duties conscientiously and with enthusiasm." [5]

MELBOURNE, VICTORIA

The first woman police in the State of Victoria was appointed in June, 1916.[6] There are now 4. They were not, as of September, 1924, sworn in nor did they have power of arrest, although the question of conferring on them such authority was under consideration. Their duties are as ˙follows: 1. Patrolling Parks, Beaches, Railway Stations, and

[4] Report of the Commissioner of Police, year ended June 30, 1923. Adelaide (R. E. E. Rogers, Government Printer), 1923, South Australia.

[5] For further comment see the *International Woman Suffrage News*, 11 Adam St., Adelphi, London, W. C., England, for July, 1924.

[6] Communication from the Acting Under Secretary, August 22, 1924.

other places where young women would be friendless and likely to be decoyed by evil designing
persons. 2. Escorting female prisoners on trains.
3. Visiting seaside camps. 4. Assisting the general
police to carry out the provisions of the Venereal
Diseases Act. 5. Keeping female witnesses under
surveillance at courts and elsewhere in cases where
they are likely to be intimidated or prevented from
giving evidence. 6. Visiting homes where children
are neglected or cruelly treated. 7. Escorting
destitute females to hospitals. 8. Assisting to place
in suitable institutions young women who are in
necessitous circumstances. 9. Interviewing women
and girls for the purpose of obtaining evidence regarding criminal offenses and sexual outrages and
assisting to trace female missing friends.

PERTH, WEST AUSTRALIA

September 1, 1917,[7] is the date of appointment of
the first woman constable in Western Australia
at Perth. There are now 6 women officers, in plain
clothes, sworn in as constables under the provision
of the Police Act of 1892. They are under the control of the Commissioner of Police and their pay
is the same as that of male members of the force.
The reason for their appointment is given as ''the
better safeguarding of the moral welfare of women
and children, particularly of girls between the ages
of fourteen and twenty-one years.'' Their chief

7 Commissioner of Police, September 10, 1924.

concern is prevention rather than punishment. Their duties are the same as those of women officers in Sydney.

HOBART, TASMANIA

Police women have been employed in Tasmania during the past seven years. At present there is only 1 woman officer. Her duties are similar to those of the women police in Sydney.

CANADA

Authoritative reports have come from five cities in Canada—Toronto, Winnipeg, Edmonton, Halifax and Vancouver, whose chief constables sent official information as of November 17 and 18, 1924, and of February, 1925.

Toronto. The first police woman was appointed and attached to the Department on June 2, 1913.[9] Since that date the number has been increased to five. They are all attached to what is termed the Staff Department, the branch of the service specially charged with laws relating to prostitution. In fact their work covers a wider sphere and is wholly preventive. They supervise parks and recreation grounds, public amusement places, fortune tellers, and handle matters of domestic difficulties which come to the attention of the police. The chief constable affirms that they are useful in so many ways

[8] Report of Commissioner of Police, forwarded by the Under Secretary, September 18, 1924.

[9] Constance E. Hamilton, President of the Equal Franchise League, attributes this appointment to the interest aroused by the addresses of Mrs. Alice Stebbins Wells. (See Chapter VI.)

that they are almost too numerous to mention and that as the population of the city increases, additional women police will be required.

WINNIPEG, MANITOBA

Women police have been employed by the City of Winnipeg Police Department since 1916. There are now 2 whose duties are to visit railroad stations, theaters, moving picture houses, dance halls and other places where the public congregate in large numbers. They also take statements of women and children. From time to time they apprehend women, especially those who may be mentally deranged.

They are considered an asset to the Department where they work in plain clothes. Their work is particularly useful in matters relating to sex offenses.

EDMONTON, ALBERTA

This department employs 2 women. The police matron who has been with them since March 14, 1917, and a woman police.

In July, 1919, 2 women police were appointed but it was necessary subsequently in the interests of economy, to reduce the number to 1. It is the duty of the women police to supervise dance halls, theaters, picture shows, and similar institutions for the purpose of seeing that these are not frequented by young girls unless accompanied by their parents or guardians. She searches women or girls in raids conducted on disorderly houses and opium dens.

VANCOUVER, BRITISH COLUMBIA

The police department of Vancouver appointed a police matron in 1912—the first woman employed in any Canadian police force. There are now 3 women police and one matron in that city.

Among the duties of the women officers are: search for missing women, girls and children: enforcing of the law for compulsory venereal disease treatment; escort and custody of women and girl prisoners; investigation of all cases involving women and children—deserted wives, neglected or delinquent children, wayward girls and the patrol of parks, dance halls, and all amusement places.

HALIFAX, NOVA SCOTIA

Since April, 1917, women police have been employed by the police department of Halifax. At present there are 2 women police and 1 matron. The chief concern of the women police are neglected or delinquent children, wayward girls and deserted wives.

IRISH FREE STATE

DUBLIN

Outside the Dublin Metropolitan Police Area, there are no women police employed in the Irish Free State.[6] In March, 1917, 2 women police were first appointed to the Dublin Metropolitan

---

[6] Communication from Secretary of the Department of Justice, November 14, 1924.

Police. This number was subsequently increased to 4 and later 6, but in 1923 the number was reduced to 4, at which figure it now stands.

These women are not attested as police constables and a week's notice on either side terminates the appointment. There is no provision for pension. Their chief duties are the suppression of prostitution and the investigation of complaints of indecency such as assaults and rape, white slave traffic, disorderly houses and charges under the Criminal Law Amendment Act. They are employed to detect cases of fortune telling, betting, gambling, and in all cases where their services can be used more effectively than those of policemen. They patrol the streets, usually in pairs, at hours deemed most desirable, mix with large crowds and visit large warehouses often at the request of the owners. They have proved very successful in detecting pickpockets and shoplifters. They point out such offenders to policemen who are usually in the vicinity and make the arrest, the women police acting as witnesses.

NEW ZEALAND

There are no women police in the Dominion of New Zealand.[10]

UNION OF SOUTH AFRICA

Women are not employed in the police of the Union of South Africa.[11]

[10] C. J. Parr, Minister of Justice, Wellington, New Zealand, November 26, 1924.
[11] Commissioner of the South African Police, Pretoria, December 8, 1924.

CHAPTER IV

CONTINENTAL EUROPE

Austria — Belgium — Czecho-Slovakia — Denmark —
Esthonia — Finland — France — Germany — Greece —
Holland — Hungary — Italy — Latvia — Lithuania —
Norway—Poland—Roumania—Sweden—Switzerland.

This chapter on Continental Europe includes the information available on the women police movement in that part of the world. There is no printed matter obtainable concerning the countries omitted and replies were not received to letters asking for information.

AUSTRIA

In this country at large there is said to be close cooperation and collaboration of the Police and the Voluntary Organizations, a situation which the women's organizations consider a justification for advocating the appointment of women police.[1] Information is available for Vienna only.

[1] Proceedings Sixth International Congress for the Suppression of Traffic in Women and Children, held at Graz (Austria) in September, 1924, and special notes on the Congress communicated by Miss Annie Baker, Secretary, International Bureau for the Suppression of Traffic in Women and Children, 2 Grosvenor Mansions, 76 Victoria Street, London, S. W. 1. Price 7s. 6d. net. (Delegates from 25 countries, 12 of whom officially represented their governments.)

VIENNA

The Chief of the Vienna Police, Dr. Bruno Schultz, approves of women police for the detective and emigration services as well as for the work which they already do, but is not convinced of their value for street patrol.[2] Police Commissioner Hans Schober, formerly Chancellor, strongly advocates women police physicians, detectives and relief officers for the families of detained or convicted persons.

In 1918, 60 women, mostly relatives of men police officers were admitted to the lower (presumably clerical) functions in the police service.[2] There are today no women in the uniformed and detective services. Of the 1200 persons employed in the other departments 400 are women, most of whom are working in the office and administrative services, and 17 are assistant directors in the offices. In the Police Relief Office, there are 3 separate divisions where women are detailed: The Juvenile Relief office, the Police Juvenile Home and the Department of Probation and Parole.

Six women are assigned to the Juvenile Relief office which is concerned with the protection of children against cruelty and neglect. The women officers investigate the cases of all such minors and make the necessary arrangements for their family and social adjustment.

In the Juvenile Detention Home, for minors, up to eighteen years, there are 4 women matrons under

[2] *International Woman Suffrage News,* May, 1924.

a woman superintendent. One woman officer in a third division acts as probation and parole officer. In May, 1924, she had 56 minors under her supervision.

Other women officers are detailed to the following duties: 1. Cooperation with Temperance Societies in the reclamation of the intemperate. 2. Work with young girls in the Morals Bureau. The work for girls under eighteen is carried on by investigators operating under women supervisors. A University woman is responsible for the work with girls over eighteen.

BELGIUM

Belgium has developed its work for the prevention of delinquency to a high degree in connection with its juvenile courts and other institutions for the care of children and adolescents. She is experimenting with one woman police at Antwerp whose program of work is not yet definitely formulated.

CZECHO-SLOVAKIA

With the possible exception of Germany, Czecho-Slovakia leads the Continental Countries in the number of women employed in actual police duties.

PRAGUE

The first woman was appointed to the Prague Police Department on January 1, 1905.[3] Very few

[3] Information received from the Czecho-Slovakian Red Cross in Prague.

were employed until 1913. Their number is now 133. Exact information concerning the assignments of all of the women is not available, but their duties are reported to be the same as those of men officers of similar grade. Rank in the Department is determined both by preliminary education and years of service.

There is a section for social work in the Prague Police Department where women are used exclusively for interviewing children and young girls, particularly in court cases involving sex offenses.

DENMARK

In Denmark agitation for the appointment of women police began as early as 1910. In 1914 Copenhagen appointed 2 women officers, 1 to the Morals Police, the other to the Welfare Department. In the former service the women police, who now number two, interview young women and girls and aid in the enforcement of the laws relating to compulsory treatment for venereal diseases. They are used only to a very limited extent in arrests and in raids on houses of prostitution.

Three women officers now attached to the Welfare Department take statements from women and girls and do personal follow-up work with them, escort women and girls who are insane or who are prisoners, investigate and attempt to adjust domestic and family difficulties, including guardianship of children, separation and divorce.

In Denmark the women police are employed on the same conditions as the men officers and are trained in the State School of Police. They are usually over thirty-five years of age and wear no uniform.

ICELAND

The Government of Iceland employs no women police.[4]

ESTHONIA

In 1924 the question of women police was discussed widely in the Esthonian Press.[5] A conference was arranged with the Department of Public Welfare, but the request for the appointment of women police was pronounced premature and was refused. At the present time, therefore, there are no women police in that country. Certain private associations employ social workers who act as protective officers, but without police power.

FINLAND [6]

The first 2 women employed in Police departments in Finland were appointed in March, 1907, in Helsingfors. The number employed in that city is now 5. In other towns, especially the larger ones, women have been added to the police force.

[4] Minister of the Interior, November, 1914.
[5] Communications from the Esthonian Red Cross, March 10, and May 7, 1925.
[6] Report from Mr. Gunnar Sahlstein, Minister of the Interior, forwarded by the Secretary of the Finnish Legation in Washington, D. C.

The women police in Finland have the following duties in relation to cases coming to the attention of the police department. 1. Handling of all cases of women, care while in detention, investigating and follow-up work. 2. Investigation and disposition of all cases of abandoned, neglected or incorrigible children. 3. Securing temporary or permanent care for dependent mothers with young children, the aged, sick and disabled. 4. Investigation of cases of domestic difficulties which involve the proper care of young children. 5. Temporary care for the insane and investigation of their cases. 6. Guarding of the women prisoners held for trial by the Criminal Investigation Department.

Nurses are attached to the police department in the larger cities. They give first aid to the sick or injured and arrange for their proper care and treatment.

FRANCE

In July, 1924, the French National Committee for the Suppression of the Traffic in Women and Children sent a questionnaire to the mayors of 30 of the largest cities in France asking for information on the subject of women police. Replies were received from 21 out of the 30. Seven mayors admitted the possible utility of women officers to the morals police, but with one exception they all made reservations or restrictions. The trend of the replies indicated that if women were to be utilized in the Morals

Police, it would be in connection with the physical examinations required of registered prostitutes.[7]

Among the arguments against the employment of women on police duties were that women were meant to be mothers and home-makers and further that women undertaking such duties would risk physical harm at the hands of the people with whom they dealt.[8]

French customs, it is maintained, would not fall into line with the appointment of women as guardians of the peace and the intervention of women police would not be well received. It is quite evident that these mayors visualized a "lady cop" stick, uniform, et al., and the French mind would naturally refuse to accept this possibility. On the other hand certain replies contained suggestions which indicate that the French are ready for official protective and preventive work for young people. One mayor proposed that women might, with advantage, form a "social police corps" whose work would be more effective than that of the agents of voluntary organizations which, he considers, do not possess sufficient means of intervention and whose action is out of proportion to their enthusiasm.

[7] Proceedings Sixth International Conference for Suppression of Traffic in Women and Children.

[8] These same arguments were encountered in France by the writer (Le Tribunal pour Enfants—Etude sur le Traitement de L'Enfance Délinquante en France—pp. 23 and 320—Les Presses Universitaires de France, 49 Blvd. Saint-Michel, Paris, 1923. Price 17f. 50c.). The second point has been disproved quite definitely in the work at the Children's Court in Paris, where a trained social worker has been attached since June 15, 1923. (Service Social pour L'Enfance en Danger Moral—près le Tribunal pour Enfants et Adolescents—11 Rue Huyghens, Paris.)

The Prefects (or Governors) of all the Departments of France in reply to an inquiry from the Government, expressed themselves as hostile to the appointment of women either in the ordinary, or in the Morals Police.

GERMANY

As nearly as can be determined from available sources of information, Germany was the first country to have a governmental employee called "policewoman."[9] The first appointment was at Stuttgart in 1903. The following cities appointed women police before 1912: Munich, Nuremberg, Leipzig, Mainz, Wurzburg, Bremen, Augsburg, Bielefeld, Dresden and Freiberg.[10] Miss Tite reports that in June, 1914, 35 towns had women police officers.[11]

In Mainz, Munich, Freiberg, Dresden, Leipzig, Bremen, Plauen, Cottbus, Berlin, and Stuttgart these women were official police officers. In Stuttgart the woman police was given an official residence in police headquarters. Among other cities mentioned by Miss Tite as having women police, presumably non-official, are Cologne, Frankfurt, Hamburg and Kiel. These appointments, with salaries

[9] Women Police. Women's Freedom League, 144 High Holborn St., London, W. C. 1, undated 4-page pamphlet.

[10] Handbuch der Gefährdetenfürsorge, A. Pappritz, München, Verlagrou. J. F. Bergmann, 1925; Die Mitarbeit der Frau bie der Polizei by Dr. of Laws, Cornelia M. Beaujon, Haag, Martinus Mijhoff, 1912. (Can be procured from Dr. Beaujon, 95 Johan van Olden Carneveltlaan, The Hague, Holland.)

[11] Policewomen—Their Work in Germany. Constance Tite. *Nineteenth Century*, June, 1914.

paid by private funds, were nearly all made at the instigation of women's organizations, the Socialist party, and religious groups, which were opposed to the system of regulation of prostitution, and which exercised a steady pressure on government authorities. The directing motive, in most instances, was to prevent young girls from being "registered" as prostitutes. In Freiberg, a woman police was appointed at the request of the women's and children's hospitals, whose officers demanded supervision, by a woman, of illegitimate children under seven years of age who were placed in boarding homes and not in the care of relatives.

In some towns at the present time women police are the appointees and agents of the magistrates; in others they are appointed by private societies and approved by the police. They are variously known as "protective officers" (fürsorgerin), "police guardians," or "police assistants," and their duties differ according to community conditions.

At first women police were delegated to the supervision and the enforcement of laws concerning prostitution.[12] They patrolled certain streets and squares, shared in nightly turns in the supervision of suspected operating and lodging houses, interrogated homeless wanderers, suspected prostitutes, and those arrested or subpoenaed on suspicion of being infected with venereal diseases, assisted at medical examinations at police headquarters, inter-

12 Notes on Graz Congress, September, 1924, International Bureau for the Suppression of Traffic in Women and Children, Miss Annie Baker, Secretary, 76 Victoria Street, London, S. W. 1.

viewed women and children involved in sex offenses, and made pre-court investigations. The entire official communication with prostitutes under supervision, as to their notification and release was carried out by women police, as was also official communication with the inmates of brothels and their woman keepers, and the weekly control and examination of account books of the girls in the brothels. Women police in this sense are no longer employed in Germany. In the police prisons in Berlin, women inspectors have for a long time supervised women and girls brought in by the police. In Mainz a woman police was appointed both for the supervisory duties and those of law enforcement, but this arrangement was considered a mistake and it was soon abandoned.

As a rule, the duties of women police in Germany today are protective and preventive in character. They act as matrons and are often in charge of detention quarters receiving children of both sexes and women and girls who are brought to the police. They do follow-up personal work with delinquent women and abandoned or neglected children, discharged women prisoners, and needy families.

There is a close cooperation between private and public agencies. In many towns there is an "exchange office" established for the use of the private and public social agencies. If a case is registered in the private organization the police assistants, unless arrest actually occurs, temporarily withdraw. Educational requirements are high for German women police. They do not wear uniform, and in general do no regular street patrol.

In Berlin the women police are assigned to the cases of children under fourteen years of age coming to the attention of the police; take statements in cases of offenses against women, girls and children; aid in the administration work of the detective service; patrol the streets, and investigate cases of kidnapping and abduction.[13]

In general, it is stated, all German towns of 50,000 inhabitants and above employ at least one woman as a protective officer or police assistant.[14] The number of towns which actually have such women officers, as given by different writers, is about 60. According to these reports, Berlin has 12 women officers; Hamburg, 11; Dresden and Stettin each 6; at least 2 cities have 3; 19 cities 2, and the remaining number have 1 each.

COLOGNE

The work of women police in this German city is of English origin, and is under the administration of the War Office of that country. In 1922 Mrs. Corbett Ashby, now President of the International Women's Suffrage Alliance, proposed to the War Office that some scheme should be outlined to meet

[13] Proceedings, Graz Congress, International Bureau for the Suppression of Traffic in Women and Children, September, 1924. (Dr. Johanus Müller, Berlin Police Department.)

[14] Margarete Dittmer, Director of Welfare Station at Police Headquarters, Berlin C 25, Alexander Street, s-6 Zimmer 219c (in communication of December 5, 1924).

the abnormal and distressing conditions in Cologne, stating that trained women police , could help matters.[15] As a result of this recommendation, Commandant Mary S. Allen, of the Women's Auxiliary Service at the invitation of the War Office visited the occupied area on the Rhine. With the assistance and cooperation of the British Commanding Officer and of the German Police, she secured the necessary information on which to base her report to the War Office. She recommended the appointment to Cologne of women police in uniform with full powers, a recommendation which was accepted.

With the help of representative German women, she selected 5 English and 3 German women, especially qualified for the work, and whose appointment was officially sanctioned by the German Government.[16] Inspector Harburn, an English woman, with years of police experience and who speaks German fluently, was put in charge of the squad. For the first time in the history of German women police, they donned uniform for their period of service in Cologne.

They work with the British military police, and also with the welfare, but not with the morals police who are in charge of the system of regulation which obtains in Germany. They are also in close touch with the German women's organizations, which give the greatest possible help. They do not deal with the regulated prostitute at all, but confine their

15 The Women's Auxiliary Service—Its Work and Ideals. 7 Rochester Row, London, S. W. 1, undated four-page pamphlet.
16 Women Police in Germany. ''The Vote,'' August, 1923.

attention chiefly to the many young girls between
fifteen and eighteen years of age, who congregate in
Cologne and the surrounding district. A large
building in Cologne was adapted for a shelter, and,
incidentally, a clearing house, and is being run by
the Salvation Army as a temporary refuge for these
girls. The official headquarters of the women police
are at the British General Headquarters. They also
have an office in the Shelter. The Station Mission
at Cologne placed a room at the disposal of the
women police, where girls arriving by train can be
taken pending inquiries.

The method which Germany will permanently
adopt for the employment of women on police duties
is by no means definitely or permanently settled.[17]
There are very definite tendencies, it is said, toward
the dissociation of women with the police as integral
members of the force and of transferring all such
work to other agencies, working, however, in close
cooperation with the police. At the same time it is
advocated that educated, refined women, physically
and mentally able to withstand the strain of such
work, are more effective, when dealing with unfortunate women and children, than are the men
officers, who, in general, are recruited from army
reserves. It seems probable that women will con-

[17] Communication, A. Pappritz, Chairman, German Branch International Abolition Federation, May 23, 1924; Dr. Jung, President,
German National Committee for the Suppression of Traffic in Women
and Children. Report of the Preparatory Conference for the Suppression of Traffic in Women and Children, London, October, 1923.
76 Victoria Street, London, S. W. 1. Price 2s. net.

tinue their work in Germany whether as official officers of police, or other governmental services, or as agents of private organizations cooperating with the police.

GREECE

The question of women police has been little discussed in Greece. No women police exist in that country where all such work is as yet little developed.[18]

Until quite recently it was felt that women police could not be instituted. But Sir Frederick Haliday, brought from England to re-organize the Greek police, is planning to appoint women to the police forces of various cities, to deal with cases involving women and girls.[19]

HOLLAND

In Holland many women are employed in Police Departments serving as secretaries, typists, telephonists, and in other clerical positions. Five of her cities employ women police in the ordinary American meaning of the term.[20]

The first woman police of The Hague, Dr. van Elzelinger, was later appointed by the Federal Department of Justice to deal with male vagabonds. By a system of selection she chooses those men

[18] Miss Doris L. Rayner, Migration Bureau, Young Women's Christian Association, Athens, October 11, 1924.

[19] Miss Helly Apostolidi, Executive Secretary, National Council of Greek Women, May, 1925. (Personally communicated.)

[20] Communicated by Marie Heinen, Assistant Director, Dutch National Bureau for Women's Work, May 22, 1924.

whom she considers capable of profiting from outdoor labor, and under her direction they are prepared to re-enter society. Her work is considered to be of high merit.

Women police in Holland do not wear police uniform. In The Hague they wear a costume resembling that of nurses. Rotterdam is the only city where the salaries are not similar to those paid the men officers of equal rank.

ROTTERDAM

The first city to thus appoint a woman to its police force was Rotterdam, where Miss D. Sanson, a trained social worker, took office on May 1, 1911. At present there are 3 other women police in that city, 2 of whom were trained nurses and the third a lawyer. These women now work in the morals and children's departments of the police. They deal with neglected and delinquent children and girls, and young prostitutes. Many of the cases are reported to the women police by the men officers, but the parents themselves often ask help when they are unable to control their adolescent daughters and social agencies have recourse to their influence. Advertising in popular newspapers is watched, and this has sometimes had very noteworthy results. Efforts to attract unwary, innocent girls to questionable employment have thus been discovered and checked, as have also certain illegal medical practices.

THE HAGUE

The first woman police officer, Miss Van Elzelinger, Doctor of Laws, was appointed in The Hague in 1913. There are now 4 other women officers, 2 of whom were trained nurses, 1 a lawyer, and 1 a teacher, before their appointment to the force. In the capital city the women police do no patrol work, but handle only such cases as come to their attention through the men officers, parents, or other interested individuals.

In the winter of 1921, The Hague instituted a Children's Police charged especially with all matters pertaining to children which come within police supervision. The staff is composed of both men and women. It is housed in a quiet building apart from police headquarters where parents and officers of child-caring agencies come freely for consultation on matters which fall within the scope of the service. About the time of its creation, the supervision of foster children was placed in the hands of the police. All foster homes reported or discovered were investigated and proper action was taken for the welfare of the children. The investigation brought to light many cases of unprotected children whose mothers were unmarried or divorced, and for whose permanent care and education plans were necessary. Over 1,000 children in 700 families were thus supervised during the first year.

Another fertile field of activity was the open spaces where families who live in vans, "park" their "houses." The children of these floating families attended school quite irregularly or not at all—a situation which was changed by the children's police. The officials of The Hague Police Department affirm that women police make contacts with these families with extraordinary ease, and that they are now well received in the homes. The mothers of incorrigible children seek out the women police for advice and guidance in the solution of their problems. A third social sore spot receiving the attention of the children's police is that of child begging, which has been handled with eminent success and particularly by the women officers. It would appear that in The Hague the most whole-hearted cooperation exists between the Children's Police and the various private and public agencies dealing with children.

AMSTERDAM

Amsterdam was the third city in Holland to fall into line and on May 1, 1920, she instituted her Children's Police and appointed women officers. In this city the women police do a certain amount of street patrol—particularly in reference to child begging. The first plan for the Children's Police in this city dates as far back as 1898. Its aim is to protect the child against itself, its guardians, and the dangers of society. Its work is preventive in character, and if necessary, repressive. The fullest cooperation exists with the other child-caring agencies. There is a staff of 30 of whom several are women who, in their advisory capacity, play an important rôle.[21]

The duties of the women police in Amsterdam include investigation of child beggars, truants, and runaways, the supervision of moving picture houses, cabarets, dance halls, and other similar places of public amusement, and the enforcement of all laws relating to the welfare of children. All members of the staff are in plain clothes. The men are selected from the regular force, and if they prove to be unfitted for the work, they are simply transferred back to the ordinary service. The women are chosen from the ranks of well-trained social workers.

BUSSON AND UTRECHT

Two towns of the Netherlands, Busson and Utrecht, employ women assistants in the Morals Bureau of their Police Departments.

HUNGARY

Hungary is reported to have women officially employed in the Morals and Children's Police, but no authoritative data as to the cities employing them, their number and status are available.

ITALY

There are no women police in Italy.[22] In some large cities a woman employee searches arrested

[21] Report of an address (date unknown) of the Police Commissioner of Amsterdam before The Hague Division of the Netherlands Association for Hospital Care, forwarded by Miss Heinen, May, 1924.

women and sometimes escorts children to their destination.

At the Third Annual Conference in Milan, October 29 to November 1, 1923, the Italian National Committee for the Suppression of Traffic in Women and Children discussed the question of Women Police.[22] It was considered that public opinion and the character of the Latin Countries were not favorable to the introduction of women police and resolutions were passed urging the appointment of women assistants in welfare and State-relief work for women and children, that these welfare bureaus should be adjuncts to police activities, but working independently.

LATVIA

The Riga Police Department employs 1 woman officer whose duty it is to "track and search out prostitutes.[23] When a woman is suspected of being a prostitute, the officer keeps watch in order to make certain, and if her suspicions are confirmed, the woman is handed over to the police.

LITHUANIA [24]

No women have been appointed as police officers in Lithuania.

[22] Proceedings Sixth International Congress for the Suppression of Traffic in Women and Children. *loc. cit.*
[23] Communication from the Latvia Red Cross, by the Secretary General, Skolasiela, Riga, Latvia, January 17, 1925.
[24] Lithuanian Red Cross, Kaunas, February 5, 1925.

NORWAY [25]

Four Norwegian cities employ women on their police forces. They wear no uniform. Their pay and conditions of service are the same as those of men officers.

CHRISTIANSAND

The first woman police in Norway was appointed in Christiansand on September 15, 1910. Her main duties are investigation in cases concerning prostitutes, vagrants, and guardianship of minors. She is also now being employed on police duties in connection with the enforcement of tobacco, chocolate and sugar excise and other tax laws.

OSLO (CHRISTIANA)

Two women have been employed in the Christiana police department since 1911. They serve in the Morals Police and have almost the same work as the male officials, even though they preferably deal with women and children.

BERGEN

The Bergen Police Department has 2 women officers appointed in 1912. They investigate cases involving women and girls, particularly those of sex offenses or vagrancy, and escort women and children who are in the care of the police. They

[25] Information from the Norwegian Department of Justice and Police, through the Consul General in New York.

have supervision of prostitutes and for this reason they do street patrol at nights.

TRONDHJEM

A woman police constable was appointed in this city in 1915. Her service is similar to that of the women police of Bergen.

STAVANGER

For some years there was a woman police officer in Stavanger, but the position was abolished as of June 30, 1923, for financial reasons.

POLAND

Although one of the youngest States of the world, Poland has recently gone far ahead in the question of women police. On April 15, 1925, 30 women police recruits began a three months' course of training in the State School of Police.[26] At the conference held at Graz, Austria, in 1924, of the International Bureau for the Suppression of Traffic in Women and Children, a motion was passed calling on each member to bring to the attention of his government, the need for women police.

Mme. Hodder-Egger, Member of the Polish Lower House, and Delegate of the National Polish Committee, carried home this resolution. As a result of

[26] Communicated by Mme. Hodder-Egger, May, 1925.

this presentation and the combined efforts of her committee and of other kindred groups, the Minister of the Interior decided to institute women police. For their selection he appealed to the various women's organizations, requesting them to propose candidates. From a list thus constituted, the National Police Selection Board, with the addition of Mme. Hodder-Egger, selected the desired 30 women recruits. They were required to be between twenty-five and forty-five years of age, to have a formal education comparable to the junior high schools in the United States, and the *école primaire superieure* in France and to have had experience in some kind of public service.

From the day of their entry into the school they receive the same pay and benefits as men police of equal rank. They will spend three months in the police school where they will follow the regular program of instruction. In addition to this, the National Committee for the Suppression of Traffic in Women and Children is providing a series of 30 lectures on social science subjects with particular reference to the prevention of delinquency and the protection of young people.

These first Polish women police will not wear a uniform when they enter service on July 15, 1925. Twenty will be stationed in Varsovie under command of Lieutenant Paleologue, a woman who rendered signal service in the Polish Woman's Legion during the World War. Ten will be sent to other cities.

ROUMANIA

The only women in the police department in Bucarest are stenographers or clerks, and at present the question of appointing women police is not under discussion.[27]

SWEDEN

About 1907, Stockholm, Sweden, appointed women police, and at present they number 6.[28] Five of them are trained nurses who wear the uniform of the "sisters" in the hospital and are addressed generally as "Sister." Although acting under police authority, they do not enjoy all the privileges of policemen, nor are they sworn in as constables, but have taken the oath to which Swedish hospital nurses subscribe.

Their duties are not defined in writing, but are said to include every kind of work for the protection of women and children. The candidates are required to have secondary school education, to be from thirty to thirty-three years of age, and to be women of discretion, tact and kindness. There is no special training required of them in preparation for their duties.

SWITZERLAND

In Switzerland the police authority, with few exceptions, is in the hands of the Cantons.[29] This

[27] Miss Christine Galitzi, Roumanian Young Women's Christian Association, Bucarest, December 4, 1924.

[28] Proceedings Sixth International Conference for Suppression of Traffic in Women and Children. Graz, 1924.

[29] Information supplied by Miss Dora Schmidt of Switzerland, August, 1924.

country during and since the World War has
maintained a strict supervision of its frontiers, and
thus undesirable foreigners have been kept out, con-
sequently conditions requiring the attention of
women police are not so accentuated as in those
countries involved in the War and whose frontiers
are less easy to control. Further, there is no large
metropolis. Zurich, the largest city, reported in
the 1920 census 248,506 inhabitants. There has
been, therefore, no strong movement for the appointment of women police, and indications are that
they will not assume what the Swiss consider the "inferior duties" of the police—"regular supervision
of the streets, dance halls and railway stations."
They are and will be educated women concerned
chiefly with the social rehabilitation of released
prisoners and the delinquent minors coming to the
attention of the police, and the cases of the aged and
the needy.

None of the cities require any specialized training
for such positions, nor are there any schools where
such vocational courses are offered. Four cities
employ women in the police departments.

ZURICH

Since 1909 there has been a police assistant, without police powers, whose duties are evidently
similar to those of a police matron in charge of detention quarters, and who also does follow-up
personal work, somewhat as a parole officer in the
United States.

GENEVA

This city appointed to its police department in 1913 two "auxiliary supervisors." The Women's Union pays half the salary of one. Their duties are care of delinquent girls, unmarried mothers, female prisoners, the aged, and of needy families, and supervision of cafés, streets, squares, and railway stations.

NEUCHATEL

A woman Inspector of Assistance has functioned in Neuchatel since 1915. The Police Inspector consults her in all cases where there is suspicion of misconduct. Her duties comprise general supervision of homes for children and the aged, repatriation, and employment.

LAUSANNE

The police department in this city pays half the salary of a woman, who is relief agent and police auxiliary. Her duties are similar to those of the Neuchatel Inspector of Assistance.

BASLE

In 1920 the position of women police assistant was created in Basle, but no appointment has been made, nor have the duties been formulated.

CHAPTER V

OTHER COUNTRIES

*Argentina — Brazil — Chile — Uruguay — Egypt —
Siam — Burma — Ceylon — China — India — Japan —
Palestine—Syria—Turkey.*

There is little information concerning women
police in countries other than the British Empire
and in Europe. In some of these countries there
exists little or no interest in preventive social measures. In others, education in the field is progress-
ing. Particularly is this true in South American
countries where women are now assuming a much
more important place in public affairs than
formerly.[1] There is promise of great things on the
part of the women of these countries where efforts
are being co-ordinated by such groups as: the
National Council of Women—The Pan American
Union, the Young Women's Christian Association,
Mothers' Clubs and various other women's organizations.

[1] The Woman's Press, March, 1925 (20 cts. per copy), 600 Lexington Avenue, New York City.

ARGENTINA

As yet the attitude of the general public in Argentina and of women themselves is unfavorable to the idea of women serving on police duties. Recently a small group advocated the appointment of women to patrol the parks in Buenos Aires, but the proposition was not accepted.[2]

BRAZIL

Women have not been employed on police duties in Brazil but they have held clerical positions in police departments.[3] Recently women matrons have been attached to detention quarters for women in at least five Brazilian cities. These appointments were made on the recommendation of a Government Police Commission of Inquiry, which visited the United States, where they had studied the work of women in police departments.[4]

CHILE

Santiago is the only city in Chile which has employed women in its Police Department. There they

[2] Miss Jane Piercy, Young Women's Christian Association, Buenos Aires, Argentina. Jan. 21, 1925.

[3] Miss Barbara Ripley, Young Women's Christian Association, Rio de Janiero, Brazil. Oct. 15, 1924.

[4] Dr. H. C. Tucker, American Bible Society, Rio de Janeiro, Brazil, October 18, 1924.

have been employed as investigators of certain cases involving women and children, and in office work. In these two capacities their work has not proved itself either to the police authorities or to the public. This situation, the General Inspector considers, is in part at least, due to the fact that the Chileans have not yet grasped the significance of the employment of women on police duties. Up to the present, women police have not been detailed to law enforcement duty.[5]

URUGUAY

There are no police women in Uruguay. At present there is no indication that a need is felt for their services, and no movement is under way for such appointments.[6]

EGYPT

There are 2 non-uniformed women police at Alexandria appointed by the British Government.[7] They meet every boat, and girls who are alone or

[5] Communication from Mr. Honorati Cienfuegos, General Inspector of the Chilean Police, dated February 10, 1923, and forwarded by Dr. Cora G. Mayers, President of the Chilean Social Hygiene Association.
[6] Miss Frances Drake, Young Women's Christian Association, March 2, 1925.
[7] League of Nations—C. T. F. E. Third Session, P. V. 3, and Vigilance Record, June, 1924, 2 Grosvenor Mansions, 76 Victoria Street, London, S. W. 1. Price 1s.

accompanied by doubtful persons are interviewed, and if necessary, are placed in the care of women of their own nationality or religion.[8] Muir Bey, the Commandant of the Police, said that he would like to appoint at least 6 women police to perform these duties. He insists on the usefulness of the voluntary organizations who are needed to take over the girls when the police have done their work.

SIAM

Women police have long been an institution in Siam, where a corps of female police is maintained to guard the Inner Shrine of the Women's Palace at Bangkok. They are uniformed but not armed, and they follow every stranger who enters the palace precincts, and remain with him until he leaves, and palace officials, including workmen and doctors, always have one of the corps in attendance.[9]

There are no women police in Burma,[10] Ceylon,[11]

[8] A later report which, although not confirmed, officially, is from a source absolutely reliable, would indicate that sometime previous to April 1, 1925, these women police were discontinued.

[9] The Vote, August 29, 1924, 144 High Holborn Street, London, W. C. 1.

[10] Miss Eva Terry, General Secretary, Young Women's Christian Association, Rangoon, October 27, 1924. Manual work has been instituted in one of the prisons for the women by the wife of the superintendent.

[11] Miss Faith Parmalee, General Secretary, Young Women's Christian Association,, Colombo, October 24, 1924. A former London woman patrol, who knows Ceylon well, tried in 1920 to obtain an appointment in the police department of Colombo. There was then, however, and there still is, no such opportunity for women.

China,[12] India,[13] Japan,[14] Palestine,[15] Syria,[16] Turkey.[17]

[12] Miss Maude E. Gill, Young Women's Christian Association, Shanghai, October 31, 1924.

[13] Miss I. Wingate, Young Women's Christian Association, Calcutta, October 23, 1924.

[14] Miss Leona O. Scott, Young Women's Christian Association, Tokyo, November 5, 1924.

[15] In Palestine there is a worker, Miss Margaret Nixon, appointed by the British Government at the urgent request of the Council of Women of Palestine, founded in 1921. Miss Nixon has rendered signal service in the field of preventive and protective measures for women and girls. Vigilance Record, 2 Grosvenor Mansions, 76 Victoria Street, London, S. W. 1, March, 1924, pp. 18 and 19. Price 1s.

[16] Miss Lettie J. Brown, General Secretary, Young Women's Christian Association, Beirut, October 14, 1924. Miss Margaret Nixon was appointed by the League of Nations as a Social Worker for Syria, but is unable to secure support for any work except that in relation to International Traffic in Women and Children.

[17] Miss Ruth Woodsmall, Executive Secretary, Young Women's Christian Association, in the Near East, December 15, 1924.

Chapter VI

THE UNITED STATES BEFORE 1917

General Considerations — The appointment of Police Matrons—Police power for women—The work of Mrs. Alice Stebbins Wells—The women police organize.

General Considerations

The movement for the appointment of women police in the United States has been influenced by certain general factors which operate in any social movement in this country and which are inherent in the political and economic life of the people as well as in the national temperament.

The chief political factor is that the federal government exercises little control or supervision over ordinary local effort, these being matters which have been expressly reserved to the States, under the Constitution. Subventions to the States by the federal government are rare.

In the domain of its regular police activities, each state is free to adapt its measures to its special needs. Outside of incorporated communities a state police force to preserve order in the open country is growing in favor. Police functions are also exercised by the county. In the past, state control of municipal police affairs has been common but, although there is still direct state control over the police of several of our cities, the tendency is toward home rule.[1] There is a great divergence among cities, even of the same state, in methods of organization and control. Further, it is generally conceded that no branch of Municipal Government in the United States is so subjected to the vagaries of party and personal politics as is the police department.[2] This is, perhaps, no more true in the women police movement than in any other part of police activities. But its influence may be particularly pernicious in that the underlying principle and effectiveness of women police are struggling to assert themselves. Every appointment based on purely party or personal reasons without reference to ability or capacity of the appointee for effective service, is not only a potential negative influence, but at times a definite obstacle to the right growth of the movement.

In the economic life of the country there is a factor which operates in every social effort, namely: the constant influx of families from older countries whose political, social and educational institutions have, for a long period of time, been static, and whose customs of living, social traditions and inherent methods of thought and action, and whose very ideals differ widely not only from those of

[1] American Police Systems. Chapter II. Raymond B. Fosdick, New York. The Century Co., 1920.
[2] See footnote 1 and Police Administration, Leonhard Felix Fuld, New York. G. P. Putnam's Sons, 1909.

their country of adoption, but among themselves.
This situation complicates any social effort and has
its full share of influence on the women police
movement. A country where traditions and life
within the family continuously encounter rude
shocks from inevitable cross currents of different
points of view in parents and children, engenders
sharp situations in the lives of young people, where
rational solution is difficult. Complicated in our
large cities by congested living conditions, the problem, at times, seems insoluble and it constitutes one
of the most pressing needs which faces the woman
police officer if she is really to prevent delinquency.

The national temperament, too, exercises its part
of influence. This is seen particularly in the fact
that, although questioning at first the value of
women in police work, the commanding officers and
the rank and file of the force, once convinced of
their value, accord generous aid in the best development of the service which women can render in
police departments.

The recent general enfranchisement of women
has had as yet no startling effect on this movement,
for women have been active for a comparatively
long time in all social endeavor. In fact, as a dis-
tinguished French Senator speaking in a Parliamentary Session said: "In the United States, in
marked contrast to older countries, the development
of the 'Cité Spirituelle' has been left practically
to women." [3]

[3] M. Hughes Le Roux, Journal Officiel, Paris, France, November 14,
1922.

In general the movement for women police in this country has been sponsored by women's groups and by private volunteer civic, state and national law enforcement, and social hygiene associations. Among the former are such national bodies as the general Federation of Women's clubs, the National League of Women Voters, the National Young Women's Christian Association and the National Women's Christian Temperance Union; local women's clubs and associations similar to the Chicago Juvenile Protective Association, the Cleveland Women's Protective Association, the Detroit Girls' Protective League and the Girls' Service Club of New York. The former type of group includes the American Social Hygiene Association, the Bureau of Social Hygiene, the Cincinnati Social Hygiene Society, the Missouri Social Hygiene Association and other kindred groups. Several influential men's clubs have been active also, notably the men's City Clubs of Chicago and Philadelphia.

THE APPOINTMENT OF POLICE MATRONS

In the United States during the last half of the Nineteenth Century (as in many countries), certain types of women's organizations manifested an active interest in securing the appointment of women for the direct supervision of women and girls who are held in custody by any government agent—police, sheriffs, superintendents of jails, detention houses, hospitals for the insane or any publicly controlled institution. These were the days before record keeping and annual reports had been generally instituted by such organizations. It is not easy therefore to obtain full information on these early appointments. In 1845 the American Female Reform Society secured the appointment of six women matrons in New York City—two at the City Prison (the Tombs) and four on Blackwell's Island—the first prison matrons in this country.[4]

Among the women's organizations the Women's Christian Temperance Union was particularly active in this field.[5] Their early records report that in the eighteen seventies prominent members of the organization in Portland, Maine, visited the women prisoners and attended court, and, in 1877, they employed a paid visitor. Soon one-half of her salary was paid by the city. The next year the city paid her salary in full and she became a police matron.[6]

Through the efforts of this same organization other cities appointed police matrons in the following order: Jersey City, New Jersey, 1880; Chicago,[7] Illinois, 1881; Boston, Massachusetts, 1883; Philadelphia, Pennsylvania;[8] Baltimore, Maryland;[9] St.

[4] Nineteenth Annual Report of the American Female Guardian Society and Home for the Friendless (1924), page 10. Woody Crest Avenue, New York City.

[5] Police Administration (Fuld), page 159. G. P. Putnam's Sons, New York, 1909.

[6] Reports of Mrs. J. K. Barney, National Superintendent of the Department of Work in Prisons, Jails, Police and Alms Homes, National Women's Christian Temperance Union, Evanston, Ill.

[7] In 1882 the number was increased to 3, and in 1885 to 10.

[8] In two years the number increased to 4 and a police committee was appointed by the W. C. T. U.

[9] Paid $10.00 per week.

Louis, Missouri; Milwaukee, Wisconsin, 1884; Detroit, Michigan; Denver,[10] Colorado; Providence, Rhode Island; San Francisco, California, 1885; Lowell, Massachusetts; Cleveland, Ohio, 1886.

The program of the various state and local committees in this department of the National Association was "Push the matter of police matrons in every city; commence at once and continue until successful."

These and other similar appointments mark the official recognition of the principle that women prisoners should be cared for by women. In 1888 the state of Massachusetts passed a law directing the appointment of police matrons in all cities of 20,000 inhabitants and over.[11] In the same year, due to the efforts of the Women's Prison Association, New York State passed a similar act.

THE FIRST POLICE POWER

There may be other individual incidents such as that in Chicago where in 1893, a woman, Mrs. Marie Owen, a patrolman's widow, was given an appointment in the Detective Bureau of the Police Department.[12] The first recorded instance on which infor-

10 "She has charge of the home for friendless women and children, is called to visit the sick and the dying at all hours of the day and night, going unquestioned into houses of prostitution, variety theaters, dance halls, and wherever needed."
11 *Lend a Hand*, iii, 161; iv, 126.
12 Communicated by Hon. Morgan A. Collins, Superintendent of Police, Chicago, Ill. This appointment was made by the Mayor, to provide for the widow of an officer. Mrs. Owen was carried as a "patrolman" for 30 years, or until her retirement on pension. She visited courts and assisted detective officers in cases involving women and children.

mation is available of a woman receiving police powers in order to deal effectively and directly with social conditions threatening the moral safety of young girls and women was in 1905 during the Lewis and Clark Exposition in Portland, Oregon. Those familiar with conditions obtaining at such expositions, together with the habits of lumbermen, miners and laborers when "off the job" and "on a spree" will thoroughly appreciate the value of these so-called "safety workers," women who were appointed to protect women, and, particularly young girls, who would naturally come in great numbers to this exposition. Mrs. Lola Baldwin, a Travelers' Aid Society Secretary, was given police powers and put in charge of this work. She had a large and competent corps of volunteers during the Exposition.

It is a recognition of the effectiveness of the results obtained in this exposition, that Portland immediately afterwards organized a "Department of Public Safety for the Protection of Young Girls and Women." Mrs. Baldwin became the first director of this new division and her incumbency outlasted those of 6 chiefs of police and 5 mayors.[18] Later this department became, by charter, a division of the police bureau. Neither the Police Department nor Mrs. Baldwin wished the women officers to be known as "police" and they were, and

[18] Municipal Police Women, by Sophia Hall, University of Wisconsin, University Extension Division, Municipal Information Bureau. Information Report No. 22, April, 1922, page 14.

are still, called "operatives" or simply "workers."
The Florence Crittendon Circle of Grand Forks,
North Dakota, was among the early groups
who advocated the need of women with police powers
to cope with social conditions contributing to delinquency. It was in 1909 that they asked definitely
for the appointment of such women, and in May,
1910, the City Council passed an ordinance creating
the position of police matron, but which carried
duties which today are considered to be those of
women police.[14]

Inasmuch as all through the early development of
the movement the terms "police matron" and
"police woman" are applied to persons performing
very similar duties, it is often difficult to determine
from the documents available, the exact scope of
the duties of these officers.

THE WORK OF MRS. WELLS

In 1910, Mrs. Alice Stebbins Wells, graduate
theological student and social worker in Los
Angeles, became convinced that the efforts of the
agents of private organizations engaged in protective and preventive work for women and children,
would yield more efficacious social results if these
agents were public officers invested with police
powers. She accordingly addressed a petition, containing the signatures of 100 influential citizens, to
the city mayor asking for her appointment as a

[14] Mrs. Pearl Blough, Proceedings International Association of
Police Women, 1916.

police officer.[15]   This appointment was made in
September, 1910, and Mrs. Wells is known as the
first regularly rated "policewoman" in this country.   Her chief duties comprised the supervision,
and the enforcement of laws concerning dance halls,
skating rinks, penny arcades, picture shows and
other similar places of public recreation.   Among
her activities were the suppression of unwholesome
bill-board displays, search for missing persons and
the maintenance of a general information bureau
for women seeking advice on matters within the
scope of police departments.[16]

Although ranking with the plain clothes men,
Mrs. Wells was permitted some functions not delegated to the men officers.   She was consulted either
in writing, or in person on the purposes, scope, and
possible value of the work of women officers, and
was given an office where she was free to keep an
office hour.[17]   A similar situation now obtains in the
case of all directors of women's work in police departments.   In 1911 the position of women police
officer in Los Angeles was placed under Civil
Service, and on October 8, 1912, there were 3
women officers and 3 police matrons.[18]

The appointment of Mrs. Wells attracted wide
newspaper comment because of the fact that she was

[15] Policewomen and the Work in America.   Maude E. Darwin, Nineteenth Century, June, 1914.
[16] The City Club Bulletin, City Club of Chicago, 315 Plymouth
Court, Chicago, Ill., October 31, 1912.
[17] The City Club Bulletin, Chicago, loc. cit.
[18] At present, this number is 20, of which 8 are jail matrons.   The
remaining 12 are attached to the Juvenile Department.

an educated woman, a social worker, and had deliberately sought and secured the opportunity to work in a police department. Naturally, many journalists presented the situation in a half-comic manner and pictured the woman police officer in caricature as a bony, muscular, masculine person, grasping a revolver, dressed in anything but feminine apparel, hair drawn tightly into a hard little knot at the back of the head, huge unbecoming spectacles, small stiff round disfiguring hat, the whole presenting the idea in a most repellant and unlovely guise. This conception, however, was not universally held and many groups of earnest women, searching for a solution of social problems greeted the idea of women police with favor, and Mrs. Wells was soon overwhelmed with requests for lectures and advice.

In 1911, Mrs. Sara Dow, President of the Women's Christian Temperance Union of Northern California, arranged a remarkable speaking schedule which was carried out to the exact letter.[19] In thirty days Mrs. Wells spoke in thirty-one cities. She visited as many more cities in California in the following years at the invitation of women's clubs, churches, parent-teachers' associations, Young Women's and Young Men's Christian Associations, and social workers' clubs.

In 1912, 1913 and 1914, 73 cities in the United States and in Canada invited Mrs. Wells to speak to 136 audiences. These cities were located all the

[19] Communicated by Mrs. Wells, December, 1924.

way from Dallas, Texas, to Toronto, Canada, and from Los Angeles, California, to New York City. The list of persons and groups who arranged these lectures, included every sort of women's group from the Current Event Class, of the Evanston, Illinois Women's Club, and the Woman's Tax Payers' League of Cincinnati, to the General Federation of Women's Clubs, and the National Suffrage Association; Baptist, Christian, Congregational, Presbyterian, Unitarian, and Methodist Churches, Councils of Jewish Women, many men's clubs, civic associations, social workers' clubs, various schools and universities and the International Association of Chiefs of Police, at its meeting in Grand Rapids, Michigan.

From 1910 to 1915 at least 16 cities had appointed women officers to their police departments.[20]

THE WOMEN POLICE ORGANIZE

At the Annual Conference of Charities and Corrections in Baltimore, in 1915, there were a sufficient number of women police in attendance to justify the creation of an association through which they might cooperate for the development of the work.[21] At the 1916 Meeting of this Association, the reports of various women officers indicated that the early women police were drawn largely from the personnel

[20] Proceedings of the International Association of Police Women, 1916. Information Report No. 88, New York State Bureau of Municipal Research; U. S. Census, 1915.
[21] See International Association of Policewomen, Chapter X.

of private social agencies in the community.[22] In many instances these agents, particularly those of the Travelers' Aid Society and the Associated Charities, were given police powers and their salaries were often paid, in part, by the police department while they still retained their position on the staff of the private agency.

At this time there was at least 1 woman supervisor of women police work in a department, Miss Annie McCully, Dayton, Ohio; 1 superintendent of a division of women police, Mrs. Blanche Mason, Seattle; 1 "senior policewoman," Miss Harvey of Baltimore; 1 inspector, Mrs. Conway, in Denver; 1 superintendent of a Woman's Protective Division, Portland, Oregon, and even 1 woman chief of police.

The Mayor of Milford, Ohio, a community of some 1500 inhabitants, in 1914, appointed a woman chief of police, Mrs. Dolly Spencer.[23] At that time gambling conditions were beyond the control of the Mayor. Mrs. Spencer, who was the general adjuster of all kinds of social problems in this small town, went "after the boys and took them out of the gambling joints to her own home." Here they were joined by their parents. By a series of small raids, she temporarily stopped gambling in Milford. She held her position as chief of police for two years, or until a new mayor took office, when the appointment was not continued.

[22] Proceedings of the International Association of Police Women, 1916.

[23] Communicated by Miss Mary E. McChristie, Referee, Juvenile Court, Cincinnati, Ohio.

The Bureau of Social Welfare of the State University of Iowa in 1916, employed a field agent, who upon request, after studies in communities, advised as to plans for general social work. In one community, for instance, of 5,000 inhabitants, a woman with police powers handled all cases of women and children involving matters within the scope of the police. In addition she was overseer of the Poor, Truant Officer, Relief agent, Supervisor of the Garden Club and Juvenile Court Agent. She had a full-time assistant and the necessary office and clerical help.

Police Officer Nellie McElroy, of Rochester, New York, had decided in 1914, that the publicity of court proceedings for girls should be avoided if possible. The responsibility of preventing future delinquency was met by a system of voluntary probation which contained all the elements of official probation. In 1916 at least 14 cities had instituted a system of voluntary probation by women police.[22]

Thus at the time of the entry of the United States into the World War, the movement for Women Police had taken root in the country, and an association had been formed "for the purpose of helping to establish and maintain a high standard both of work and of workers, and to advance as members of the police department its general service to the community," and at least 30 cities employed women in their police departments.[22]

[22] Proceedings of the National Association of Police Women, 1916.

CHAPTER VII

THE UNITED STATES FROM 1917 to 1922 *

The Commissions on Training Camp Activities of the War and Navy Departments—Committee on Protective Work for Girls—Section on Women and Girls—The Interdepartmental Social Hygiene Board.

Immediately upon the entrance of the United States into the World War, the energies of the women of the country, like those of the men, were diverted from their ordinary activities into the various channels which would assist in the winning of the war.

Events following mobilization gave an impetus to the movement of women police and furnished a basis upon which more general demands were later made for the appointment of women officers by police departments. Since the primary object of forming an army is that men may be trained and put into the field in the highest possible state of efficiency, it would seem reasonable that those in

* See *a. in Social Hygiene;* July, 1917. Wm. F. Snow, M.D.; October 1917, Bascom Johnson, Franklin Martin, M.D.; April, 1918, Walter Clarke; July, 1918, Timothy Newell Pfeiffer; October, 1918, Wm. H. Zinsser, Katharine Bement Davis; April, 1919, M. J. Exner, M.D. *b.* Reports of the Commissions on Training Camp Activities. *c.* Reports of the Interdepartmental Social Hygiene Board.

command of mobilization should attempt to discover and correct all the conditions which are likely to impair fitness. Based on previous experience, it was to be expected that a certain proportion of the army would be incapacitated for service each year because of syphilis and gonorrhoea. If this enormous waste were to be prevented and we were to be able quickly to send an effective army over-seas, protective measures had to be applied, and applied immediately.

COMMISSIONS ON TRAINING CAMP ACTIVITIES OF THE WAR AND NAVY DEPARTMENTS

"Even before the United States entered the Great War, governmental and civilian experts began laying plans for the control of gonorrhoea, syphilis and chancroid. The most powerful of these pre-war stimuli came from the American Social Hygiene Association, a voluntary civilian organization that for a number of years had been gathering scientific information and laying carefully organized plans for the control of the venereal diseases." [1]

"Within six weeks after America had entered the Great War, there was enacted into law by Congress a policy in regard to prostitution and the liquor traffic in connection with men in the service that was wholly unique. Under the provisions of Sections 12 and 13 of the Selective Service Law, zones were

[1] *Manual for the various Agents of the United States Interdepartmental Board.* Washington, Government Printing Office. 1920.

created around military and naval establishments, within which houses of prostitution were forbidden and traffic in alcoholic liquors barred. The sale of liquor to soldiers and sailors everywhere was forbidden.

"The Commissions on Training Camp Activities were charged by the Secretaries of War and of the Navy with the duty of seeing to it that the environments of training camps were kept free from the vicious conditions traditionally surrounding them."[2]

The National Government announced "that alcohol and prostitution which had heretofore been regarded, or largely tacitly recognized, as necessary evils in connection with army life, were no longer to be tolerated; that a government which drafted its young men to fight and perhaps die for it could no longer permit them to be surrounded by crude and vicious influences from which many would return home maimed in body and soul."[3]

The Commission availed itself of representatives of several civilian law enforcement groups who were to study actual conditions around the camps, in relation to prostitution and alcohol and to formulate, in cooperation with military and local civilian authorities, a plan for the carrying out of the program of the Commission. Out of this effort grew the Law Enforcement Division. The Commission,

[2] Social Hygiene and the War.—Timothy Newell Pfeiffer—*Social Hygiene*, July, 1918.
[3] "What Some Communities of the West and Southwest have done for the Protection of Morals and Health of Soldiers and Sailors," by Bascom Johnson, Social Hygiene, October, 1917, Vol. III, No. 4.

in order to "enlist the special interest and support of women individually throughout the United States"[4] in the control of the situation around training camps, in relation to young girls, established a Committee on Protective Work for Girls.

Committee on Protective Work for Girls. This committee was composed of persons of national reputation who at first planned to undertake the entire responsibility for the girl problems, in connection with military camps, including both the problems of delinquency and protection. Girls were following the wave of emotionalism which was sweeping the country and making a hero of every man in uniform. Counteracting influences were required to utilize the energies thus gathering momentum and turn them into constructive channels.

At its first meeting the Committee outlined and proposed to communities, where military camps were located, a program which included:[5]

a. The creation of girls protective bureaus with a woman in charge who should direct the work of women protective officers having police power, and whose functions would include: 1. Patrol Work. 2. Supervision of amusement places. 3. Personal work with girls, and 4. Aid in law enforcement.

b. Provision for proper detention quarters for girls and women.

c. Appointment of women probation officers.

[4] Report of the Chairman on Training Camp Activities, 1918, Washington, Government Printing Office.

[5] Girls in Khaki, by Winthrop D. Lane, "The Survey," December 1, 1917.

d. Securing of necessary legislation on related matters, and,

e. Promotion of educational work in the community.

The committee proposed, in addition to efforts in connection with establishing its program in communities, to carry on a wide educational propaganda to the end that the intelligent handling of girls by every agency coming into contact with them should become a permanent practice in every community.

In order to provide immediately, instruction for protective workers, the schools of social service in Boston, Chicago, and New York offered courses which took the form of institutes where specialists could present quickly the salient facts which protective workers should know together with a program of action and a point of view which would form the basis for a right perspective on the pressing problems encountered.[6]

In April, 1918, the Commission transferred to the Section on Women's work of the Social Hygiene Instruction Division the responsibility for a program on education for women and girls.[7] The Committee on Protective Work for Girls then concentrated its efforts in the creation of proper detention homes and reformatories. About this same time the Sec-

[6] Protective Work for Girls in War Time. Maude E. Miner. Proceedings National Conference of Social Work, 1918.

[7] At least 14 of the important private organizations were actively cooperating with this Section. See Social Hygiene and the War by Walter Clarke—*Social Hygiene*, April, 1918.

tion on Reformatories and Detention Houses was created as a part of the Law Enforcement Division of the Commission.[3] Its work was to secure additional facilities for the custody and rehabilitation of women and girls whose commitment to an institution is found necessary for the protection of the Military and Naval Forces of the United States against venereal diseases.[4]

These functions having thus been delegated to other authorities, the Committee on Protective Work was free to concentrate on special educational work looking toward the creation of properly organized local agencies which would undertake "protective work" for girls.

As early as 1918 six field workers had been appointed to organize the work in separate geographical communities. In the efforts to influence communities to create protective bureaus for work with girls the need was clearly seen for a closer cooperation of all organizations interested in girls. To meet this need, therefore, a comprehensive program of work had been drawn up in February, 1918. Until this date the attention of the Committee had

[3] Work of the Section on Reformatories and Houses of Detention. Martha P. Falconer. *Proceedings National Conference of Social Work*, 1918. When interested groups are working for the appointment of women police officers in this country, one of the planks in their program has invariably been that of providing proper detention houses for women and more recently it is being advocated by some that these houses should be under the direction of the Women's Division of the Police Department. There can be no doubt that the work of the Section on Reformatories and Houses of Detention has had a large part in bringing about this particular situation.

largely been directed toward the end of protecting young girls from sex delinquency.

Meantime in steadily increasing numbers, not only young girls but older women had already classed themselves under one of several categories which public service workers denote by such titles as "charity girl," "patriotic prostitute," and "clandestine prostitute." Further, "Procurers"—in some instances the husbands of the victims—were plying their trade in sections around military encampments. These conditions required rapid and drastic action, if the changes of physical disability through venereal infections were to be reduced to a minimum. Therefore about May 1, 1918, the Committee on Protective Measures began concentrating on the definite supervision of women and girls who were consistently and persistently seeking to break through the Government's laws concerning prostitution. The name of the Committee was changed to "Section on Women and Girls of the Law Enforcement Division."

The Committee on Protective Work for Women and Girls already had 60 protective officers in or near 21 training camps, 11 embarkation centers, 5 naval training stations and 5 large cities in the vicinity of the camps. To secure the funds for the payment of these workers there existed a close cooperation between federal and local governmental authorities and private civic and national groups.

The Section on Women and Girls. The newly organized section formed 9 administrative fieldwork districts with each under the direction of a fixed post representative who should exercise "eternal vigilance." In July and August, 1918, 70 new workers joined the field staff and during September and October, 62 more were added. Of these 141 workers, all of whom were directly responsible to the Section on Women and Girls, only 40 were paid by the Commissions. The salaries of the others were provided by private citizens whose interest and cooperation had been secured by the agents of the Commission. Eventually the number of field workers reached 198, 77 of whom were paid from Federal funds and 121 by funds raised through the efforts of the Section.[9]

The three-fold purpose of this section was first, to supplement the work of the Section on Vice and Liquor Control; second, to assist the Army, Navy and the Public Health Service in their campaign against venereal diseases; and third, to work with individual girls in the effort to curtail the sources of supply to prostitution. This program has much in common with current thought as to the functions of women police officers. The first function—that of supplementing the work of the Section on Vice and Liquor Control, included education for better laws and ordinances against prostitution. In the discharge of the second function—cooperation in combating the venereal diseases,—the officer saw to it

[9] Through the courtesy of police departments, these workers were provided with an official badge. They did not have police powers which as a matter of fact were seldom needed in the work.

that women and girls infected with syphilis and gonorrhoea received regular treatment at the clinics. In speaking of the third function, that of work with individual girls, the director of this section says:

"The work with individual girls, who have had but one or two sex experiences, is the hopeful point of attack upon prostitution. The 'charity girl,' the 'patriotic prostitute,' and the runaway and incorrigible girls with sex experiences may, by intensive individual treatment, be diverted from the life of professional prostitution. Wherever there is an existing social agency which is equipped to do intelligent work with these girls, they should be referred at once. Where there is no such agency, it is the duty of the Fixed Post Worker and her assistants to build up the girl's character through such resources of education, health, recreation, employment and religion as may be found in the community."[10]

INTERDEPARTMENTAL SOCIAL HYGIENE BOARD

On July 9, 1918, the President signed the Chamberlain-Kahn Act which created the Interdepartmental Social Hygiene Board to consist of the Secretary of War, the Secretary of the Navy, the Secretary of the Treasury as ex-officio members and of the Surgeon-Generals of the Navy, the Army and the Public Health Service, or their ap-

[10] Outline of Organization and Methods. Section on Women and Girls Law Enforcement Division. Jane Deeter Rippin. War and Navy Department Commission on Training Camp Activities.

pointed representatives.[11] This Board, in December, 1918, was authorized to take over the Section on Women and Girls of the Law Enforcement Division of the Commission on Training Camp Activities, and 58 persons—9 supervisors and 49 field agents were transferred to work under its direction. On April 1, 1919, the Section on Vice and Liquor Control was also transferred to this board whose work in the so-called "Protective Social Measures" followed the general policies of the Law Enforcement Division of the Commission on Training Camp Activities.

In 1921 decreased appropriations made it necessary to reduce materially the number of workers formerly employed to deal with individual cases of women and girls leading promiscuous sex lives.[12]

In March, 1922, the Board proposed a program of work which was embodied in the Jones-Kahn Bill and whose purpose was to transfer the law enforcement activities of the Board to the Department of Justice. Congress adjourned without passing this bill, and on June 30th, 1922, the Board discontinued these activities.

The permanent results of the Committee on Preventive Work for Women and Girls, the Section on Women and Girls of the Law Enforcement Division, and the Interdepartmental Social Hygiene Board cannot be statistically measured. Much of the actual social effort which today is directed toward

[11] Publication No. 193, 65th Congress, Chapter XV, July 9, 1918.
[12] Publication No. 193, 65th Congress, loc. cit.

securing women police owes its origin directly to the influence of the activities organized and vigorously fostered and developed by these groups which sought to develop community responsibility through local committees. Through the actual demonstration of case work by trained workers, representative citizens, in many communities, learned for the first time of the delinquency which existed in their midst and city and county officials have at least been convinced to some extent that a *protective* and not a *detective* program, was or might be made, effective in the hands of the right women officers.[13]

[13] 1. Specific Problems in Camp Communities. Jane Deeter Rippin. Proceedings, National Conference of Social Work, 1918.   2. Discussion, by Miss Virginia M. Murray. Proceedings, National Conference of Social Work, 1919.

CHAPTER VIII

THE UNITED STATES SINCE 1922

General Statistics — Boston — Chicago — Cleveland — Detroit.

GENERAL STATISTICS

The number of women police is by no means static —it is continually changing. Some cities discontinue their services, some add to the number already employed, and other cities are instituting their services. Different cities apply different titles to women employed on similar duties, and at times women performing widely divergent duties are designated by the same title in different cities. For instance, in New York City the name "policewoman" is applied both to women who are assigned to definite matron duty and also to others who are discharging law enforcement, patrol and special service functions. Quite frequently also the same descriptive terms are used in several cities to denote work which in reality differs greatly. All of these factors, and yet others, render it difficult, if not wholly impossible, to present, at any given moment, absolutely accurate and true information on the women police movement in the United States.

The first questionnaire on the subject of women police which is a matter of record, was sent out in 1919 and 1920, by Lieutenant Mina C. Van Winkle, Director of the Women's Bureau of the Police Department of Washington, D. C., after she became president of the International Association of Police-women. At its annual meeting in 1920, in New Orleans, this Association distributed copies of a tentative digest of the replies received.

In 26 of the 30 states reporting, women were employed in the police departments of cities.

Of the cities to which the questionnaire was sent, 146 replied. Of these 146 cities, 56 employed a total of 175 women in their police departments. It was known, that among the cities that did not reply some did employ women police. For instance New York City, which did not reply, had at least 30 patrol women, and perhaps 50 or more police matrons bringing the possible total to at least 275. The proportion of these 275 who were women police and police matrons is not known.

In the cities reporting, the salaries of the women police or matrons ranged from $900 to $2,100 a year with 59 per cent between $1,000 and $1,500.

Thirty cities required, and 26 did not require civil service examinations for appointment as women police. In only 21 cities was some form of social service training deemed essential for effective police work by women, while 35 required "no special training." Although in some cities serious consideration had been given to the question of the formulation of a general program of work for their women police, on the whole these functions were not clearly defined.

The International Association of Policewomen is now completing the tabulation of returns in a recent questionnaire covering a wide range of information on the employment of women on police duties.

Preliminary reports from the results of this questionnaire indicate that the pay of women in police departments in 148 cities ranges from an initial salary of $65 to $105 and a maximum salary of from $150 to $205 per month.[1] The largest percentage of monthly salaries are between $100 and $150. In 19 of these 148 cities appointment is by civil service and, in at least 38, social service experience is considered essential for women police.

In order to present facts concerning the numbers of women police and police matrons, together with the date of the first appointment to those two posts in the different cities, a request for such information was sent to the police departments of a list of cities.[2] Replies have been received from 268 cities. In each city reporting the employment of women in police departments, every effort has been made to learn if they are women police or police matrons.

[1] The information does not state if these figures refer to salaries of both police matrons and women police.

[2] This list was compiled from such sources as the Tentative Digest of the 1920 questionnaire referred to above, newspaper and magazine articles, correspondence and the list of membership of the International Association of Policewomen. The list included the 100 largest cities in the United States.

The statement presented, however, may not give a true picture because it has been difficult to know the exact duties of the persons employed. The term police matron is here used to designate a person employed to give physical care and supervision to women and children detained in the custody of the police. "Women police" is used to designate those persons performing the preventive functions of the police as outlined in Chapter XI.[3]

In the 268 cities from which information is available, the following facts obtain:[4]

> 58 cities employ no women in their police departments.
> 210 cities employ women in the following capacities:
>> 22 employ 1 person for both matron and women police duties;
>> 65 employ matrons only;
>> 52 employ women police only;
>> 71 employ both matrons and women police.

It would thus appear that 145 cities employ women police, in 22 of which the women police also act as matrons, and that 158 cities employ police matrons, in 22 of which the matrons perform preventive functions also. In other words, in 145 cities of the United States women are employed in the execution of the preventive functions of the police.

[3] It is possible that there are misinterpretations of the replies and that changes have occurred in some cities since the date of writing. It is earnestly requested that persons having such corrections or new information will submit it to the author.

[4] For names of individual cities see Appendix I.

The 210 cities employ at least 355 police matrons;[5] 395 women police and 22 women who perform both functions in police departments. One can say, therefore, that at least 417 women in the United States are today executing the preventive functions of the police.

Of the 58 cities who at present employ no women in their police departments, 8 have had women police and 2 have had police matrons, but have discontinued their services. The reasons given for this are either that funds have not been appropriated for salaries, that the city authorities have not been convinced of the value of the women on the force, or that there is not enough work to justify their employment. In 3 of the 9 cities there are police matrons. In 3 others of the 58 cities having no women on continuous service, 2 have given police power to women serving in other social agencies, and a third employs special women police in summer time for the patrol of the public parks and bathing beaches.

Of the 100 largest cities, no information has been made available from 4. Of the remaining 96 the following facts are reported:

    4 employ no women in their police departments.
    2 employ 1 person as police matron and woman police.
   24 employ police matrons only.
   10 employ women police only.
   56[6] employ both matrons and women police.

[5] The number employed in Milwaukee is not available.
[6] Two other cities, Milwaukee, Wis., and Norfolk, Va., did employ women police, but have discontinued their services.

Thus, in at least 92 of the 100 largest cities, women are employed in some capacity in police departments, and in 68, women are engaged in the execution of the preventive functions of the police.

Before the entry of the United States into the World War in 1917, according to the returns of the Chiefs of Police in these 268, 36 cities employed only women police, 100 employed only police matrons and 12 employed 1 officer for both duties, while in 25 cities both matrons and women police were employed. Accordingly where now 210 cities employ women in police departments there were 173 before 1917. Today in at least 145 cities women are performing preventive police functions and before the war this fact obtained in 73 cities only—an increase of 72 cities.

The war period provided not only new experience in law enforcement problems in relation to the prevention of delinquency, but it also presented situations in which the protective and preventive functions of the police were necessarily stressed. To meet these situations it brought into this field types of trained women from related activities who came to the work with various points of view.

Since the war there have been increased efforts toward the formulation of the functions of women police and experiments as to the forms of organization under which their work will be most effective. Since 1917, at least 8 cities have created definite women's divisions within their police departments.[7]

[7] Charleston, S. C.; Cleveland, Ohio; Indianapolis, Indiana; Wash-

In 5 others this service is supervised by a woman of educational and social service training higher than that of the rank and file. It is being demonstrated that good women police officers must be selected for other qualifications than those which, up to the present, have been demanded of men officers.

That the movement, in general, is becoming more coherent and articulate is shown by the brief history of the International Association presented in Chapter X.

As concrete illustrations of the efforts to develop the movement locally, a narrative description of its history in 8 selected cities follows:

BOSTON, MASSACHUSETTS *

Agitation over the appointment of women police officers in Boston began at least as early as 1912.[8] About this time the Massachusetts White Slave Traffic Commission in a report to the Legislature called attention to the increasingly large number of young girls between the ages of twelve and eighteen to be found, in every city, roaming about the streets and parks at night. To remedy these conditions, the report recommended the appointment "of well

ington, D. C.; Detroit, Michigan; Wichita, Kansas; New York, and Knoxville, Tennessee. Two of these cities, New York and Indianapolis, have discontinued this division as a separate administrative service.

*Manuscript read by Chief Inspector John A. McGarr, Miss Nichols, Mrs. Robert Words and Miss Helen Pigeon.

[8] Policewoman Movement in Massachusetts, by Marian C. Nichols. The Massachusetts Society for Social Hygiene, Bulletin April, 1920.

qualified women—as adjuncts of the police system."
This question was formally discussed in the various
civic associations. Continuous efforts were made to
secure legislation on this subject, and in 1914 Miss
Marian C. Nichols, Secretary of the Women's
Auxiliary of the Civil Service Reform Association,[9]
was largely instrumental, through the Boston City
Federation, and the Massachusetts State Federa-
tion of Women's Clubs, in securing the passage on
May 12, 1914, of a general law providing for the
appointment of women as special police officers in
Massachusetts.

Haverhill was the first city in the State to take
advantage of this power and the first woman police
officer in Massachusetts was appointed in that city
in 1915. Worcester and Holyoke followed in 1917
and in 1918 Lowell, New Bedford, Lynn, and Springfield appointed women officers to their police departments.

The War and Navy Department Commission on
Training Camp Activities maintained during the
war its corps of women protective officers in Massachusetts, one of whom was detailed to Boston as in
other centers where army and navy men were
stationed or through which they passed frequently
in groups. Miss Mabel Blake [10] was the Commission's first supervisor for New England. She
was later succeeded by Miss Mary E. Discoll.[11] In

[9] 3 Joy Street, Boston.
[10] Now of the Harvard University School of Education.
[11] Now a member of the License Commission of Boston.

Boston the work was largely centered in the patrol
of the Boston Common, and near vicinity, frequented by army and navy men whose presence in
uniform had the usual attraction for young girls
and whose pay envelopes were of interest to the
commercial prostitute.

In accordance with the general plan of procedure
of the Commission, the supervisor aroused the interest of private organizations to the extent of securing the salary of several special workers for the
City of Boston.

The Boston War Camp Community Service submitted to the mayor of the city on April 30th, 1918,
a Report of a Survey conducted by 21 experienced
social workers, agents of various Boston organizations, over a period of 6 consecutive nights through
the latter part of March and early April. As a result of these combined independent observations
recommendations were made that at least 6 experienced social workers should be appointed in Boston,
as plain clothes women and police officers, who
should function directly under the Commissioner
and from central control. In 1919 the Boston
Society for the Care of Girls, the Boston City
Federation, Boston Section of the Council of
Jewish Women, Boston League of Women Voters,
The Florence Crittendon League, the Massachusetts
League of Women Voters, the Travelers' Aid
Society, the Women's Municipal League, the
Women's Auxiliary of Massachusetts, and the Civil
Service Reform Association, organized a mass meet-

ing addressed by Lieut. Mina C. Van Winkle, Director of the Women's Bureau of the Metropolitan Police Department of Washington, D. C., and at which a plan for a Women's Bureau was proposed and endorsed.

Although the state law permitted municipalities to appoint women as special officers to their forces, a special empowering act was required to make women eligible as regular members of the police force of the city of Boston. The Boston City Federation prepared a bill to this end, and with the aid of other organizations went out to secure its enactment. They were so successful that on March 29, 1920, they had the satisfaction of sending delegations to witness the signing of the Boston Policewomen Act by Governor Calvin Coolidge. On December 21, 1920, the Civil Service Commission held an examination for policewomen in the service of Boston and other cities in the State. Of the 94 women who took the examination, 27 passed and of this number 11 were eligible for the Boston service. Six were appointed, of whom 1 had previously been a police officer in another city, 2 had been stenographers, 1 a nurse, and 2 had been housewives.

Before instituting the work of women officers, the Commissioner of Police, Edwin V. Curtis, commissioned Chief Inspector John A. McGarr to study the functioning of women officers employed in the police departments of St. Louis, Chicago, Washington and other cities. He decided that the Boston women officers should function directly from the office of the Chief Inspector, under his personal direction. This plan still prevails.

The first detail of work to which the women officers were assigned was that of accompanying special plain-clothes officers in an attempt to make a "clean-up" of certain cabarets which were thought to be tolerating and actively abetting solicitation by commercial prostitutes. Arrests were made and a number of proprietors were convicted and their licenses revoked.

At present one woman officer is assigned to this duty. Another with a representative of the "Better Business Men's Association," visits the public auction rooms and buys from the stock as any customers would do. Their purchases are then appraised by experts. According to the findings of the appraisers, licenses to operate auction rooms are continued or revoked. The outside expenses connected with these investigations are met by the "Better Business Men's Association." Two are detailed for the patrol of the Common, dance halls, and certain streets, with the double object of "picking-up" women prostitutes and of exercising a general supervision over the public conduct of young girls. The instructions of the women are that if they observe a young girl conducting herself in public for the *second* time in such a way as to indicate a lack of decency or a possibility of ignorance on the girl's part of the consequences of her actions, to quietly warn her. If the same girl is observed for the *third* time to be thus conducting herself, the woman officer is to accompany her to her home and to report the facts to the girl's parents. In all possible instances friendly supervisory contact is maintained with the girl and her family.

There is no formulated plan of work for the women police in Boston. They are not assigned permanently to any duty but undertake such work as is considered advisable from day to day by the Chief Inspector. The work of women officers, who now number five, is not kept as separate records, but is absorbed in the general reports of the Department.[12]

CHICAGO *

For some years prior to 1912, many civic and social organizations, notably the Juvenile Protective

[12] Communication from Chief Inspector John A. McGarr, February 5, 1925.

*The manuscript of this Section was submitted for comment to Superintendent of Police Morgan A. Collins, Miss Jessie F. Binford, Superintendent of the Juvenile Protective Association; Mrs. Gertrude Howe Britton, Superintendent and Director of Social Service, The Central Free Dispensary, Rush Medical College, Chicago, Ill.; Mr. J. T. Moss, Chief Probation Officer, Juvenile Court, and to Mrs. Joseph T. Bowen, President of the Juvenile Protective Association, who comments thus: "In looking over the article, I gather the idea that women police are doing a fine work. They have been, however, a grievous disappointment to us all. They are under Civil Service, but the standards for these examinations are not high enough to secure a group of trained women. Over and over again the Chiefs of Police have been asked to secure higher standards for these examinations, but, somehow, it has never been accomplished; as a consequence, the women police have never been a vital power in the city, possibly because they have never been competently directed by other than police officials whose conception of their duty is that of ordinary policemen on their beat. The women police here are assigned to

Association, Jewish and Catholic Social Agencies, the Chicago Woman's Club and the Men's City Club had engaged actively in a campaign to secure women police. Qualified persons to speak on the work of women police elsewhere were brought to Chicago. Among them, in 1912 and 1913, were Mrs. Alice Stebbins Wells, of Los Angeles, and Raymond B. Fosdick, of New York City. There seemed to be a conviction on the part of many organizations that the time had come for the appointment of women police in the City of Chicago.

In 1910, Chief Justice Olson of the Municipal Court of Chicago had appointed a committee of women trained in social work, who were later known as the Mayor's Committee,[13] to study the functioning of the Municipal courts and to make recommendations for their improvement. One of the suggestions made by them was that the city should appoint women police officers to take the statements of women and children who came to the attention of the police department and to be present in court when cases of women and children were heard.

[13] The Mayor's Committee—Gertrude Howe Britton, Juvenile Protective Association, Chairman; Minnie Loew, Jewish Social Agencies, and Leonora Z. Meader, Catholic Social Agencies.

different precincts or to courts, stations, etc. They should be under one competent head who has been trained along certain lines of social work, who has some vision of what is necessary for the protection of young people and who has authority and executive ability to carry out well-defined plans of prevention and protection. There is very little cooperation between our women police and private organizations; they are too often used to perform work which should be done by the men on the force; and they are seldom seen in dance halls or theaters.''

Acting on this recommendation, Mayor Harrison instructed the Corporation Counsel to draft an ordinance instituting women officers in the Police Department. The Women Police Ordinance was passed by the City Council December 30th, 1912, and amended on January 27, 1913.[14] The number of women officers was not fixed by law but is determined by the amount of appropriations voted by the City Council for the purpose of their salaries. Appropriations were made in 1913 for the employment of 13 women officers for a period of one year.

The Mayor's Committee on Women Police—which functioned for nearly three years or until the advent of a new administration—advised in the selection of their work. The first 10 women were appointed on March 19, 1914. The next year the city voted to increase the number to 30 and to place the position under Civil Service.

Before the women police ordinance was passed, Mayor Harrison had given police powers to Mrs. Mary Boyd,[15] an officer of the Juvenile Protective Association, who was to patrol the bathing beaches with the object of protecting young girls.

Chicago now has 30 women officers whose assignments are as follows:

[14] Section 1, amending paragraph 1907, and Section 2, amending paragraph 1908, of the Chicago Code of 1911.

[15] Mrs. Boyd was one of the first women police appointed and is still a member of the Department.

[16] Communicated peersonally by Hon. Morgan A. Collins, Superintendent of Police.

Superintendent's Office: 2.

Special work which includes: visiting and cen-
soring of cabarets, public dance halls, and
moving picture theaters; investigation of
abortion practitioners; investigation of advertisements offering employment, of "lonesome clubs"[17] and of clairvoyants; warning
and apprehending of commercial prostitutes
who solicit for trade in public places.

Morals Court[18] : 2.

Act as escorts for the women defendants and
remain in court for the hearings.

State Attorney's office: 2.

One attached to Social Service Department for
the preparation of Grand Jury cases of rape
and crime against minors. The second is detailed to the Juvenile Division of the State's
Attorney's office. In Cook County all war-
rants on charges of rape must have the
recommendation of the State's Attorney.
The woman officer takes the statements of
girls and women involved in such charges.

[17] For instance, "AAA means you; join my Lonely Hearth Club;
best results; members everywhere—Chicago, California, Canada
stpd. env.). Lonesome? That's your fault,—Write . . ."
[18] It is the general practice of this court that each woman defen-
dant before trial shall pass a physical examination with particular
reference to infection by syphilis or gonorrhoea. The 2 women
police officers are charged with their escort from the Detention
House to the Iroquois Hospital for contagious diseases. (SPECIAL-
IZED COURTS DEALING WITH SEX DELINQUENCY. A Study
of the Procedure in Chicago, Boston, Philadelphia and New York, by
George E. Worthington and Ruth Topping. Frederick H. Hitchcock,
Publisher, New York, 1925.)

Municipal Beaches and Piers: 6.
  For patrol.

Missing Persons and Detective Bureau: 1.

Precinct Stations: 17.
  For duty under the Commanding Officer.

Matron duty has been imposed on women police by some commanding officers, but in general they are assigned to such duties as investigation of complaints of sex offenses and crimes against children; cases where juveniles are involved as defendants or as delinquents; patrolling of suspected small gambling stores near public schools, moving picture houses, dance halls, streets and other public places with a view to the apprehension of prostitutes openly plying their trade.

All women officers are also subject to call, as the necessity arises, for the guard of women witnesses held for court testimony. This involves continuous 24 hours on duty as the officer is responsible for the appearance of the witness when called.

Quite separately from the Police Department, the Commissioners of Lincoln Park have for several years employed 15 women police from June to September.[19] These women are appointed on the recommendation of qualified persons. They patrol the parks and bathing beaches to the end of protecting women and children from annoyances and

[19] Communicated by Harry Klatzco, General Superintendent and Manager, March, 1925.

to enforce the rules covering matters relating to the use of the park and the beaches, such as for instance, the type of bathing suit allowed.

An effort was made in 1919 to associate the women officers closely with the work of the Juvenile Court. After this court was instituted in Chicago in 1899, the cases of juveniles of both sexes which came directly to the attention of a police precinct station, were investigated by men police officers designated for this purpose and known as "juvenile officers" or "police probation officers." They file petitions, serve summonses and notify witnesses to appear in court. This work is directed by a sergeant of police attached to the office of the chief probation officer of the Juvenile Court.

On November 26, 1919, at the request of the chief probation officer, acting in conjunction with the sergeant of police, 3 women police officers were assigned to this service to prepare for presentation to court the cases of delinquent girls coming to the attention of the police department.[20]

The plan of cooperation, as proposed, gave joint supervision of the work of these new women officers to the head of the investigation division of the probation department and to the sergeant of police. The chief probation officer reports that the results of this experiment were excellent. The sergeant of police, however, after some near difficulties had arisen, considered it imperative that he should have

[20] Communicated by Joseph T. Moss, Chief Probation Officer, Cook County Juvenile Court, Chicago, Ill., January, 1925.

complete control of these women police probation officers and should direct action in all cases in order to protect police department interests. This plan practically nullified any social control of these cases, which it had been hoped might be brought about and a protest was made by the chief probation officer. On April 5, 1920, the women police probation officers were returned by the Superintendent of Police to their regular assignments and the men police probation officers in the precinct now investigate the cases of girls as well as boys who come to the attention of the precinct and decide whether or not a petition shall be filed.

An independent social investigation however is made by a woman probation officer of the court in each case in which a petition is filed.

CLEVELAND, OHIO *

Since its establishment in 1901, the Juvenile Court has been functioning as a socialized court in Cleveland with both men and women probation officers, and until the last few years was the only court using women probation officers. Among the earlier efforts which had a bearing on the development of women police in Cleveland was a survey of dance halls made in 1911 by a committee of citizens. Following their report, an inspector of dance halls, paid by city funds, was appointed. His functions were in-

*Information supplied by Miss Sabina Marshall, Executive Secretary, Women's Protective Association; Miss Grace Treat, and Mrs. Keppele Hall, of the Women's City Club.

spection, regulation and licensing of dance halls.
In 1916, these responsibilities were transferred to
the police department. A second step was made
when, during his term as Mayor, Mr. Newton D.
Baker appointed a woman as head of the Sanitary
Bureau of the Board of Health, whose personnel
consisted of 30 men police officers. This established
in Cleveland the idea of a public bureau officered
by a woman.

Definite efforts towards the securing of women
police began in the spring of 1915, shortly following
the abolition of the segregated district by Mayor
Baker, who acted on a report of a survey made
under the auspices of the Federated Churches.

The acute situation following this event brought
out, with startling clearness, the need of women
officers to deal with girl and women cases coming
to the attention of the Police Department and the
adult court. Three well-known men holding important positions, Allen T. Burns, then the Director
of the Cleveland Foundation, Cheney Jones, of the
Humane Society, and William Winants, Assistant
Director of the Department of Public Welfare, together with Miss Belle Sherwin,[21] of the Welfare
Council, presented the matter to the judges of the
Juvenile and Police Courts. To cope with the
situation outlined, the chief justice appointed Miss
Sabina Marshall as a probation officer to deal with
girls and women who were first offenders. During

[21] Miss Sherwin is now President of the National League of Women
Voters.

the latter part of 1915, a committee of women
formed under the chairmanship of Miss Sherwin,
attended court hearings daily for two weeks. Their
findings confirmed those of the probation officer and
demonstrated definitely the need of preventive and
protective work for girls in the city. They immediately undertook to raise funds for the salary
of a trained social worker who would deal with
women and girls coming to the attention of the
police department. In the early part of 1916, the
mayor appointed Miss Marshall to the police department as a special investigator. She was given
a police badge, but no power of arrest. This step
was made through a committee headed by Mrs.
Malcolm McBride. Free office space was assigned
for the hearing and investigation of girl cases.

About the time that this bureau, under the special
investigator, was opened at the Central Police
Station, a tragedy concerning a sixteen year old
girl, reported in full in the press, stirred public
sentiment deeply, and a second committee of women
undertook to raise funds for protective work for
girls. The two committees learned of each other
and consolidating their efforts they formed, in 1916,
the Women's Protective Association of Cleveland,
of which Miss Marshall became executive secretary,
a position which she still holds, and where she has
also served as a police officer. The organization
was the pioneer body active in urging the appointment of women police and the development of the
two movements is, over a period of time, in-

separable. The office at the Central Police Station
was maintained as a branch until the appointment,
by ordinance, of women police. The Association
has constantly kept the need of women officers before
the church, civic and social groups, and had never
ceased to bring the matter actively to the attention
of public officials.

A Vice Bureau had been created in the Police Department in 1916. The staff was composed of 30
policemen officered by a lieutenant. Women and
girls arrested for prostitution or vice complaints
were permitted to sign a waiver and, on their
promise of future abstention from prostitution, they
were released with a warning. It was found that
many girls between fourteen and twenty-one were
being thus dealt with by the vice bureau. Shortly
after the appointment of the special investigator, the
vice bureau was ordered by the chief of police to
report to her all cases involving young girls. Soon
an assistant was added and both women continued
the work as probation and police officers. Their
duties were largely those of police officers.

The trustees of the Women's Protective Association recommended, and secured, in 1918, the appointment of a woman probation officer, paid from
city funds. In that same year, Sterling House was
established for temporary care and observation of
women and girls coming to the attention of, and released by the police.

During the war period, the office of the special
investigator, which was located in police head-

quarters, became the clearing house for girls' problems in Cleveland. The need of protective work rapidly outgrew the budget of the organization, and an appeal endorsed by the War and Navy Department Commission on Training Camp Activities, which had already appointed the special investigator as their agent, was made in 1918, to the Cleveland Mayor's War Board. This board granted $1,000 a month to the Women's Protective Association during part of 1918 and the period of demobilization. When the Interdepartmental Social Hygiene Board took over the work of the Commission, the same arrangements were continued in relation to the special agent, but new offices were opened outside of the police building.

The office at the Central Police Station, with no rental charge, became the branch office of the Women's Protective Association until its withdrawal on the appointment of women police in July, 1923. The judge of the juvenile court out of his experience with cases brought before the court, realized the need of women officers, and had given probation powers to those doing protective work under the Mayor's War Board. They also were authorized as deputy dance hall inspectors.

The first attempt to secure in law the appointment of women police was made by Miss Helen Albro, of the Women's Protective Association in the summer of 1917, when an ordinance creating a woman's bureau with 29 officers was presented to the city council. The ordinance was not passed. In the

meantime, Mrs. Jane Deeter Rippin, and Miss
Maude E. Miner (Mrs. Alexander Hadden) were
brought by the Women's Protective Association to
address a meeting of the Men's City Club, which
was largely attended by both men and women. In
1920, a hospital and health survey of Cleveland was
made, which recommended the creation of a woman's
bureau in the police department, whose functions
should include street and park patrol, inspection of
tenement houses and the handling of women's and
girls' cases coming to the attention of the police.
The report recommended that the bureau should be
officered by a woman, directly responsible to the
Chief of Police.

Further steps were taken at the end of 1920, when
a committee of the Women's Protective Association
approached the mayor who expressed himself in
favor of the appointment but who left office without
such action being taken. On September 26, 1921,
an amendment to the police regulations was passed
by the City Council reading as follows:

"Provided that women shall be eligible to appointment in the discretion of the Director of Public
Safety, and a separate list of women shall be established by the Civil Service Commission."

The chief of police in his annual reports of 1921
and 1922 recommended policewomen. In 1922 new
impetus was given the movement by women's
organizations, notably the Women's City Club, who
through its court committee, with Mrs. Keppele
Hall, as chairman, began actively working for a

women's division in the police department. This work began with an unsuccessful appeal to the mayor, to use his influence on the authority of the permissive ordinance to have created in the police department a Woman's Bureau headed by a woman. He did order prepared, however, the list provided for in the ordinance. In an effort to prevent the introduction of women into the police department on the same basis as are the men and working as individuals under men officers, and with no constructive social program, Miss Virginia N. Murray, General Secretary of the New York Travelers' Aid Society, was asked to go to Cleveland for an intensive educational campaign of some two weeks. Her coming was made possible through the cooperation of the American Social Hygiene Association and the Travelers' Aid Society. Miss Murray did much to create an overwhelming sentiment in favor of a Woman's Bureau among the women of the city.

In June, 1922, the secretary of the Civil Service Commission, acting with a citizens committee of men and women, prepared a set of examination questions for this post. One candidate passed the examination and was regularly appointed to the police department. At a second examination, 3 additional women passed and were similarly appointed. These women officers worked directly under the chief of police and the chief inspector and were detailed for the most part on girls' and women's work. During the Christmas season they were detailed also as store detectives, and in one or two instances relieved for the matrons in the jail. One woman was made a clerk in the recording room at police court, to relieve a man for regular police work.

In November, 1923, a new Council was elected, two of whose members were women who worked unremittingly for the establishment of a Women's bureau.[22] The Women's City Club seized upon this situation and arranged to go before the new Council at an unofficial meeting in December. Here the need of a Woman's Bureau was presented to them by three qualified persons—Miss Sabina Marshall, of Cleveland, Deputy Commissioner Eleonore Hutzel, of the Detroit Police Department, and Lieutenant Mina C. Van Winkle, Director of the Woman's Bureau of the Metropolitan Police Department of Washington, D. C. The movement was supported wholeheartedly by all the organized Women's Clubs in the city and an ordinance was prepared and presented to the Council, and was referred by that body in January, 1924, to their judiciary committee. Finally, after many hearings and much discussion, an ordinance was passed in April, 1924, establishing a Women's Bureau in the police department.[23] The

22 Miss Marie Wing, formerly with the Young Women's Christian Association and the Consumers' League, and Mrs. Helen Green, formerly with the Women's Christian Temperance Union.

23 "There shall be, and is hereby established in the Division of Police, a Women's Bureau, to be commanded by a woman, appointed by the Director of Public Safety. She shall receive not less than Captain's pay and be directly responsible to the Chief of Police. There shall be in the Women's Bureau, in addition to the commanding officer

salaries were provided as a regular part of the police budget for 1924. The 4 women officers had received, and still receive, the regular pay of patrolmen. The ordinance creating the Bureau has provided that the Director should receive "not less than captain's pay."

On January 1, 1925, the Woman's Bureau was established under the immediate direction of a woman ranking as captain. This new captain, Miss Dorothy D. Henry, is a Cleveland woman, a university graduate, with several years' experience in social service case work and community agencies.

The 4 women officers appointed in 1923, form the nucleus of the new Bureau. Appropriations for the salaries of 15 women officers have been passed by the Council, and efforts are being made to secure the additional 11 women to complete the allowed number.

Captain Henry's present office is located in a little used building which it is hoped will eventually be assigned entirely to the Woman's Bureau as headquarters.

thereof, fifteen policewomen of rank below the commanding officer. The purpose of the Women's Bureau shall be to do preventive work with women and children, and to deal with all cases in which women and children are involved, either as offenders or as victims of offenses. The Women's Bureau and the members thereof, shall be governed by the general police rules of the Division of Police." (Section 187, Code of 1924. No. 62835. See the City Record, Cleveland, April 31, 1924.)

DETROIT, MICHIGAN *

Due to the efforts of the Women's Christian Temperance Union police matrons were appointed in Detroit in 1885. In 1914 the Girls' Protective League began discussing the necessity for women police officers in dealing with individual girls detained by the police for "investigation." [24] In many cases the League staff were being called in for consultation and for personal and social adjustments when the girls were discharged from custody.

In 1916 the League directors gathered all the available information concerning women police and began a definite campaign to create public opinion a campaign which they pursued vigorously until the desired result was obtained. In fact, the eventual creation of the Women's Division in the Police Department was due almost entirely to their efforts. They brought to Detroit in June, 1917, Mrs. Alice Stebbins Wells through "whose wise counsel much impetus was given the movement. The information she was able to give and the fine spirit of understanding did much for the League's attitude in the months that followed." [25]

In November, 1917, they petitioned the Common Council for appropriations to pay the salaries of

*The manuscript of this section was submitted for comment to Miss Mary E. Hulbert, Social Service Director, Girls' Protective League; Miss Eleonore L. Hutzel, Deputy Commissioner of Police, and Miss Virginia Murray, Secretary, Travelers' Aid Society, New York City.

[24] A term applied when a supposed prostitute is brought in by the police, but without sufficient charge for a court appearance.

[25] Report of Miss Hulbert, for the League, January, 1924.

3 women officers. The Council called for a conference with the Board, who to re-inforce their position brought from Camp Custer, Miss Virginia N. Murray, then a field supervisor in the federal Commission on Training Camp Activities. The desired appropriations were voted. Commissioner of Police, James Couzens, however, stated that no women officers would be appointed until the Corporation Counsel could give a decision relative to the legality of such action. Mr. Couzens resigned as Commissioner in July, 1918, to become Mayor of Detroit.

He appointed, in January, 1919, as Commissioner of Police, Dr. James Inches, then serving as Commissioner of Health. In his farewell to his staff and his corps of nurses he said "if women will be the help in the Police Department that nurses are in the Health Department, I will appoint a hundred of them."

Shortly afterwards he met at dinner, in the home of a Director of the League, representatives from this organization. As a result of this conference, Dr. Inches agreed to appoint a woman officer to interview all women and girls held in the Police Detention House. In March, 1919, he appointed Miss Josephine Davis—a graduate of Michigan University and a member of the staff of the Girls' Protective League, who had cooperated in many instances during Dr. Inches' administration of the Health Board. She established and carried on in the department, a program of social adjustment with the women who were taken into custody by the police. The money for this salary was taken from what is known as the "auxiliary fund" a fund maintained for the purpose of carrying auxiliary (not regular) officers.[26]

Among the persons whose recommendations aided in forming the program for this venture were Lieut. Mina C. Van Winkle, [27] Miss Clara Burnside,[28] Miss Mary E. Driscoll,[29] Mrs. Martha P. Falconer,[30] and Mrs. Maude Miner Hadden.[31]

The League again brought Miss Murray to Detroit, and she outlined a program of work. The Common Council made a special appropriation of $3,000 for her salary, and in January, 1921, Commissioner Inches appointed her Director of a Women's Division. During this year Miss Murray, who still remained General Secretary of the New York Travelers' Aid Society, spent two weeks of each month in Detroit. Miss Davis became supervisor of case work. Fourteen women officers were appointed during the first six months of the year at a salary of $1,600, taken also from the "auxiliary fund."

In July, 1921, the Commissioner did not appoint

[26] Report of Deputy Commissioner Hutzel.

[27] Washington, D. C. Director of Woman's Bureau, Department of Police.

[28] Indianapolis, Ind. Formerly Director of the Woman's Bureau, Department of Police.

[29] Boston, Mass. Commissioner of Licenses.

[30] New York City. Then of the American Social Hygiene Association.

[31] New York City. Then of the New York Probation and Protective Association.

a possible 20 uniformed men patrol officers but allowed, in the budget for 20 women officers at a salary of $2,000 each.[32]

In May, 1922, Miss Eleonore Hutzel, for twelve years Director of the Social Service at the Detroit Women's Hospital and Infant's Home was appointed Director of the Women's Division, an office which she still holds, but with the added rank of Deputy Police Commissioner. This rank was given her after the City Charter of Detroit was amended in March, 1923, to provide, in law, for a woman director of a Women's Division, and who should rank as Deputy Commissioner.[33]

The fact that provision is made by charter for a woman director as long as there are women officers, and the fact that there are now 30 confirmed officers in the Women's Division, who cannot be discharged unless charges are preferred, and then sustained against them by the police trial board and Common Council, would seem to assure sufficiently the continuance of women officers. The greatest security

[32] For method of selection and type of woman, see Chapter XIV.

[33] "The Commissioner shall appoint four deputy commissioners, one of whom shall be skilled in police duties and shall have charge of the police work of the department, one who shall have charge of the office administration, one who shall have charge of the Bureau of Public Safety herein provided, and one who shall be a woman and have charge of the Women's Division. He shall also appoint such other clerks and assistants as may be necessary. The Commissioner shall designate the Harbor Master and Sealer of Weights and Measures and such other officers as may be required; he shall prescribe their duties, and subject to the approval of the Common Council, fix their compensation." (Amendment to the Detroit City Charter, March, 1923. The amendment was brought about largely by the efforts of the officers and directors of the Girls' Protective League.)

of the Women's Division according to Miss Hutzel
lies in the fact that both the community and the
police department, as a whole, have accepted the
fact that the Women's Division fills a real need. As
long as there are girl problems, there is no more
question of its abandonment than there is of abolish-
ing the traffic division as long as traffic problems
exist.

The Detroit police department is administered by
a Commissioner of Police appointed, under the
charter, by the mayor. Under the commissioner are
four deputy commissioners, each responsible for his
own department, but not responsible to each other.
The Deputy Police Commissioners serve in the following capacities: 1st Deputy Commissioner—
Superintendent. 2nd Deputy Commissioner—Secretary. 3rd Deputy Commissioner—Assistant Superintendent. 4th Deputy Commissioner—Director—Women's Division.

In actual operation of the work of the Women's
Division the director finds herself dealing with the
commissioner in matters of policy—but with the
superintendent, who is chief executive officer in all
matters of inter-departmental detail.

The Women's Division does protective work with
women and girls; functions within the department
on all cases involving young girls; maintains a
bureau of information for women desiring information from the police department; investigates complaints made against women and girls, juvenile and
adult; conducts search for missing women and chil-

dren; supervises the Women's Detention Home, where all women held by the Police Department are cared for, patrols the streets and other public places of commercial recreation which are open to women. The Women's Division refers all cases to other social agencies for follow-up treatment work;

ORGANIZATION

The work of the Division is divided in the following manner:

(1) Complaints and Records. (2) Investigation —Adult and Juvenile. (3) Missing Girls and Women. (4) Patrol. (5) Women's Detention Home. (6) Law Enforcement.

Complaints and Records. The Supervisor is responsible for all complaints received and for all files. An information desk, where complaints are received, is maintained at the office of the Division. An officer is in attendance from 8:30 A.M. to 7 P.M. After 7 P.M. complaints are taken by the officer on duty in the Women's Detention Home. Juvenile complaints are taken at the office of the Juvenile Department. Officers taking complaints are trained experienced workers so that 50 per cent of all cases received are either disposed of or are referred to the social agency doing that type of work without being referred to the investigation department. The supervisor meets the public as they come to the office, takes reports of officers reporting in (each officer reports in every hour), assigns stenographers and checks all correspondence and files. An officer from this department interviews each young girl and each new offender admitted to the Women's Detention Home.

Investigation—Adult Service. The Supervisor is responsible for case work. Officers on duty 8 A.M. to 10 P.M. Investigates all complaints made on women and girls over seventeen years. Makes cards on every case; face sheet and summary when indicated.

Officers investigate according to methods approved by social agencies. Investigation is continued until diagnosis is made at which time the case is referred to the proper agency or individual. When investigation shows that court procedure is indicated the Supervisor of this department refers the case to the Law Enforcement Department for court work, but continues her plan for social adjustment.

Investigation—Juvenile Service. The Supervisor is responsible for case work. Officers on duty 8:30 A.M. to 5:30 P.M. Investigate all complaints made on girls under seventeen years, neglected and dependent children. Has special office located in Juvenile Detention Home. Proceeds as Adult Department.

Missing Girls and Women. Supervisor (same as adult investigation) responsible for case work. Officers on duty 8 A.M. to 10 P.M. Investigation made until girl is located, at which time case becomes one for social adjustment and is handled as any other investigation case. The officer making the investigation on the missing complaint continues to work on it until the case is disposed of. All out of town missing juveniles are referred to Wayne County Juvenile Probation Department unless counterindicated, and case is referred by them to the Juvenile Probation Department of residence county for adjustment.

Patrol. Supervisor responsible for work of patrol officers. Cards or Case Records kept on each individual dealt with. Officers on duty 7 A.M. to 2 A.M. (Saturdays and Special Holidays, 4 A.M.)

7 A.M.–9 A.M.—Patrol districts made of rooming houses and questionable hotels, interurban station, employment agencies, comfort stations, and early performances at moving picture theaters.

9 A.M.–Noon.—Restaurants and cafeterias, public rest-rooms in department stores, hotels, railway stations, general delivery entrance to post office and downtown streets.

Noon–9 P.M.—Patrol downtown streets, rest-rooms, comfort stations, general delivery post office, moving pictures, theaters, small parks, 5 and 10 cent stores (looking for missing girls),[34] streets around high schools and small stores near schools.

9 P.M.—4 A.M.—Patrol, in the interest of young girls, downtown streets, small parks, interurban station, moving picture theaters and other places; observe for employed children, enforce ordinance in regard to children on streets, inspect dance halls

34 Attracted by display of cheap jewelry and other accessories.

and other places of commercial recreation open to women (mostly dance halls) enforce 1 o'clock closing for dance halls.

N.B. One patrol officer spends all of her time investigating complaints which come to the office, which do not concern special individuals but are indicative of bad social conditions.

Women's Detention Home. Supervisor responsible for care of women in custody of the police. Officers on duty 8 A.M. to 12 M. All women prisoners are finger printed and records are kept showing the number of arrests, dates and charges.

The 13 matrons—on duty twenty-four hours a day, in 3 shifts—give physical care to the women in custody, escort them to and from court and to local institutions. They also accompany men officers when a woman is transported from city to city. One matron is assigned to duty with juveniles, whom she also chaperons during court sessions when they are witnesses in criminal cases.

Law Enforcement. Supervisor (same as patrol) responsible for all court records. Officers on duty 9 A.M. to 5 P.M. Records kept on all cases. In accordance with an order from William P. Rutledge, Superintendent, certain immorality cases involving women and girls must be referred to the Women's Division. The cases referred by the men's department, as well as the cases with which the Women's Division makes contact direct, are handled by special officers trained in court procedure and investigation for court.

Procedure in Court Cases in the Detroit Police Department may be divided into three classes:

(a) Certain immorality cases as incest, rape, seduction, bastardy, indecent liberties with a female child, assault on a female child, assault to rape, enticing a female child under sixteen years for marriage and contributing to the delinquency of a female child, must be referred to the Women's Division. Men officers assist the Women's Division in its efforts to locate and apprehend the offender, if a man, but they take no responsibility for the case and have no dealings with the girl. It is in violation of the Police Rules for a man officer to take one of the above mentioned cases into court. Petty larceny cases involving young girls are also included in this group.

(b) Other immorality cases in which young girls are involved: Men officers *may* refer these cases to the Women's Division. They are not, however, required to do so. The procedure in the event that the case is referred is as in Group A. In the event that the case is not referred and a young girl is involved, the men officers are required to refer the girl to the Women's Division for social adjustment. The plans of the Women's Division must, however, wait on the release of the men officers.

(c) All other cases are handled by the officers assigned to the case. In the event that a young girl is involved the procedure is as in Group B, when the case is not referred to the Women's Division.

Women officers refer to the Precinct or the Detective Bureau any cases which come to their attention which do not involve young girls and women.

Women officers are at all times available to the Men's Department if needed for work on special cases. The request for a woman officer must come from the Commanding Officer of the Precinct to the Director of the Women's Division.

The present staff of the Women's Division consist of the Director and 31 women police. During the years 1923 and 1924, the cases handled by the different departments were as follows:[35]

	Number of Cases	
	1923	1924
Investigation Department:		
Adult..	820	1426
Juvenile....................................	1312	1777
Missing Girl Department.......................	1051	1360
Patrol Department............................	1168	1480
Law Enforcement Department—Cases in Court...	540	789
Special Officer—Narcotic Division...............	....	94
(Assigned to work July 1st, 1924)		

The police department has 13 matrons working under the Director of the Women's Division. In addition to caring physically for the women prisoners in the custody of the police, they escort them to and from court or to local institutions and accompany men officers when they escort women to and from another city. One matron is assigned to the same duty with juveniles and also chaperones them during court sessions.

[35] Annual Report, 1924, Police Department, Detroit, Michigan.

CHAPTER IX

THE UNITED STATES SINCE 1922 (*Continued*)

New York City—Portland, Oregon—St. Louis—Washington, D. C.—State Women Police of Connecticut.

NEW YORK CITY

In New York City among the first of the peace-time organizations which saw and attempted to solve the social problems created by the massing of large numbers of soldiers and sailors in the city during the war, was the New York Probation and Protective Association through the Girls' Protective League and its branches.[1] On July 4th and 5th, 1917, 40 representatives from the membership of the branches met in conference to discuss "how can we do more to protect girls in war time."[2] After investigation the League made a report to the New York Police Department concerning conditions near certain recruiting stations, small parks and subway stations. As a result of these representations, additional police officers were stationed in these districts.

[1] Now the Girls' Service League of America.
[2] New York Probation and Protective Association Report for the year ending September, 1917.

In June, 1917, the Mayor's Committee of Women on National Defense had called a conference of interested agencies to consider the "Girl Problem in New York." [3] As a result of their deliberations they organized a special section of Social Welfare with a Committee on Protective Work for Girls, of which Miss Stella Miner, of the New York Probation and Protective Association, was made chairman.

In order to determine and to demonstrate clearly the kind of program needed for effective protective work for girls in New York City, this Committee in July, 1917, placed in the field 2 women especially trained in methods of work for girls and who were given police powers. The time of these two women was devoted to searching out individual girls to the end of preventing delinquency and to discovering conditions conducive to delinquency. Workers from the Girls' Protective League assumed responsibility for follow-up work with girls who came to the attention of the two protective officers.

During the first two months the 2 officers with police powers had dealt with 708 girls. The Committee on Social Welfare considered that this situation justified a request that the city pay salaries for 6 protective officers with police powers who should work within the police department. These salaries were included in the budget, and passed by the Board of Estimate and Apportionment with the approval of the Mayor. The Board of Aldermen, however, dis-

[3] Protecting Girls in War Time. Stella A. Miner. *Proceedings New York City Conference of Charities and Correction,* 1918.

proved this expenditure and the item for salaries for protective officers failed of final passage.

The Girls' Protective League had already adopted a plan of assigning 1 protective worker to each of 7 selected districts for the purpose of following up and befriending the girls discovered by the two protective officers. Now that the money for the salaries was not forthcoming, the association met this situation by special appropriations together with money provided by several other social agencies and by certain individuals. Until their disbandment at the end of 1917 the work was carried on under the official auspices of the Committee on Social Work of the Mayor's Committee of Women on National Defense.[4] After this time the work was under the direction of the Girls' Protective League. Miss Miner as chairman was directly responsible for the organization and supervision of the work of the women officers, which included scouting on the streets, in the parks and around the camps, armories, recruiting stations; visiting dance halls, moving-picture theaters, amusement parks, and investigating furnished room houses, places of employment, restaurants, railroad terminals, tenement hallways and other places where conditions had been criticized.

Until August, 1918, when official policewomen were appointed by the city, these protective officers were given police powers.

[4] Annual Report, New York Probation and Protective Association, 1918.

Meanwhile, in the winter of 1917, Mrs. Mary E. Hamilton entered the Missing Persons Bureau of the Police Department as a volunteer, where she was joined early in 1918 by Mrs. Ethel H. Gay.[5] In January, 1918, the newly appointed Commissioner of Police, Richard E. Enright, named as Fifth Deputy Police Commissioner, Mrs. Ellen O'Grady, formerly a probation officer attached to one of the Magistrates Courts of Brooklyn. Mrs. O'Grady was the first woman deputy commissioner appointed to duty in the New York and probably in any police department. She received full rank and full pay. The work of the Fifth Deputy Commissioner's office was considered to be vitally important as it aimed to eliminate delinquency by building up strong forces for removing temptation and for the protection of children and youth.[6]

Her principal duties, as outlined by the departmental reports, comprised:

(a) Supervision of all conditions relating to White slave Traffic.

(b) Crimes and offenses affecting women and girls.

(c) Social Welfare.

(d) Protection of Juveniles.

In line with this innovation, 10 policewomen were added to the Force. Eight were assigned to duty under the Fifth Deputy Commissioner and 2 to the Bureau of Missing Persons. These first 10 police-

[5] Now Mrs. Harry H. Corbin.
[6] Annual Report, New York Police Department, 1920, page 235.

women did not enter under Civil Service. They were appointed in accordance with the Laws of 1917 authorizing the appointment of special police during the war, or as the Commissioner states it: "In August, 1918, under chapter 651 of the Charter, 10 women were appointed to serve as the first police-women in New York City."[7] The salaries were provided from a special war emergency fund. The number of policewomen was subsequently increased to 20. In May, 1920, the State Legislature passed a bill making their appointment permanent. They enjoy all the rights and privileges of police officers except pension benefits.[8]

By this same enactment the designation of "policewoman" was changed to "patrolwoman" and provision made for the appointment under the Civil Service of additional persons to a total of 30 as patrolwomen "for the increased moral protection of women and minors, for the prevention of delinquency among such women and minors, and for the performance of such other duties as the Police Commissioner may assign to them." The patrolwomen are subject to general provisions of the charter covering salaries, pensions, appointments and removals of the members of the police force. No woman is eligible for appointment as patrolwoman who, on date of filing her application for civil service examination, is under twenty-one or over thirty-five years of age.

[7] Annual Report, Police Department, New York City, 1919, page 56.
[8] Laws of New York, 143rd Session, 1920, Vol. 2, Chapter 501, pages 1312, 1313.

As long ago as May, 1888, the Commissioner of Police in New York City, had appointed police matrons.[9] On May 11, 1920, the Charter of New York City was amended by Legislative Act, and the rank and grade of policematron was abolished.[10] The policematrons then in the department became known as policewomen with all the rights and privileges of patrolmen. For purposes of pension benefits the time served as policematron counted as if it had been served as policewoman. The policewomen are appointed by the Police Commissioner. The law requires that all appointees to the position of policewoman shall have the endorsement of 20 women of good standing and residents of New York City.

Actually, the Civil Service Commission holds examinations for policematrons, and appointments as policewomen are made from the list thus established.

On December 13, 1920, Deputy Police Commissioner O'Grady resigned after nearly two years of service and the Third Deputy Commissioner, Joseph A. Faurot, temporarily took charge of the work of this branch of the Police Department.[11]

[9] Under authority of Legislative Enactment which required the Commissioner of Police of the cities of New York and Brooklyn to provide separate detention quarters for women and to designate Police Matrons for the care of women held in the custody of the police. This was due largely to the efforts of the Women's Prison Association, 110 Second Ave., New York City, through its Executive Secretary, Miss Alice Woodbridge. (Annual Report, 1888.)

[10] Laws of New York, 143rd Session, 1920, Vol. 3, Chapter 705, p. 1785.

[11] Annual Report, New York Police Department, 1920, p. 234.

On April 4th, 1921, the Police Department opened a Woman's Precinct, which was located in an old police station which had been cleaned and remodeled. Mrs. Mary E. Hamilton was placed in charge of the Precinct. Several lieutenants were temporarily assigned to the Woman's Precinct for the purpose of instructing patrolwomen in the proper method of making official records as well as of handling the different conditions that came within the scope of the department.[12]

On May 12, 1921, an Honorary Deputy Police Commissioner, Mrs. George W. Loft, was appointed. She was assigned to supervise the activities of the Woman's Precinct and the Special Duty Division. These combined divisions comprised a force of 59 men and 35 women who devoted their entire time and efforts to doing protective and preventive work for the youth of the city.[12]

On June 21, 1921, the patrolwoman in charge of the precinct was assigned to Headquarters Division. She was succeeded by Captain John C. Amon, who remained in charge until the Woman's Precinct was discontinued.

In the spring of 1922, the Honorary Deputy Police Commissioner having completed the organization of her precinct, turned her attention to the question of providing special instruction designed to help her women officers in the better discharge of their duties. In May of that year, in cooperation with the

[12] Annual Report, New York Police Department, 1921, pp. 92, 93, 94.

New York Office of the United States Interdepartmental Social Hygiene Board, she organized a course of lectures in Police Women's work in relation to Social Hygiene. The lectures included well-known experts in the field. The subjects treated covered the general phases of protective and preventive social measures; the services of women police and methods of work, venereal diseases and prostitution.

In December, 1922, Mrs. Loft resigned the office of Honorary Deputy Police Commissioner. The Woman's Precinct was kept open until September, 1923, at which date it was closed.

With the closing of the Woman's Precinct, the center of activity of the women police was transferred to the various departmental services. Their assignments were made in about the same manner as were those of the men officers. They reported for duty to the officer commanding the Division, Bureau or Precinct, to which they were assigned.[13]

There are at present 100 women in the police department of New York City, 70 of whom are policewomen and 30 of whom are patrolwomen.[14] Both groups receive the same annual pay of $1,769 mini-

[13] For example: Police Department . . . Temporary Assignments . . . POLICEWOMAN—Elizabeth Ray, 13th Division, Women's Bureau to 37th Precinct, for 10 days, from July 22. PATROL-WOMEN—Rae Nicoletti, 12th Division to 13th Division, Women's Bureau, for 2 days, from July 24. From 13th Division, Women's Bureau to 37th Precinct, to Aug. 1.—Helena Brady, Frances Driscoll.—New York *Times*, July 25, 1925.

[14] Communication from Commissioner Enright, March 28, 1925.

mum, and $2,500 maximum at the end of five years service.

Women members of the force have been assigned to four general forms of duty: search for missing persons, special service, matrons and welfare duty. In the special service division the women work on assignment under the direction of the commanding officer of the special service or plain-clothes division of the department.

Welfare duties include supervision of dance halls; patrol of the streets, parks, and other public places to the end of preventing juvenile delinquency; the suppression of activities of professional abortionists and persons practicing medicine illegally; investigation of complaints of parents that their daughters are incorrigible: investigation of the activities of fortune tellers; of employers who act in an indecent manner toward young girls applying for work; of complaints against a certain type of individual frequenting motion picture shows and attempting to converse with women who sit beside them, and of cases in which women and children are involved, either as victims or as offenders.

As of December 31, 1924, and of May 5, 1925, policewomen and patrolwomen were assigned to duties as follows:

December 31, 1924 [15]	Number of Policewomen	May 5, 1925 [16]
Matron Duty......................	42	36
Missing Persons Bureau..............	1	1
Special Service Division..............	25	27
Women's Bureau....................	2	6
Precinct Welfare Duty..............	0	0
	Patrolwomen	
Matron Duty......................	0	3
Missing Persons Bureau..............	2	2
Special Service Division..............	15	13
Women's Bureau....................	13	11
Precinct Welfare Duty..............	0	1

The Women's Bureau is located at Headquarters
and its work is under the supervision of Mrs. Mary
E. Hamilton, who was appointed March 8, 1925, as
Director.[17] "The purpose of the Women's Bureau is
to provide a central office where women and girls
seeking aid, advice and assistance relating to police
service may apply and discuss their problems and
troubles with women officers." [18]

Commissioner Enright is of the opinion that "investigations made by this department (Police Department of New York City) have demonstrated

[15] The City Record Civil List Supplement, Employees of the City of
New York and of the counties contained therein, from July 1, to
December 31, 1924.

[16] Communication from the New York Police Department, May 5,
1925.

[17] Excerpt from Special Order No. 75, promulgated by order of
the Police Commissioner, March 31, 1925: "Patrolwoman Mary E.
Hamilton, 13th Division, is designated as Director of the Women's
Bureau at Police Headquarters. She will have supervision over the
work of the Women's Bureau and policewomen assigned thereto,
effective as of November 1, 1924."

[18] Communication from Police Commissioner Richard E. Enright,
March 23, 1925.

that prevention of crime is the first duty of the police and any experiment or innovation which tends, however remotely, to the prevention of crime may be of incalcuable value. That the evils of juvenile crime and prostitution may be more effectively prevented and controlled by policewomen than policemen is no longer a matter of speculation." [18]

WOMEN POLICE RESERVES

In the ferment of public feeling which followed the sinking of the *Lusitania* it was believed in New York City that an auxiliary to the police force might be of value. A body of citizens volunteering their service for this purpose organized in 1918 under the name of the Police Reserves. In June, under the direction of Captain Charles H. McKinney of the Police Department, a Woman's Branch was organized, and a Women's Police Training Corps launched, the difference between these two groups being that the Training Corps was composed of the younger women, from eighteen to twenty-four, who could devote more time to special training, and "it was hoped that they would be the trained and paid policewomen of the near future."[19]

By December 31st, 4949 women were enrolled, more than one-fifth of whom volunteered to continue on duty after the war, and 1,300 of this number still remain as an auxiliary to the Police Department. They are divided for organization purposes

[19] Boston *Evening Transcript*, May 18, 1918. Interview with Inspector John F. Dwyer, of the New York Police Department.

into units, that of Manhattan and the Bronx, is commanded by Major Jean Dean Barnes, and counts 500 members. The Brooklyn and Queens unit of 800 members has as its commanding officer, Major Mary Farrell. Major Barnes defines their functions and adds: "May I stress to the limit of capital letters that *we do not do police work.*' We only know what to do and how to do it when we are faced with an emergency." [20]

To quote Inspector General McKinney, under whose direction the Women Police Reserves function, "The duties of the Women Police Reserves are those of peace time officers. The organization is composed of women who willingly give their time to the work which they like. They act as informal agents of their neighborhoods in such matters as the relieving of temporary distress, particularly that caused by illness, accident, fire or intensely cold or hot weather, and the adjustment of family discords. They are at all times prepared to render emergency service to the community." [21]

PORTLAND, OREGON *

Portland, Oregon, was the first city in the United States to organize a Women's Division in its police department. This occurred in 1905.

[20] The Women's Police Reserves by Major Jean Dean Barnes, *Police*, November, 1924. Police Publishing Company, Inc., 461 Fourth Avenue, New York City; 25c. per copy.

[21] Personally communicated, February, 1925.

*Information concerning this city was communicated by Miss Martha Randall, Superintendent Women's Protective Division, Portland. Also see Chapter VI.

In 1909 the city charter was revised and the early women's department was renamed "Women's Protective Division of the Department of Public Safety, Bureau of Police," with a corps of three workers. Until 1912 their offices were in the Young Women's Christian Association Building.

By 1918 a nurse was added to the staff which in 1920 numbered 14. Mrs. Lola Baldwin, who had served from the time of organization resigned as superintendent in 1922, and Miss Martha Randall, the present incumbent was appointed.

The staff now consists of 10 "workers" generally spoken of in the press as "Operatives." In addition to the superintendent and five patrol officers there is an assistant superintendent, a graduate nurse who is also a deputy health officer and who handles the sick, arranges for mental examinations and carries out the venereal disease program of this Bureau, an inspector of dance halls, a stenographer and a record clerk.

The Women's Division has the use of a touring car and two men officers are detailed to drive the car and assist in arrests when needed. The office hours are from 8:30 A.M. to midnight every day in the year.

Since it is the oldest established social service agency in the city, except the former Associated Charities, now the Public Welfare Bureau, the Women's Division acts as a community clearing house for many and varied matters which after consideration, it refers to the proper agency.

Besides the general preventive and protective work with women and children, the Division makes the investigations for cases coming up in the Domestic Relations Court.

ST. LOUIS, MISSOURI *

The first formulated public suggestion and request for the appointment of women police in St. Louis, was proposed at a meeting of the Social Service Conference in January, 1915, at which time the Conference had as its guest, Honorable Samuel Mc-Pheeters, President of the Board of Police Commissioners. This Conference had brought to St. Louis, from Los Angeles, Mrs. Alice Stebbins Wells, to speak on the work of women police, and during her visit she addressed a number of groups interested in the subject. About this time Mr. Raymond B. Fosdick of New York City also spoke at the City Club, and addressed meetings at other places in the city emphasizing the need of women police.

Senator Kinney, in the same month, January, 1915, introduced into the Missouri Legislature a bill to permit the appointment of women police. This bill was passed and became a law in June of that same year. It was not until May 15, 1916, a year later that St. Louis appointed her first four women police, who constituted the staff of the first Policewomen's Bureau of the police department of St. Louis. In 1918 eleven more appointments were

*Manuscript read by Lieutenant John A. Brandenburger.

made, and a woman supervisor, Mrs. Catherine
Fertig, was appointed to direct the work of the
Bureau. After several months it was decided to
abandon this form of organization and the women
were transferred to the Detective Bureau, in which
they became a separate service, and since that time
they have been directed by a man detective sergeant
who is directly under the jurisdiction of the chief
of detectives.

The women police are listed in the official report
of the department as "18 Matrons (Policewomen)." [22] In this same report the Chief of Police
says:

This report would be incomplete without a word of praise
for our Policewomen's Department. Especially efficient
have been the ladies in tracing persons reported missing
and in restoring them to their relatives. Their visits to
the picture shows, dance halls and other places frequented
by young girls have been numerous, and complaints of
unseemly conduct at such places have been greatly mini-
mized as a result.

This Bureau, which at present is composed of
18 policewomen, 2 of whom are negroes, is under the supervision of Lieutenant John A. Brandenburger. They are under civil service, and are
not required to wear uniforms. Among the qualifications and requirements for appointments are
that they must be women of high moral standing
between the ages of twenty-four and thirty-four

[22] Annual Report Police Commissioner, St. Louis, 1924.

years who must have completed at least four years of secondary school education. After appointment they are placed on probation for a period of six months, during which time they are required to study police rules and regulations. If they successfully pass the test they are promoted to the rank of a policewoman. Fourteen of the women police are at present assigned as follows:

One—To the Venereal Disease Clinic.
Two—Patrol Duty at Union Station.
One—To the congested business district to look for shoplifters, and especially for women wanted by the police.
Two—To a detail consisting of the answering and the follow-up of letters of inquiry, usually for missing relatives, and to investigate conditions reported by anonymous letters.
Two—To office duty in interviewing women and girls for the purpose of general advice and social adjustment.
Two—To the follow-up of desertion and non-support cases. These two women police make many arrests for the Prosecuting Attorney.
Two—Sometimes four—to patrol duty in public parks, picture shows, and on various occasions at dance halls.
Two—Negro women police are assigned to handle all negro cases.

In addition to the above specified duties all women police have general instructions to visit, in passing, the motion picture houses, dance halls and other such places of commercial recreation. They are sometimes called upon to deal with disorderly conduct or to investigate bad conditions which have been reported to the police.

The women officers are also at times assigned to cases with the Narcotic and Homicide Squad, under the Mann Act, Dyer Act, and those involving postal matters. Assistance in raids is another duty to which women are detailed as the need arises. Another general custom is that a younger woman be detailed with a recent male recruit to the force, who is not yet known to the keepers of houses of prostitution, in order that they may together secure evidence that a house is disorderly, or that liquor is being sold on the premises. The work of the Woman's Bureau includes investigation of fortune tellers, suspicious advertisements, medical practitioners who have no license, and the protection of women traveling alone. In general, all cases affecting the moral and physical welfare of women and girls are handled by the women police officers.

In 1924 the women police dealt with 2,687 girls and women who were involved in court cases either as victims or as offenders. These involved 432 cases of abandonment of a wife or children or both; 132 violations of laws relating to sex offenses, rape 32, felonious carnal knowledge 27, violations of Mann Act 20; 621 incorrigible children; 966 (adults 788, juveniles 178) violations of City Ordinance relating to venereal diseases, and 254 petit larceny.

They report 3,714 visits of inspection as follows: Cafés 3; dance halls 38; picture shows 734; railroad stations 717; stores 1,740. Various miscellaneous duties performed were: Investigations: (a) at request of letters of inquiry 2,471; (b) of cases 6,151; [23] (c) houses or hotels referred by Morality Squad 7; securing employment for 76 persons; referring to other agencies 2,824 cases; locating 5,368 missing persons; attendance in court on 1,286 cases; recovering stolen property to the amount of $6,336.57.

The Department employs 11 matrons who search and supervise generally all women held in the custody of the police.[24]

On May 28, 1924, a Conference on the Work of Women Police was held under the auspices of the St. Louis Committee on Protective Work by Policewomen composed of representatives from such organizations as Missouri Welfare League, Missouri Social Hygiene Association, College Club of St. Louis, Big Sisters of St. Louis, League of Women Voters of St. Louis, Women's Chamber of Commerce, Hospital Social Service, The Young Women's Christian Association, Jewish Women's Council, Salvation Army, Neighborhood Association, Epworth League of St. Louis, Junior League of St. Louis, Eighth District and the Missouri Federation of Women's Clubs.

The questions actively discussed were the history and the organization of the Policewomen's Bureau of St. Louis, and its work: the general need and opportunity for protective work by women police, and

---

[23] Character of ''case'' not indicated.
[24] Communicated by Major Elias W. Hoagland, Chief of Detectives, St. Louis Police Department, February 18, 1925.

finally the service which women police should perform in the preventive and protective field.

The Conference recommended additional women police for St. Louis, special training for women officers, a central detention home for women and girls, an active campaign for the securing of more wholesome public recreation for young people, and finally that delegates be sent from St. Louis to the annual meeting of the International Association of Policewomen at Toronto, in June, 1924.

Among the social agencies pursuing a program of constructive effort in this field, is the Missouri Social Hygiene Association, whose committee has incorporated in its program of activities a "close cooperation with the policewomen in their protective social measures program." [25]

WASHINGTON, D. C.[*]

The Metropolitan Department of Police of Washington, D. C., as do all governmental services in the District, exists by Congressional enactment and appropriations. The development of its Woman's Bureau has, therefore, a special national significance in relation to the appointment of women police in the United States. Indeed its present director, Lieutenant Mina C. Van Winkle, in her search for solutions of local problems and in the formulation of the general functions of the Washington

[25] Program for 1925, Missouri Social Hygiene Association, 2221 Locust Street, St. Louis, Mo.
[*]Manuscript read by Lieutenant Mina C. Van Winkle.

Woman's Bureau, has constantly kept in mind this possibile reaction and influence on the general movement.

It is worthy of note that the Woman's Bureau in the Washington Police Department was instituted as a separate administrative service on the initiative of the superintendent of the department.

Raymond W. Pullman became Superintendent of the Police in Washington, D. C., in April, 1915. He had no previous experience in police work, being by profession a journalist. His appointment was due to two fellow journalists who were, at the time, Commissioners of the District of Columbia, and who knew Major Pullman's deep interest in police problems. The year of his appointment he attended the annual Conference of Charities and Correction, held in Baltimore, Maryland, and it was afterwards recalled that he had listened with intense interest to the address of Mrs. Alice Stebbins Wells on "Women Police." Later, in Washington, following a lecture by Mrs. Wells, he was active in the open discussion of the subject.

In his report to the Commissioners in 1915, he said: "Throughout the United States, cities have discovered the advantage of having a limited number of policewomen to work in connection with the regular force in handling certain kinds of cases which are brought to the attention of precinct commanders or headquarters. Women, it has been found, are better able to do investigation work in cases in connection with wayward girls, juvenile delinquency, and in preventive work accomplished through conference with mothers of children who are being led into committing serious offenses."

Congress, in the Appropriations Bill following this report, voted the salaries of 2 women police and, in the appropriations of 1917, salaries for 2 additional women officers were voted, making a total of 4.

"The Woman's Bureau of the police department," says a Commissioner, "was established by the Commissioners to do a very great deal of special work that women can do infinitely better than men can do. The salary of women officers, first appointed, was lower than that of the regular force and it was very difficult with the salary paid to get the people who could do the work." [26]

Commissioner Louis Brownlow, searching for a method by which women could be employed on regular police salaries considered that the Act of 1906, providing for the personnel of the police department contained no sex qualifications for regular members of the force. He consulted a lawyer, the auditor of the District, and finally the Comptroller of the Treasury, all of whom agreed with him. The 4 women were then appointed to the regular force as privates of class 1—with pay of that grade. Since that time there have been no special Congressional appropriations for women officers. They are added to the force as any police officer would be

[26] Hearings on Bill H. R. 7983, Part 1 (Hon. Louis Brownlow, District Commissioner), Washington Government Printing Press, 1919.

chosen and their salaries are paid from the general departmental appropriations. The women officers may be members of the Police Relief Association.[27]

In his report for the year ended June 30, 1919, the superintendent says: "In the District of Columbia it was seen that not only could women do much of the work that heretofore had been given only to men, but that a certain class of duties such as work for the welfare of wayward girls and checking delinquency among girls could be carried on more easily by women than by men. Accordingly the Major and superintendent planned for the establishment of a Woman's Bureau in the summer of 1918, and succeeded in getting Mrs. Marian O. Spingarn, an experienced social worker, to accept the position as director of the proposed Women's Bureau.

Mrs. Spingarn was appointed as detective sergeant on September 17, 1918, and started the organization of the bureau. On October 15, 1918, she had a nucleus of four members of the bureau. In February, 1919, she resigned as Director, and Mrs. Mina C. Van Winkle, who had been a member of the Bureau since October 7, 1918, was made director. During the period of September 15, 1918 to July 1,

[27] The Police Relief Association is a cooperative benefit organization conducted by members of the Metropolitan Police Department. It is one of the oldest organizations of its kind in the United States, having been originally formed on November 16, 1869, and has been in existence ever since that date. Each member of the Department belonging to the Relief Association pays into it a monthly assessment of $2.00 and upon the death of a member the beneficiary receives immediate financial relief to the sum of $1500.00. (Communicated by Lieutenant Mina C. Van Winkle.)

1919, the Director of the Woman's Bureau states that its greatest emphasis had been put on case work.[28]

The women officers, as is the case with practically all recruits, men or women, to the Department of Police, came to their new task without previous police training. The needs of the hour were so urgent that only a very small part of the day could be devoted to the securing of special professional information. However, the second director of the Woman's Bureau instituted training for the women officers and invited the police officers to lecture on their respective special duties. They were instructed in court procedure by the District Attorneys and their assistants. Facts concerning the activities of the District Public Charities were given by the Secretary of the Board of Charities. Other qualified persons informed the women police of the work of the Board of Children's Guardians and of the Juvenile Court, emphasizing particularly the relation between these agencies and the Police Department. Psychiatry as an essential adjunct of courts and the part of the police in the control of venereal disease infection and prostitution formed subjects of other lectures. The Woman's Bureau accepted naturally, as a basic element, training in police practice as gained by daily experience. In addition it saw the necessity for general and specific knowledge on the part of the women if they were

[28] Report of the Woman's Bureau of the Metropolitan Police, District of Columbia, for 1919.

to fulfill the purpose of a woman's work in the police department.

Since the number of women officers was not limited, Superintendent Pullman, in the early days of the Woman's Bureau, had urged Lieutenant Van Winkle to secure 30 or 40. In her first report to the Superintendent of the work of the Bureau, for the year ending June 30, 1919, the Director said: "It has been rather difficult to secure the full quota of policewomen allowed, because of the low salaries, long hours, and the desire of most women to have at least one day's rest in seven. The staff has never been large enough to have a special detail for night work. The policewomen who are on duty all day investigating and aiding in the prosecution of court cases are compelled to go on duty at night and remain out until midnight and after."

At that time qualified women had been, and were still, receiving in governmental departments and in private agencies, concerned with war activities, salaries which the police department could not offer. In spite of very strenuous efforts to find extra women officers, the Woman's Bureau was unsuccessful in this regard.

In August and September, 1919, the Woman's Bureau was involved in a Congressional investigation of the entire police department, on the occasion of the presentation of Bill H. R. 7983, to increase the pay of members of the department. It was alleged that the investigation grew out of a campaign carried on in a Washington newspaper against the police department because of certain law enforcement activities.[29]

During the investigation the committee members were bombarded with letters from the women's organizations, State and National, who sprang to the defense of the Woman's Bureau. The result of the investigation was complete exoneration of the department as to its methods, and appropriations for increase in salary for all its members including the women officers.

Major Pullman died in February, 1920. The two superintendents who have succeeded him have shown a sympathetic interest in the Woman's Bureau. The last two administrations of the District Commissioners have not actively furthered its fullest development. In 1920 they moved that the number of women officers be kept at 20 and further that the Woman's Bureau be prohibited from asking for an increase in number of workers. This motion was carried in spite of the fact that each year the police department returns to the Treasury unspent moneys which have been received for the year's work.

An incident which indicated the inherent strength of the Woman's Bureau was the trial of the Director before the police trial board on April 7, 1922, on a charge of "insubordination." [30] This charge grew out of the Director's refusal in accordance with her obligations to release, before she could

29 Hearings Bill H. R. 7983, page 49.
30 Voice of the People, Baltimore, Maryland, April 22, 1922, page 28 (price 5c.).

examine into the case, two young runaway girls held
in the Detention Home.[31]   At Lieutenant Van
Winkle's trial 62 women's organized groups were
represented.   "Women from all parts of the country
offered assistance and support to Mrs. Van Winkle.
They beseiged their Congressmen and the Commissioners in behalf of the threatened Woman's
Bureau.   Clergymen, child welfare groups, lawyers
and associations interested in civic betterment did
the same.   Meetings of women's organizations in
Washington talked of nothing else up to the moment
of the trial."[32]   The trial board found Lieutenant
Van Winkle "not guilty" but went on record as be-
lieving that she had not a proper conception of
the cardinal principle of discipline which must pre-
vail in a police department, an expression of
opinion from which Lieutenant Van Winkle appealed to the Supreme Court of the District of
Columbia.   On June 12, 1923, this court ordered that
the only part of the findings of the trial board which
should not be stricken out was that in which the
Board found Mrs. Van Winkle "not guilty."

In 1919 the women officers were put under Civil
Service.[33]   The Director and other members of the
Woman's Bureau, whom she may designate, sit in
on the ratings of the examination papers of the
candidates for the position of women police.   There

[31] Manual, Metropolitan Police Department, Sec. 4 (b), Functions
of the Woman's Bureau "To deal with all matters relating to lost
children, and cases of females of whatever age, unable to give proper
account of themselves."
[32] A Policewoman on Trial, *The Survey*, July, 1922.
[33] See Appendix 1.

is also a preference list for each post in the Bureau. Other qualifications being equal, the candidates who have had social service training are given the preference.

On January 2, 1925, the Commissioners of the District moved to permit an increase of 3 officers thus bringing the possible total to 23.

The Woman's Bureau exists as an Administrative Division in the Metropolitan Police Department at the pleasure of the Superintendent and the District Commissioners.[34] The present organization of the Bureau and House of Detention together with the duties of women officers are definitely set forth in detail in the 1923 Manual of the Department.[35]

The Woman's Bureau has the same general status as a police precinct so far as its records and rules are concerned, but it serves the whole city and is under the command and immediate supervision of a Woman Director who "shall be a trained Social Worker," and who shall also have charge of the House of Detention.

The functions of the Woman's Bureau are "to deal socially and legally with all delinquent women and children." Women officers are governed by rules laid down for the guidance of privates and by the general rules of the department, in so far as such rules are applicable and consistent with the special class of work performed by policewomen.

[34] Hearings on Bill H. R. 7983, Part 2, page 65, Washington Government Printing Office, 1919.
[35] Manual of the Metropolitan Police Department, District of Columbia, 1923, Chapters XII, XII-A, XII-B, XII-C.

Efforts have been made to secure an Act of Congress which will establish the Woman's Bureau in law as it is now in fact. The last proposed bill would create, in law, the position of a director with the rank of assistant superintendent and who is a qualified social service worker; one assistant director with the rank of captain; one case-supervisor, one patrol-supervisor, and a number of privates (of either sex) 45 of whom shall be women. All ranking officers shall be women. Necessary clerical help is provided for in the Bill.[36] The Bill was not passed and renewed efforts will be called for in a future Congress.

Each year the Bureau would submit its own budget including such operating expenses as railway fare for the escort of women and girls who are returned to their homes or are taken to institutions. This expense at present, even for District of Columbia girls, escorted to institutions where they receive free care and treatment, is a charge as private funds, often supplied by the director or the staff.

WORK OF THE BUREAU

The privates of the Woman's Bureau now function in the following manner:[37]

Under Supervisor of Case Work: 1 officer—missing persons detail; 1 officer—interview persons detained in the House of Detention, and attend court session; 1 officer—follow-up work; 1 officer—in-

[36] Senate Bill S 4308.
[37] Woman's Bureau Report, 1924.

vestigate new cases ; 2 officers—work with colored persons.

Under Supervisor of Patrol: 2 officers—store and market patrol; 2 officers—Union Station details (night and day shift); 2 officers—moving picture houses and theaters (night and day shift); 1 officer —night patrol and rescue duty to 8 A.M.; 3 officers —general patrol duty and miscellaneous assignments.

Because the increase of work was so pressing that neither the lieutenant nor the sergeant could supervise all of the detail involved in case work and patrol, it was necessary to select the two most experienced women police to undertake to specialize and supervise in these two divisions of service. The supervisor of case work is obliged to give much extra time without additional financial compensation. Although the supervisors should be free to give all of their time to the supervision and training of the workers and to direct special investigations, they themselves are obliged to serve with the women in their division.

The problems of the officers on patrol duty are as follows: (1) Truant children in the moving picture houses and elsewhere. (2) Children "parked" in moving picture houses by their mothers who then seek their personal pleasures or shop unencumbered. (3) Degenerate men and objectionable women who frequent motion pictures. (4) Objectionable details in films. (5) Private and public motor vehicle drivers who lure young girls

astray, serve as procurers and consort with
prostitutes. (6) Unlighted canoes and other small
craft on the Potomac. Camps along the Potomac
conducted by objectionable persons who harbor
young girls. (7) Unlicensed dance halls conducted
as schools where young girls without means of support
are "employed" as "teachers" through whom
decent young boys are seduced. (8) Mashers.

A complaint desk and a complete record system
function regularly.

Policematrons are appointed by the United States
Civil Service Commission in open competitive
examination in general household duties and simple
first aid. The position requires kindly women, who
are sensible, and equipped with good health and
strength. The present number of matrons is 6—
with 3 eight-hour shifts.

The following statistics indicate the work done
by the Woman's Bureau in 1924:

Complaints made directly to the Woman's Bureau		902
House of Detention inmates interviewed (in many of these cases investigations and adjustments were made by the Woman's Bureau)		1747
Cases investigated and adjusted (other than the House of Detention cases)		594
Arrests:		
Under 17 years of age:		
White	121	
Colored	106	
Total		227
Over 17 years—under 21 years:		
White	86	
Colored	54	
Total		140
Over 21 years:		
White	203	
Colored	52	
Total		255 622

DISPOSITION OF CASES

One hundred and ninety persons were fined, 23 committed to jail, 10 are awaiting action of the Grand Jury, 4 cases were nolle prossed, 3 were dismissed, 8 are pending, 6 were committed to institutions for the insane, 45 to Gallinger Hospital for treatment, 152 juveniles were released to parent or guardian, 21 were committed to the Board of Children's Guardians, 1 to the National Training School for Boys, 39 to the National Training School for Girls and 16 to Industrial Schools, 78 were placed on probation and 11 are under suspended sentence. Two girls were entered in the House of Good Shepherd, 1 in the Industrial Home School, 1 case was released to the Immigration authorities, 3 to Maryland authorities, 6 to Virginia authorities, 1 to West Virginia and 11 were sent out of the District to their homes.

STATE WOMEN POLICE OF CONNECTICUT *

Connecticut is the only state in the Union which has tried the experiment of appointing women police as state officers. The first appointments were made on August 17, 1917, after the formation of the large temporary war training camps at New Haven and Niantic, where the men of the Connecticut National Guard were assembled for federal service.

*Information secured from reports in the files of the former Supervisor of State Women Police in Connecticut—Valeria H. Parker, M.D.

The usual influx of women prostitutes from adjacent large cities created an urgent need for a counter influence in the form of recreational facilities for the men, and protective work in behalf of the younger women who were attracted to these localities. While much was done by voluntary effort the fundamental situation could be met only with police authority.

The suggestion for the appointment of women police was offered to the State Council of Defense by its Committee on Sanitation and Medicine, and on Health and Recreation following a joint meeting with the State Horse Guards at the Capitol. After the State Council had agreed to pay the salaries of the women police, they were accepted by the State Police Commission. Six women police were authorized and Dr. Valeria H. Parker, Chairman of the Health and Recreation Department of the Council received the first commission and was made Supervisor of the State Women Police Corps with no fixed post of service. Two of the other five women police were stationed at New Haven, near the Yale Camp; one at Niantic, one at New London, and one in Hartford. Offices were maintained in each of these cities, thus giving opportunity for private interviews with girls and women.

Appointments and dismissals were made by the Supervisor with the approval of the Superintendent of State Police, to whom she was directly responsible for the work of the women police.

The duties of the women police included general

law enforcement, but special attention was paid to the enforcement of laws concerning prostitution and the use of liquor in the vicinity of camps and naval bases. At first considerable difficulty was experienced in obtaining the cooperation of the local authorities, and in one city it was found advisable that a Federal Agent should be given special detail in the locality.

The work done in New London was so effective that a movement for the appointment of similar workers was started in the neighboring city of Norwich. A group of its social workers sent a request to the State Council of Defense, showing that, after the cleaning up of New London, there had been a large overflow of vice into Norwich, and that the sailors and soldiers were coming into their city. The Council added a seventh woman police officer for Norwich.

The women police made as few arrests of young girls as possible. They practiced voluntary probation, holding arrest in suspension on the condition that the girl would report at stated periods, that they should work regularly and lead an orderly life.

Among the tangible results of their efforts were the elimination of a number of unsatisfactory baby farms, and the improvement of conditions in others; the closing of several disorderly houses; the suppression of a great deal of illegal liquor traffic and the departure of a large number of professional prostitutes discouraged by the lack of possibilities for trade, induced not only by repressive measures but by the creation of opportunities for the men to have clean amusement in the camps. At the end of the first year the monthly report reads:

REPORT OF POLICEWOMEN—AUGUST, 1918

SUMMARY OF CASES

Girls and Women:

Cases investigated	66
Girls sent or taken home	39
Visits made to homes	112
Girls arrested	13
Reports made by girls on probation	99
Girls committed to institutions	13
Work found for girls	15
Work of girls supervised	5
Girls physically examined	20
Cases referred to doctor or hospital for treatment	16
Pregnant girls assisted	14
Cases of girls followed up	161
Cases referred to hospitals and dispensaries	19
Boys' Cases	8
	589

Vice and Liquor Cases:

Cases of illegal liquor selling	5
Immoral houses investigated	9
Visits made to cafés, theatres, etc., getting evidence	69
Pro-German cases	22
Court cases attended	29
	134

Two assignments of women police stationed at New Haven, illustrate how their services were used by the police department.

In a certain district in New Haven, over a period of time, men had persisted in forcing their attentions on women who happened to pass that way. Some of these men were residents, but a fair percentage were of a floating population, such as railroad employees, and men traveling for various sorts of enterprises. They were not army or navy men, and the condition was well known in the city. The Precinct Captain and the City Attorney worked out a plan of action in which 2 women police, sufficiently disguised to cover their identity, walked in this section every night for two weeks. According to the plan, when men spoke, for the third time, to them, they stopped and listened to them, knowing that the captain and another officer were nearby, and they allowed themselves to be escorted to one or another hotel, proposed by the men, registered and went up in the elevator; at the hotel room door the captain and his aide appeared, speaking roughly to the women police, ordered them to "get out of town immediately." The woman police, be it admitted, went each time with trembling knees and were so exhausted after each arrest that they "got out" of the hotel and neighborhood with exemplary speed. They never appeared in court. Arrests were made every night for two weeks and the situation was cleaned up. So carefully was the plan followed, so earnest and so straightforward were the police and city attorney, that to this day the "news" has not leaked out which concerned the women police, even though the city press carried the "news" of the nightly arrests and daily convictions.

The second assignment concerned a certain hotel which, in reality was a closed club frequented largely by students and commercial prostitutes, where a plan was again so carefully conceived and executed, that not only this place, but as a by-product, another even more pernicious place, was put out of business.

Again the faith was kept by all concerned, and this time two city attorneys, the New Haven police, a student, an army man and 2 women police worked together. Such instances as these demonstrate that highminded women police have been used to great effect in such assignments with no attendant publicity, and with no need for their appearance in court. Many such cases are probably known to those concerned and remain hidden from the public except in rare instances where as in this case, the information is stumbled upon.

After the cessation of war activities a Bill was introduced into the Connecticut State Legislature which proposed the appointment of women to the State Police as a permanent institution. The Bill was sponsored by the State League of Women Voters and by other women's organizations, but it failed to pass the Legislature and, the Connecticut State Women Police Service terminated March 1, 1919. Its promoters and sympathizers consider that it demonstrated the social value of a mobile corps of women police who are free to move about in an entire State and who are not subjected to the influences of strong local politics.

CHAPTER X

THE INTERNATIONAL ASSOCIATION OF POLICEWOMEN

In June, 1914, at the time of the National Conference of Charities and Corrections,[1] Mrs. Alice Stebbins Wells, policewoman of Los Angeles, California, asked and secured from the Secretary a place in the 1915 program for the presentation of the subject of women officers in police departments. On May 17, 1915, the women police in attendance at the Conference organized their Association of which Mrs. Wells was elected president. As then stated, the objects of this Association were "to act as a clearing house for compilation and dissemination of information on the work of women police, to aim for high standards of work and to promote the preventive and protective service by police departments."[2]

Before launching this organization Mrs. Wells had enlisted the good will and support of the Inter-

[1] Now National Conference of Social Work.
[2] Proceedings, International Association of Policewomen, 1916.

*The organization was so named, according to its first president, because it was hoped that women police of all countries, where such officers were employed, would find, in this organization, a medium for mutual expression and exchange of experience. At the present time the membership is largely composed of women from Canada and the United States.

national Association of Chiefs of Police through its president Richard Sylvester, and had secured a copy of the constitution of this Association using it as a model for the women's organization. A copy of the "objects" of this later association were submitted to and approved by the police commissioners of Baltimore, the Conference City. On her return journey to Los Angeles, Mrs. Wells, as president of the new association, reported officially its formation to the Convention of the Chiefs of Police, then in session at Cincinnati, Ohio.

At the first meeting of the Association after its organization women police were present from 14 states—12 officers with all expenses paid by their cities. The membership roll of the Association included women officers from 22 states and Canada.

Although ten years have elapsed since this meeting it is still necessary today to advocate some of the suggestions made at this time. Among them were: (a) work of women police officers should be largely preventive and protective; (b) need of trained women is urgent; (c) courses of instruction or Institutes of Social Sciences, in Schools for Social Work, with field work in police departments are needed; (d) proper legislation should be secured for the appointment of women police; (e) women's divisions should be established within the police department and officered by a woman with rank not lower than that of captain; (f) careful records should be kept and monthly reports of work should be made to the Department; (g) simple civilian clothes of dark color, preferably navy blue, should be worn on ordinary duty; certain special duty might require a uniform; (h) exchange of women officers by municipalities would provide for enlarged experience and would make for standardization of work and methods.

It was suggested that an Educational Committee be appointed by the Association and that it should prepare: (1) a course of reading; (2) minimum educational and professional standards for women officers; (3) arrange for the presentation of the work of women police before as many as possible of the regional, state or national conferences in related fields, particularly before women's club gatherings; (4) publish periodical bulletins.

The actual activities, as reported to the Conference by the various delegates, embraced practically all of the functions which enter into the proposed programs of work for women police today.

The Association, as organized, called for a definite educational program. Nine district vice-presidents —8 covering the United States, and 1, Mrs. James Robinson, of Saskatchewan, Canada—were appointed to act as special agents in all matters pertaining to the movement in their respective territories.

In addition to these district vice-presidents, there were three standing committees, Education, Program and the Auxiliary Committee. In 1917, Miss Damer-Dawson, of England, accepted membership on this last named committee. Through correspondence, Mrs. Wells was in close touch with the English women interested in the movement. The results of the work in the United States were used as a means of arousing public opinion in England.[3]

In 1918 the Association elected as its president, Miss Annie McCully, of the Dayton, Ohio Police Department. She, however, entered war service, the vice-president of the Association left the field of police service, and Mrs. Wells generously carried on the work of the Association until the 1919 conference.

During the years 1916 to 1919 the attention of the members and of the officers of the Association, as happened generally in organizations of this character, was directed to activities connected with the World War. At its first Annual Meeting after the war, held in Atlantic City, in June, 1919, the discussion of the few members present was based on experience gained in the protective work during the war.[4] Under the Chairmanship of Miss Maude E. Miner (Mrs. Alexander Hadden) a section of the Conference of Social Work considered the relation of the police to delinquent and near-delinquent women and girls. It strongly urged that women should deal with the problems of such women and girls. At a session of the Annual Meeting of the Association it was moved that such workers should be regularly appointed women police and not officers

[3] For instance, ''Nineteenth Century,'' June, 1914, and ''Women Police,'' Women's Freedom League, 144 High Holborn Street, London, 4-page undated pamphlet.
[4] See Chapter VII.

of private protective associations with police powers.[5]

Former annual meetings had informally endorsed the creation of women's divisions in police departments. This session was the first to recommend, in the form of a motion, the establishment of a Woman's Bureau in each department which should be headed by a woman director.

The Association at this meeting elected as its President, Lieutenant Mina C. Van Winkle, Director of the Woman's Bureau of the Metropolitan Police Department of Washington, D. C.[6] One of the first official acts of the new president was to send out a questionnaire for the purpose of securing information on the status of the work of women police throughout the country. A Tentative Digest of the replies to the inquiry was presented to the 1920 Annual Meeting held in New Orleans.[7] This report added impetus to the growing movement, and a Committee was appointed to study and report on the functions of the parole officer, the probation officer, the protective officer, and the women police with particular reference to their respective places in a community plan for the prevention of delinquency. The report was presented at the meeting of the National Probation Association held in Milwaukee during the 1921 Conference of

[5] Minutees of the 1919 Conference.
[6] Chapter IX, Washington, D. C.
[7] *Tentative Digest of the Work of Women Police in the United States and Canada.* A second questionnaire was sent out in 1922-1924. The information is now being compiled by the Association, Star Building, Washington, D. C.

Social Work.[8] This meeting was attended by persons working in all four groups. Acting on this report it was moved that the sense of the meeting was that where women police are trained social workers preliminary investigations made by them should be accepted by the Juvenile Courts, and that probation officers should be responsible for follow-up work in probation cases after court action.[9]

The 1922 Conference held in Providence, Rhode Island, indicated that women police had reached a significant place in the field of social work.[10] Speakers discussed the work of the woman police officer in cooperation with probation departments and with institutions caring for delinquents, her methods of work and her contribution to general child welfare and protective and preventive social measures in relation to delinquency.

In this same year, Lieutenant Van Winkle, as President of the Association, was invited by Lady Astor to go to England to assist the English women interested in saving the principle of women officers in police departments which was jeopardized by the Geddes Report.[11] During this visit Mrs. Van Winkle studied the movement in England and in some of the Continental countries where women police are employed.

[8] This report with some modifications appeared in the *Journal of Social Hygiene,* 370 Seventh Avenue, New York City. Single copies 10c. June, 1924, under the title, ''Functions of Police Women'' by Henrietta Additon.

[9] Communicated by Lieutenant Mina C. Van Winkle, April 6, 1925.

[10] *The Survey,* July, 1922.

[11] See Chapter I, Women Patrols.

In the 1923 Washington Meeting the Association reaffirmed the principle for which it had stood.[12] Here a resolution was adopted affirming the belief of the association that: (a) ''Where women are employed in a police department they shall function in one unit as a Woman's Bureau, and shall have a woman in charge who shall be known as the director of the Woman's Bureau and shall be immediately responsible to the Chief of Police, or to the Commissioner of Police, or to the Commissioner of Public Safety, and she shall have rank equal with other such officers as are immediately subordinate to him.'' (b) ''That policewomen shall carry out a preventive and protective program which will include social protection of women and children.'' (c) ''That policewomen shall deal with all cases in which women and children are involved, either as offenders or as victims of offenses.''

The formal and more general activities of this Association have been limited by the fact that its officers and members have been compelled to concentrate their efforts and their time on the building up in their own communities of the work of women police. The two presidents, Mrs. Wells and Mrs. Van Winkle, have both given unstintingly of their time, during their incumbencies, to forward the movement. The ten annual conferences have provided the possibility of interchange of thought on the various phases of the work and the printed re-

[12] Bulletin No. 2, May, 1924, International Association of Policewomen.

ports of addresses are of value to the students of the movement in this country. In addition to the responses for general lectures and advice on the subject of women police, the Association has attempted, so far as its limited funds would permit, to act as a clearing house for information and for the placing of women officers.

The present president has continuously sought help from other groups interested in this movement, notably the General Federation of Women's Clubs, the Bureau of Social Hygiene and the American Social Hygiene Association.

Through its Committee on Institutional Relations of the Division of Social and Industrial Conditions of the Department of Public Welfare, Lieutenant Van Winkle appeared on the Program of the General Federation of Women's Clubs at its Bi-annual Meeting in 1924, at which meeting it was "resolved that the General Federation of Women's Clubs cooperate with the International Association of Policewomen, in the development of Women's Bureaus in Police Departments, officered and manned by trained women."[13]

Miss Julia Jaffray, Chairman of the Committee on Problems of Delinquency, is now working through this committee to create intelligent consideration by women's clubs of the work of police-women.[14]

The American Social Hygiene Association, par-

[13] Communicated by Miss Julia Jaffray, Chairman of the Committee.

[14] Formerly the Committee on Institutional Relations.

ticularly through its Departments of Protective and Legal Measures, has been interested in the woman police as an important factor in a community program for the protection of its young people and for the prevention of delinquency.

The International Association of Policewomen has accepted the cooperation of the American Social Hygiene Association in this part of the program. The Annual Meeting of the International Association of Policewomen, held in Toronto, June, 1924, authorized the appointment of a committee of six whose functions should include the formulation of a plan of cooperation with the American Social Hygiene Association and other organizations in an endeavor to enlarge the field of activity of women police.

This Committee of Six has revised the constitution and outlined definite policies of action which were accepted at the annual meeting held in Denver, Colorado, in June, 1925.

Acting on the authority granted at the Toronto Conference, the President with the advice of the Committee of Six appointed a Field-Executive Secretary to carry out a constructive program of work in the field in cooperation with other organizations.[15] An office is maintained in Washington, D. C., where information and advice may be obtained.[16]

[15] Dr. Mary B. Harris (resigned July 1, 1925), International Association of Policewomen, Evening Star Building, Washington, D. C., Room 420, Pennsylvania Avenue and 11th Street.

[16] International Association of Policewomen. Minutes 1924 Annual Meeting.

At the Annual Conference of Social Work, held in Toronto, Canada, in June, 1924, the Association of Policewomen was for the first time an integral part of the General Conference. They held their meetings in the group of agencies for the prevention and treatment of delinquency, and their special group meetings were arranged as were those of related groups.

The 1924 Annual Meeting re-elected Lieutenant Van Winkle as President. Deputy Commissioner Eleonore L. Hutzel, Director of the Women's Division of the Detroit Police Department, was elected Vice President, and Police Officer Ruth Saunders, of the Richmond, Virginia Force, was made Secretary-Treasurer. In addition to these officers, seven regional directors were chosen.[17]

The Constitution as revised by the Committee of Six, sets forth as the objects of the Association "to fix standards for the service of policewomen, to secure the appointment of qualified policewomen, to encourage the establishment of Women's Bureaus in Police Departments and to promote such service internationally."

The Constitution as revised provides that membership shall be open to official women police, policematrons, and interested individuals; that an executive committee composed of the officers of the Association shall be responsible for the fiscal policy; that there shall be seven regional directors who shall be qualified women police in active service and

[17] Minutes, 1924 Annual Meeting.

an International Council of not less than 50 members who shall advise with the officers on request. The Committe of Six will act in an advisory capacity.

The present membership of the Association numbers at least 179 of which the majority are women police in active service. The Association's annual dues are $1.00 and subscription to the Monthly Bulletin is $1.50 in addition.

Chapter XI

COMMUNITY PROBLEMS AND THE POLICE

Legitimate police functions—Public agencies—Private protective agencies—The police department: Women police.

The average person accepts the police departments as a part of the established order of things, and their functions as static. As a matter of fact, the police are a fairly recent institution and many changes have occurred in their functions. The modern police force of the Metropolis of London dates only from 1828. This was the first modern urban police force in the world. The man police officer was first a volunteer, then inadequately paid by a committee and finally employed full time on full pay and forbidden to engage in other remunerative work.[1]

Thus the modern police developed from a group of civilians with no qualified administrative head and no definite organization or discipline to a semi-military body with a trained directing head whose business it is to create an organization and to maintain discipline.

[1] *Police Administration*—Leonhard Felix Fuld.

Legitimate Police Functions

Today among the activities which are accepted as legitimate functions of the police are the protection of life and property, the preservation of public order and the prevention and detection of crime. There is an increasing tendency to accept as a matter of course, the punitive functions of the police, and to place the larger emphasis on the preventive functions.[2] Indeed, there is a rapidly growing sentiment that the ultimate goal of all police work should be the prevention of crime and delinquency.

The preventive function of the police may be compared to the same function as exercised by health officials. These latter recognize, in a program for the prevention of communicable diseases, two primary factors: (a) The protection of the individual susceptible to a disease from contact (exposure) with persons suffering from it, and (b) the dissemination of information relating to the manner in which this disease can be prevented. These

[2] See: Leonard Dunning (Oxford Graduate, 12 years District Inspector of Police in Ireland; Assistant Head Constable, Liverpool, England, for 9 years; 10 years Head Constable in Liverpool, and since 1912, one of H. M. Inspectors of Constabulary), A. Par. 17. Reports of the Committees on the Employment of Women on Police Duties. Cmd. *877* and Cmd. *2224.* Richard E. Enright, Commissioner of Police, New York City, since January, 1918, Annual Reports, 1920-1922. Arthur Woods, Commissioner of Police, New York City, April, 1914, to January, 1918, *Crime Prevention*, Princeton University Press, Princeton, 1918, price $1.00. Leonhard Felix Fuld, *Police Administration*, 1909, G. P. Putnam's Sons, New York. Raymond B. Fosdick, *American Police Systems*, Century Company, New York City, Constitution, Article 1, Section 2, International Association of Chiefs of Police.

measures are embodied in a well rounded constructive health program.

This same reasoning can be applied to the anti-social diseases of crime and delinquency, efforts for whose prevention are within the scope of police activities.[3] There are persons who for some reason —voluntary or involuntary—are criminals and delinquents and there are social conditions which experience has taught us are conducive to anti-social conduct.

Preventive and protective social measures are thus concerned on the one hand with the protection of children and young people against contact with anti-social conditions and with persons known to be criminal or delinquent, and on the other hand with constructive activities which are believed to provide immunity to crime and delinquency. Both parts of this program—the preventive and protective—are necessary and are not far from being equally difficult in their execution.

In order to understand more clearly the possible contribution of the police in the effective discharge of these functions, it is desirable to survey briefly the social agencies whose program of work embraces activities which can be considered as preventive and protective social measures in relation to delinquency, and specifically, in the United States, to

[3] Anti-social conduct is that which hinders the development of groups and of their individual members in accordance with standards which are generally accepted by the group as normal physically, morally and intellectually. Thus what would be anti-social in one group, might not be so in another.

know the accepted functions of these agencies where they actively operate.[4]

PUBLIC AGENCIES [5]

SCHOOLS

The first definitely preventive and protective public activity is encountered in the schools, which have instituted attendance officers, visiting nurses and, during the past few years, particularly in the elementary schools, the visiting teacher, and, in the secondary schools, advisors or deans for boys and girls. Still more recently the school psychiatrist has appeared on the scene and is increasingly considered an essential factor in the correct social diagnosis, and hence, in the treatment side, of the preventive and protective program.

The concern of the school attendance officer is the children who absent themselves from school. His duty is to apply the school attendance laws.

The primary functions of the visiting nurses are: (a) to examine children on entry, either direct or through transfer into the school to which she is attached; (b) To examine children referred to her

[4] In no one locality do all—and in some localities none—of these agencies function satisfactorily. In actual practice public and private agencies may perform the same tasks. In this brief general presentation only the "high spots" are discussed.

[5] In this brief survey those accepted health agencies whose educational activities in pre-natal, first infancy and childhood care have a direct bearing on the physical vigor of young people which in itself forms the foundation of all social efforts, are not considered, for the police, as such, are not concerned with their program.

by teacher or principal as possibly ill; (c) To visit children reported by parents or attendance officer as retained at home by illness. In this last situation her province is to satisfy herself whether or not the child is really ill, and if so, to insure the proper medical attention through the family physician, or a physician attached to the proper health service.

The attendance officer and the school nurse found that they were not able to control the fundamental causal factors of absence from school, be the direct reason illness, ignorance or willful neglect on the part of the parents. Further, numbers of children were yearly failing either to adjust themselves to school discipline and were becoming problems in the field of delinquency, or did not advance to a higher grade. In the efforts to find a solution to these problems, the school introduced the psychologists. After several years of experimenting the psychologists found that this maladjustment could not be dismissed with an intelligence test alone, but that if school discipline were to be maintained, and anti-social conduct prevented, the unadjusted child must become the object of very special individual study and treatment in his home as well as inside the school.

It was at this point that the visiting teacher was considered essential.[6] She is a trained social case-

---

[6] *The Problem Child in School.* Narratives from Case Records of visiting teachers, by Mary B. Sayles, with a ''Description of the purpose and scope of visiting teachers' work,'' by H. W. Nudd. Price $1.00. *Joint Committee in the Prevention of Delinquency.* 50 East 42d Street, New York City.

worker to whom are referred for study and possible treatment those children who seem incapable of adjustment in school. Her function is to discover the causes of this maladjustment and to eradicate or overcome them as completely as possible. The science of mental hygiene has come to her aid in the person of another social agent—the psychiatrist— who is now quite generally contributing to the solution of the problems of unadjusted school children. The psychiatrist is first of all a physician who has graduated from an accepted medical school, and who has added to his basic medical training an extensive experience in the diagnosis and treatment of departures from mental health. He soon discovers that in most cases of maladjustment there exists definite emotional and physical as well as intellectual causal factors. The function therefore of the psychiatrist is to study the individual child in the light of his whole make-up, physical, mental and emotional.[7]

PLAYGROUNDS

School, city, and privately administered playgrounds provide for school and adolescent children wholesome, constructive and wise recreational activities which are unquestionably vital factors in any program for the prevention of delinquency.

[7] *Personality and Social Adjustment*, Ernest R. Groves, Longmans, Green and Co., 1923; price $1.40. *Your Mind and You—Mental Health*—Dr. George K. Pratt, Funk & Wagnalls, New York City, 1924; 30c.

COURTS

In spite of these efforts numbers of children find their way to the Juvenile Courts.[8] The Judge in formulating his sentence is deeply influenced by the physicians' reports on mental and physical conditions which are considered a most important part of the "evidence" in the case. The other public agents attached to the court and concerned with the prevention of delinquency and readjustment of the delinquent, are the court investigator and probation officer, often one and the same person. The investigation, in principle, includes the study of the social condition of the individual with the idea of finding those elements which may provide a basis for an adjustment looking toward the rehabilitation of the individual and his return to society as a useful, happy, and self-respecting member.[9] If he is placed on probation the same officer who made the investigation may act as probation officer. His function is to help the individual to properly adjust himself to his personal and social environment. In many instances the environment must be changed, a duty which devolves upon the probation officer.

If an individual is sent to an institution and later released on parole a new officer comes into action—the parole officer. His obligation is to help the

[8] Youth in Conflict, Miriam Van Waters, Ph.D. The New Republic, Inc., 421 West 21st Street, New York City. (Paper cover, price $1.00; board cover, $1.50.)
[9] The same general system applies to courts for women and girls over the juvenile court age.

parolee to find his rightful place in the economic and
social life of the community, either as a member of
a family or as an individual member of society.

The roster of public agencies in this field would
be incomplete without the mention of the Children's
Bureau which was established in 1912 in the Federal
Department of Labor and Commerce. Quite logi-
cally its early undertakings were concerned with
the study of child labor in its many phases. This
branch of the government service has now made
its own place and it is doubtful if the public thinks
of it in other terms than the Federal Children's
Bureau and as though it had an independent administrative existence. Perusal of its publications
list shows clearly that its activities have been
oriented in the direction of preventive and protective social measures.

Private Protective Agencies

Not only in New York City and in other large
cities in the United States, but in numberless
smaller towns, in addition to the officers paid by the
government and selected by civil service examinations, private religious associations maintain officers
at the juvenile and, frequently, at the other courts.
These associations are known under such names as
"Big Brothers" and "Big Sisters" and ordinarily
represent the 3 religious faiths, Catholicism,
Judaism, and Protestantism. The intent of the functions of these officers is exactly the same as those

performed by the government agents but with more emphasis on church affiliations.

Privately administered institutions—religious or lay—for delinquents also maintain parole officers whose functions are similar to those of parole officers who are paid agents of the state.

In addition to the agents functioning from the schools, courts and institutions for delinquents, there are goodly numbers of persons working from and through a wide variety of private public service institutions which may be designated under the general term of "preventive and protective social agencies."

Among the more generally known preventive and protective social agencies in addition to other religious and church groups, one finds the Young Men's and Young Women's Christian and Hebrew Associations, the Catholic Associations; the Societies for the Prevention of Cruelty to Children, the Children's Aid Societies, the Travelers' Aid Societies, and an ever-increasing social force in associations known under such names as the Juvenile Protective Association; Girls' Protective League, and the Girls' Service League of America.

The work of the religious organizations is similar in character and is notably protective and preventive. They seek to throw around the adolescent, influences which are conducive to clean living and thinking and thus prevent antisocial conduct.

Such organizations as the Children's Aid Societies and the Societies for the Prevention of

Cruelty to Children, in so far as they remove children from unwholesome influences, can undoubtedly be classed among agencies for the protection of children against possible delinquency.

In the United States during 1923, the Travelers' Aid Society through 133 of its local branches extended aid to 1,840,923 persons arriving at the railway and steamship terminals. At least 99,259 of these were under sixteen and 180,221 persons were between sixteen and twenty-five years of age. A proportion of these might easily have become offenders against the law or victims of the unscrupulous if timely aid had not been extended to them.[10] One might say that the function of the Travelers' Aid Society in relation to children and young girls traveling unaccompanied by older people and who show evidence either of a definite desire to escape notice or of seeking information or of bewilderment, is preventive and protective in the sense of our basic definitions.

Many of the private organizations occupy places of high trust and the general lay public often, quite likely, does not differentiate their functions to any great degree from those of public agencies. However, in the execution and in the conception of their functions there is a difference.

Two marked dissimilarities are the limitations in program making and the choice of individuals in whose favor they may direct their efforts. The

[10] National Travelers' Aid Bulletin, May, 1924. National Association of Travelers' Aid Societies, 25 West 43d Street, New York City.

government institutions, schools, courts and custodial or re-educational institutions must deal with all individuals who come within the scope of the duties imposed upon them by society and which are clearly outlined by law. The private agencies can limit their activities and can choose how many and what types of individuals shall become the objects of their investigation and treatment.

Those associations, in this country, which we have designated as private protective agencies, combine certain characteristics of the other agencies already discussed with some special features of their own. Administratively they may not be governed by a church although quite often distinctly religious in tone and manifesting the highest regard and respect for the church.

Three lines of endeavor are in general followed by these private protective agencies. Some of them act as receiving centers where any girls who have problems may find a friend.[11] She may come of her own volition, or she may be sent by a third person, who, at times, may ask the officer of the association to call on the girl in her home. In either event, the association functions as an agency doing personal individual work with girls.[12] Other protective associations, in addition to this work, provide, in their own buildings, limited temporary sleeping quarters and wholesome constructive

[11] One hears very little of private protective agencies, as such, for boys.

[12] The Girls' Protective League, 9 Cadillac Square, Detroit, Mich., is a good example of this type of organization.

recreation and study facilities in the form of clubs for the adolescent girl.[13]

A third group of agencies which may or may not engage in one or both of the above activities are primarily interested in community conditions which influence inevitably the conduct of growing boys and girls, or as Dr. William F. Snow might put it "in growing humans." [14] Public recreation—municipally or privately owned and administered, free or commercial, juvenile court procedure, detention facilities for young girls, women and children accused of delinquency or crime or merely abandoned or neglected, are some of the things which claim the attention of such organizations.[15]

In addition to these agencies, there are large numbers of social settlements and small clubs and groups within the churches as well as the Boy and Girl Scout movements, all of which are engaged in providing for the adolescent boy and girl the educational recreation which is advocated as a potent factor in the prevention of juvenile delinquency.

It might seem that with the multiplicity of "organizations" there could not possibly be even a small fraction of a function left unprovided for. But does the general program of functions being dis-

[13] The Girls' Service Club of New York well illustrates this particular feature of protective work.

[14] California's New Industry, *Growing Humans*, William F. Snow, M.D., November, 1910. Bulletin of California State Board of Health.

[15] Among these organizations may be cited the Juvenile Protective Association of Chicago, the Women's Protective Association of Cleveland, Ohio, and the Women's Cooperative Alliance of Minneapolis, Minnesota.

charged by these already existing social agencies
cover all the essentials in a thoroughly effective
attack on the problems of the prevention of juvenile
delinquency and crime?

With the possible exception of the recreation
supervisors and the agents of the Travelers' Aid
Society, the private agencies which we have discussed have two characteristics in common: (a)
The individuals whose welfare forms the object of
their activities are persons who come to their
attention in the routine of their work. In rare instances the individual may come of his own volition
and practically never do the organizations actively
reach out individuals as such, although perhaps,
constantly promoting their program in public;
(b) The worker rarely has direct legal authority
by which he can protect the individual either against
the results of his own ignorance or misguided in-
stincts or against exploitation by unscrupulous
persons.

The great problems then of the preventive and
protective agencies have been and are, first, the
fact that too often the individual does not come to
them until he has passed the state where he is yet
susceptible to voluntary constructive character
building and, second, the continued persistence of
those social conditions which contribute to the
undermining of the individual character.

Thus in the field of prevention of delinquency, the
general functions which are not yet satisfactorily
solved by these agencies are:

(1) Active searching out of individuals who are in danger of becoming official delinquents either as offenders or as victims coupled with the actual securing of their withdrawal from such surroundings and their placement in contact with positive constructive protective and preventive social forces.

(2) Searching out and classifying general social conditions which contribute to delinquency.

(3) Study and proposal, and the enforcement of remedies for these conditions.

THE POLICE DEPARTMENT

The only public body already legally constituted in *all* communities whose functions do include *all* of these duties is the Police Department. Its personnel is at present largely composed of men officers.

WOMEN POLICE

The appointment of women to police forces has been advocated as one means of securing a more effective execution of preventive functions as suggested on page 204. A goodly number of the directing heads of police forces and many policemen have opposed such appointments. In the United States no concerted opposition has arisen within police departments, whose attitude has been rather that women have yet to prove themselves good police officers. There has been an organized movement in Great Britain where the Police Federations of

England, Wales, and Scotland have placed themselves on record as opposed to women police. Their action in each instance, according to the testimony of its promoters, has been motivated by the fear that the entry of women into police forces would militate against the welfare of the men (A-1558 ff.).

It is in vain that one searches for evidence which indicates that such opposition arises because of administrative difficulties (A-344 et ff.). The evidence shows that the average policeman considers as "police duties" the strictly punitive functions and they are, therefore, convinced that women are not fitted for police duties. Advocates of women police reply that where women have proved themselves unfitted it is either because the wrong type of woman has been chosen, or because they have been ordered to perform duty as punitive agents— a duty for which they are neither fitted nor desirous of executing.

Dispassionate study of available documents discloses that in but rare instances have women police been appointed for the execution of a definitely outlined program of work. Under such conditions, it is perhaps not fair to class ineffective work as a complete failure. It has been said that women police have not always cheerfully executed the orders of superior officers, when such orders were contrary to what they held to be their moral obligations; a situation which might create some administrative adjustments. It is a question whether this fact should be used as an argument solely against the appointment of women police, or also in favor of the creation of a more socialized police practice.

It is particularly important to keep clearly in mind that in those countries where the appointment of women police has received serious consideration the promoters have invariably stressed the fact that women should be used *primarily* in the execution of the preventive functions of the police.

This attitude seems to have been determined not only by the fact that women police produced excellent results in this branch of the service during the war, but that they are by nature fitted to assume those functions whose chief concern is with the conduct of young people and particularly with that of young girls and children.

Social conditions are forcing an ever-increasing number of women and young girls out of the seclusion and security of home life and supervision into the whirlpool of the public world.[16] This situation demands conscious social guidance. The scale of pay, the conditions of work and the long wait for possible promotion in police departments have not been such as to attract men of unusual training, qualifications or ideals for the *prevention* of delinquency. They have been selected for an entirely different type of duty, whose chief concern is the protection of life and property and the preservation of public order.

[16] "The Work of a Policewoman," Eleonore L. Hutzel, *Proceedings 1919 Annual Meeting of the American Prison Association.*

In addition to the statement that women are fitted by nature to assume these duties, a second reason for their appointment is advanced. The great bulk of the work in the proposed preventive and protective measures program, is concerned with individual women, adolescent boys and girls and younger children.

In public as well as in private social service agencies the method of dealing with individuals commonly known as "case-work" has been tacitly adopted as the mode of procedure—a form of work for which women are peculiarly fitted when it involves the social adjustment of girls, women and children.[17] Today they form by far the largest percentage of such case workers. Men have not yet professionally entered this form of work in great numbers, and there is no indication that they will do so in the near future.[18] It is maintained that for this reason alone the entry of women into police departments is particularly essential if a preventive program is to be effectively applied.

[17] Social Education of the Maternal Instinct, Mme. Pieczynska, Third International Congress of Moral Education, Geneva, 1923. *Rapports at Memoirs* Institut J. J. Rousseau, Taconnerie, 5—Geneva, Switzerland.

[18] For instance, nurses, visiting teachers, psychiatrists, probation and parole officers and the agents of myriads of private special agencies are notably women.

CHAPTER XII

PROGRAM OF WORK

*General Considerations—British Opinion—Opinion in
the United States—Present Tendencies in Program of
Work: The Information Service; The Patrol Service; general background, supervision of public conduct, "mashers," commercialized prostitution, procurers, traffic in
women and children, shoplifting, résumé of patrol service
—Investigation Service: missing persons; Court Service:
attendance at court, relation of court to probation—Detention Service—Paper Work—Résumé.*

GENERAL CONSIDERATION

Generally speaking the work of women police has
not *developed*; it has largely just happened. It has
shown certain traits and tendencies, however, which
with proper care and direction may produce a new
variety of police work which will have a marked influence on our social philosophy in relation to police
functions. For this reason society can well afford
to treat it seriously and to give it a fair chance for
a healthy development.

So far, the services of women police have been
largely directed toward, or used in the effort—con-

scious or not—to substitute a social control or guidance over the public conduct of young people who seem devoid of such direction or help from those persons directly responsible for their character training and their social conduct. There is, as yet, no body of reliable, tested, related factual experiments which can serve as a basis for a universal program of work for women police.

In those countries where social conditions are similar in the different localities, and particularly in those countries where the police are either officers of the central government or partially subjected to its control or supervision, it is possible that all of the women police might follow a uniform program of work.

In the United States, police functions, with few exceptions, are exercised by individual municipalities or states. Further, no community resembles another either in its delinquency problems or in its organized facilities to cope with them. These two conditions render it nearly impossible, and certainly impractical, at present, to propose one program of activities for women police which could be universally applicable.

BRITISH OPINION

No country, with the possible exception of Great Britain, has attempted officially to formulate such a general program. And on close scrutiny this program resolves itself into a listing of possible duties and which, admittedly, will not be the same in all communities.

Withdrawn from the political, social and philosophical considerations which form their setting, the recommendations from the two Home Office Committees appointed to study the employment of women on public duties, are that women should be appointed to police departments to perform such duties as: interviewing of women and children involved in police cases, particularly those of indecent assault; conducting the necessary investigations and preparing the evidence in such cases; attending court when women and children are tried; supervising: (a) employment agencies, (b) licensed lodging houses, (c) public parks and open spaces, (d) public amusement places, acting as policematrons when women and children are detained by the police and where this would not be against the interests of men officers, performing clerical duties.[1]

This list of duties with a few additions, and with some reservations particularly in relation to clerical duties, has been quite universally endorsed by interested persons in Great Britain and the Dominions.[2]

OPINION IN THE UNITED STATES

No such thorough study as that in Great Britain has been made in the United States. Published

[1] Report of Committee, 1920 (Cmd. 877), Par. 14, 20, 21, 22, 27, 28. Report of Committee, 1924 (Cmd. 2224).

[2] Sir William Horwood, A. 29; Council of Women of Great Britain and Ireland, Reports and Publications. Parliament Mansions, Victoria Street, S. W. 1, London; The Women's Auxiliary Service, 7 Rochester Row, Westminster, S. W. 1, London, Reports and Publications.

opinions even are not numerous. Several experiments have been made, or are under way, but the vastness of the territory involved and the differences in social conditions and points of view encountered have militated against rapid progress in the formulation of a standardized program of work for women police. At present there exists a forceful effort toward concerted action by those interested in the healthy growth of the movement. There is in reality so great a similarity in the programs proposed here and in Great Britain that, for practical discussion, one may consider them, in the main, as identical.[3]

In these two, and in most other countries, the fundamental principle in the formulation of the duties of women police, has seemed to be that women and girls, as well as men, who find themselves in any situation requiring or involving the advice or intervention of the police department, should have the possibility of attention from police officers of their own sex.

[3] *The Functions of Policewomen*, Henrietta Additon, Journal of Social Hygiene, June, 1924, 370 Seventh Avenue, New York City. Policewomen Here to Stay, H. B. Rogers, *Police Journal*, 110 West 54th Street, New York City, October, 1923, price 30 cents. Purpose and Scope of a Woman's Bureau, Mina C. Van Winkle, *Police Journal*, November, 1922. Work of a Policewoman, Eleonore L. Hutzel, *Proceedings Prison Association Conference*, 1919. The Policewoman—Her Service and Ideals, Mary E. Hamilton, New York; Frederick A. Stokes, 1924. Woman's Place in the Police Plan, Mary E. Driscoll, *Policewoman's News*, November-December, 1920. Metropolitan Police Department, Washington, D. C. Manual 1923.

Present Tendencies in Program of Work

In several cities in the United States where all the women members of the police force have functioned in a regularly constituted woman's division under the direct supervision of a woman, the tendency has been to follow a program of work which involves several distinct services such as: Information, Patrol, Investigation, Court, Detention and Paper.

THE INFORMATION SERVICE

The Information Service acts as a clearing house for organizations or individuals seeking advice or service on matters falling within the scope of police departments.

It is advocated that, in smaller communities, a woman officer be at the desk at some one hour or period of the day and which should be known to the community. At this time she could do the desk and office tasks required in her day's routine. Special provisions could be made for the handling of emergency cases.[4]

PATROL SERVICE

General Background: The varied activities of women police on patrol elude definite codification

4 In Detroit a woman officer is on duty at the information desk from 8:30 A.M. to 7 P.M. Between 7 P.M. and 8:30 A.M., complaints or other matters are taken care of by the officer on duty in the Investigation Department. A skilled officer at the information desk in that city during 1924, disposed of fifty per cent of the cases coming to her attention, either by giving the advice sought, or by referring the visitor to the social agency best equipped to render the service required.

or even detailed formulation.[5] One writer has caught them in a colorful description, "The Police-woman," she says "must walk about the streets where the bright lights, jazz band and the very atmosphere prove to be so alluring to the very young girl. She must watch out for this young girl and apprehend[6] her when she first plays truant from her work or school to go to the moving picture house or dance hall. She must locate the large group of children that are to be seen upon the streets begging, and bring about the social treatment needed with these cases."

She "must be on duty at night observing upon the streets and in the parks, watching out for the runaway girl, the street-walker, and the commercialized woman [prostitute] who solicits for her trade upon the public streets . . . she must be friendly and helpful to the unfortunate drug fiend and derelict and to the forlorn outcast who walks upon the streets."

It is generally conceded that these *are* legitimate functions of women police on patrol, as well as others, such as continuous supervision of dance halls and general amusement places including motion pictures and burlesque shows. Each community has its unwholesome and questionable public amusement places, known under a variety of names, and which are susceptible to general supervision by women

[5] For description of such activities in Detroit, Michigan, and Washington, D. C., see Chapters VIII and IX.

[6] "Apprehend" is a strong term. "Counsel" is more in accord with actual practice.

police on patrol. That which actually characterizes the women and men patrol officers among social agents in the field of preventive and protective measures in delinquency, and which is their distinct contribution, is that they are *legally* charged with the *active* searching out of conditions which tend to produce juvenile delinquency and those minors who frequent places where these conditions obtain.

They can be of inestimable value to other social agencies whose functions have already been outlined. They can materially assist the work of each if close cooperation is given all along the line. For instance, they can aid the attendance officer in his work with those minors habitually truant from school. They can supervise as no probation or parole officer can do, those probationers who are inclined to frequent questionable public amusement places at night. The visiting teacher may find that one of the great difficulties in the adjustment of a school child lies in the conduct of an older sister or brother over whom she nor any other social agent except the woman police officer has either control or influence.

Most workers in private protective social agencies welcome heartily the presence of women patrol officers for whom they have long felt the need.

Supervision of Public Conduct: There is a marked tendency toward using women patrols to supervise and control the social conduct between the sexes. Their exact relation to problems of public indecency, misdemeanors, such as solicitation, in

public places for the purposes of prostitution, and,
the more serious crime of traffic in women and children is as yet undefined.

Their activities in this field require actually so
large a proportion of their time, that they deserve
special consideration here. This is not the place,
however, to attempt to discover why boys and girls
of today have markedly free and easy relationships,
which are often in bad taste and which, at times,
result in open disregard of public decency and in
individual unhappiness. Nor is it the place to discuss possible remedies for such conditions. These
two subjects must be left to sociologists, educators,
philosophers, and social and mental hygienists.[7]
The important point here is that a great proportion
of the girls under eighteen years of age who are
brought before the courts, have had some sex experience—a fact which women police are called
upon to face and which today forms invariably the
prime factor in the demands of women's organizations in any given community for the appointment
of women police.

The practical question is how far are women police
to go in handling this situation. Shall it be her
duty, while on patrol, to interfere actively in the

[7] Your Mind and You—Mental Health—George K. Pratt, M.D.
(Chaps. 1, 5, 6, 7 and 8), Funk & Wagnalls, New York, 1923; 30
cents. The Sex Factor in Human Life, American Social Hygiene
Association, 370 Seventh Avenue, New York City, 1921; price $1.25.
Mental Hygiene and the College Student, Frankwood E. Williams,
M.D.; Paper No. 1. Mental Hygiene. April, 1921; paper No. 2.
Mental Hygiene, April, 1925. 370 Seventh Avenue, New York City.
Changes in Social Thought and Standards which Affect the Family,
Porter R. Lee. *Proceedings, Conference of Social Work*, 1923.

public social conduct of young people when they are not actually breaking a law, but when their actions are such as to predicate in her mind, in the near future, delinquency before the law?[8] Both in Great Britain and in the United States the answer has been affirmative. Naturally this is a delicate task and one requiring very special qualities and tact in the woman who undertakes it.[9] To carry it out successfully requires that the community should offer adequate means for wholesome recreation[10] and proper facilities for sex social education in the schools.[11] These constructive measures are absolutely essential in the handling of the situation.

Subway Mashers: A second task in this domain which has at times been performed by women police is that of suppressing the activities of "mashers" who operate ordinarily in crowded public conveyances. There is divergence of opinion and feeling both as to the utility and the advisability of assigning women police to this duty. As yet no

[8] This raises the question as to whose and what "standards" of conduct are to serve as a basis for action by the woman police officer in any given situation—a question which demands a thorough and impartial discussion. (See footnote 7.)

[9] See type of women desirable, Chapter XIII.

[10] The Playground and Recreation Association of America, 315 Fourth Avenue, New York City. *Normal Course in Play* (Chapter I. The Community Recreation Program); price $2.00. *Why a Year Round Recreation System* (free on application). *The Theory of Organized Play* (Chapter II, The Present Need for Organized Play). Bowen & Mitchell, A. S. Barnes & Co., New York City, $2.40.

[11] *The Teacher and Sex Education,* by B. C. Gruenberg, Ph.D., American Social Hygiene Association, 370 Seventh Avenue, New York City, 1924; 25 cents. *High Schools and Sex Education,* B. C. Gruenberg, Ph.D., Public Health Service and Bureau of Education, Washington, Government Printing Office, 1922; 50 cents. *Sex Education,* Maurice A. Bigelow, New York, Macmillan, 1919; price $1.60.

fixed methods have been worked out to handle this situation.

Commercialized Prostitution: There is by no means unanimity of opinion on the question of the employment of women police for the enforcement of laws relating to commercialized prostitution. Indeed, there is extreme divergence of opinion as to how far the police force, as such, should go in attempting to suppress prostitution.[12] One thing only is quite clear—the police force will go no further than active public opinion actually demands.

Inside the police departments themselves the method of dealing with commercial prostitution depends on the laws, ordinances and regulations of the particular city or state. The evidence required varies in different courts and therefore the methods of procedure are not similar. The enforcement of such laws generally devolves on a special group within the police.[13] The ordinary police work in this domain embraces the following activities: (a) Observation on the streets, in hotel lobbies

[12] "As far as the organized police force of a city is concerned, not prostitution itself . . . should be punishable . . . but all such manifestations of it as properly belong under the head of public nuisance—street walking, soliciting from windows, prostitution in tenement houses." Police Administration, Leonhard Felix Fuld, page 406; Niles, Alfred S., The Police Department and the Social Problem. *Proceedings National Conference of Charities and Corrections,* 1915.

[13] Specialized Courts Dealing with Sex Delinquency—A Study of the Procedure in Chicago, Boston, Philadelphia and New York, George E. Worthington and Ruth Topping; Frederick H. Hitchcock, New York, 1925. "Under present conditions practically all sex delinquents are brought to court by the police. . . . The majority of such arrests are made by members of the Special Plain Clothes Division of the Police Department."

or elsewhere of women soliciting men; (b) the arrest of such women as are seen soliciting several different men; (c) visiting, for the purpose of obtaining evidence of prostitution, the rooms or other localities where the woman has taken her supposed client and (d) evidence that taxi chauffeurs, bell-hops, elevator or telephone operators in hotels or apartment houses, or other persons are "go-betweens" for prostitutes.

Will society in the long run gain or lose by the assignment to these duties of women officers? With the small number of women police actually on duty in our cities today, can their services be utilized to greater effect elsewhere? Experiments have not yet yielded answers to these questions which are either satisfactory or final.

Those advocating the definite assignment of women police for such duties are influenced by such considerations as: (a) the protection of men officers against a too constant contact with prostitutes (179); (b) the fear of false accusation by prostitutes against men officers; (c) a more strict and equitable enforcement of laws relating to prostitution which, it is maintained, would eliminate more successfully solicitation in public where it may result in the delinquency of young people (2453); (d) the protection of inexperienced youth against solicitation by prostitutes (2528).

The arguments used against the assignment of women officers to these duties are: (a) that the special contribution of women in police departments is in the direct prevention of delinquency among young persons and that the number of women officers is too small even for this duty; (b) that the confirmed commercial prostitute rarely changes her way of living except for reasons more profound than the possible influence of a woman officer or other women; (c) that "they (the experienced and hardened prostitutes) would at once turn around and try to molest the women police" (1185); (d) that the women officers would soon lose their power of effectiveness in the duties for whose execution they are on the whole best qualified;[14] (e) that without an honest willingness on the part of decent citizens to face the whole question of prostitution, women officers would probably be little more effective than are men officers.[15]

In the United States, the situation in Detroit illustrates some of the problems encountered by the police in the effort to enforce the ordinances concerning commercialized prostitution, and shows the actual attitude of the women police. In order to convict a woman in Detroit as a common prostitute, it is necessary that the man who was a party to the act testify that he had sexual intercourse with the woman and that he has paid her for it.[16]

[14] It is feared that the constant dealing with "repeaters," often hardened, would inevitably build up a technique and an attitude of mind detrimental in the handling of young persons.

[15] "What we have got to get people to accept is the fundamental idea that prostitution is a dirty bad habit and thoroughly bad form, and unsocial and cruel." Miss Neilans, *Proceedings Imperial Wembley Congress of Social Hygiene*, 1924, 120 Dean Street, Oxford Street, London, W. 1.

[16] The Statutes in Detroit, used by the Police Department in its

Very few men are willing to give this testimony. If the man is willing to testify and a conviction is secured the common practice is for the woman to appeal the case. The special clause in the Recorder's Court Law provides for an appeal for jury trial. "This necessitates a delay of several weeks with a result that by the time the case comes up on appeal the witness is seldom available." [17]

The Women's Division of the Detroit Police Department has always interested itself in the problem of prostitution, but it has not been active in the enforcement of the Disorderly Act, as the small number of women officers are needed to do protective work with young girls. Executives of the Department are of the opinion that men officers can enforce this act as well as women officers, and that an arrangement whereby young girls found by the men in disorderly houses are referred to the women for adjustment is at present the best solution. [18]

Since the organization of the Detroit Women's Division the director has worked and is now work-

efforts to control prostitution are: Disorderly Act, 7774—Public Acts 1915, under which women are charged as common prostitutes; Bawdy House 1571, Public Acts 1915; Enticing to become a prostitute, 15494, Public Acts 1915; Pandering, 389, Public Acts 1919; Injunction and Abatement; Soliciting ordinance effective October 20, 1924.

[17] The 1924 Report shows 19 arrests under the Bawdy House Act; no arrests were made for enticing; 66 arrests under the Pandering Act; 36 houses were closed under the Injunction and Abatement Act, and orders issued against three individuals.

[18] The Detention Quarters of Women are under the direction of the Women's Division, and inevitably each prostitute arrested by the men officers, thus passes—but only "passes" through the machinery of this division.

ing with other executives of the Department to secure more adequate statutes and to create an enlightened public opinion on this matter.

Procurers: Again, a fourth problem is that presented by the activities of procurers, particularly in relation to minors. There is common accord that this is not only a part of the preventive functions of the police, but rightly a special charge on the women officers on patrol.

Traffic in Women and Children: When procurers function between States they are classed as traffikers.[19] In the international bodies, created to study and to cope with the social aspects of commercialized sex relations, it is at present officially accepted as a basis of negotiation that prostitution *per se,* is a matter for national and not international control. It is, however, maintained that international traffic in women and children *is* a subject, whose treatment is susceptible to, and even requires a system of international control based on mutual acceptance of formulated principles.

In its international aspects it is warmly contended on both sides of the proposition that in those countries where houses of prostitution are licensed by and subject to the supervision and control of the police, these houses could not be kept filled with the countries' nationals alone and therefore they would inevitably become commercially unprofitable if their

---

[19] Such interstate traffic within the borders of the United States comes under the Mann White Slave Traffic Act, June 25, 1910; Public Acts of Congress No. 277.

owners were prohibited by law to employ prostitutes of alien nationality.[20]

The most advanced program for dealing with international traffic in women and children is the Convention of the Second Assembly of the League of Nations.[21] This Convention particularly provides for punishment—both in successful and unsuccessful attempts—of traffickers in women and in members of both sexes under twenty years of age. In the case of adult women this means prostitution by force or by fraud and in the case of minors with or without consent.

Articles 1, 2, 3 and 6 bind the contracting parties; to centralize all information on this subject, to maintain a supervision at points of embarkation and debarkation to the end of detecting traffickers, to record the declaration of women and girl prostitutes of foreign nationality and to supervise agencies recruiting women and girls for employment in foreign countries.

In the United States the authority placed in charge of this work is the Commissioner General of Immigration. There are no women officers in this

[20] League of Nations Publications; Advisory Committee on the Traffic in Women and Children, Geneva, Switzerland; Publications, International Bureau for the Suppression of Traffic in Women and Children, 2 Grosvenor Mansion, 76 Victoria St., London, S. W. 1.

[21] "This Convention has been signed by thirty-three states, eighteen of which have up to the moment ratified, and three states which have not signed the convention have adhered to it." Dame Rachel Crowdy, *Proceedings of the Imperial Social Hygiene Congress*, Wembley, 1924, National Council for Combating Venereal Diseases, 129 Dean Street, Oxford Street, London, W. 1; *Journal of Social Hygiene*, December, 1924, 270 Seventh Avenue, New York City.

department, particularly concerned with this question, detailed to handle such cases.[22]

In order to aid in a more adequate enforcement of this Convention, the League created an Advisory Committee on the Traffic of Women and Children.[23] At its second session held in March, 1923, this committee moved as follows: "The Advisory Committee, having regard to the useful work done by women police in countries where they have been employed, recommends that women as well as men should be employed among the police engaged in dealing with prostitution." [24] The resolution was circulated to all State Members of the League for their information. "It was not, however, taken up by any of the governments." [25] In a plenary session during the Fourth Assembly in September, 1923, the question of women police was presented to the League of Nations in a forceful manner by Dame Edith Lyttleton.[26] She urged the various delegates to bring to the attention of the governments of their individual countries the social value to be derived from the activities of properly qualified, trained women police.

[22] Communication from Commissioner General W. W. Husband, Bureau of Immigration, Washington, D. C., February 11, 1925.
[23] On December 10, 1924, the name of this committee was changed to "Committee on Traffic in Women and Protection of Children." Monthly Summary of the League of Nations, December, 1924.
[24] Resolution No. 8, League of Nations Publications, 0225 N. 125, 1923, IV.
[25] Communication from Dame Rachel Crowdy, League of Nations, January 27, 1925.
[26] League of Nations Official Journal, Special Supplement No. 13, Geneva, 1923, pp. 51 and 52.

At its third session held in April, 1924, the Secretary reported that "Replies concerning women police had been received from various governments. None of these had been positively in favor and one government had gone so far as to state that the proposal was impracticable because the only women who would undertake such work would be those belonging to the prostitute class." [27]

The Committee "took note of statements [28]—on the subject of women police—and decided to postpone any further consideration of this question until its next session." [29]

At this same session, the Committee—among other recommendations relating to this traffic in connection with migration—proposed that "it considered desirable that competent women should be specially charged to take care of the interests of women and children on all emigrant ships." [30]

[27] League of Nations Publications, C. T. F. E., Third Session, p. IV.

[28] Statements were submitted by delegates from several States.

[29] League of Nations Publications, C. T. F. E., 218.

[30] At its fourth session in 1925 a useful discussion took place in the Committee as to the value of women police. The British delegate stated that the English Committee had expressed its opinion that the efficiency of the police service had been improved by the employment of women. The French delegate gave the reasons why his government did not see its way to apply this measure.

The following resolution was passed: "The Advisory Committee has had under consideration the resolution on the subject of the employment of women police adopted by the Congress at Graz convened by the International Bureau for the Suppression of the Traffic in Women and Children in September, 1924. The Advisory Committee is impressed by the experience gained in several countries showing that women can give effective and valuable service in police work, especially in the prevention of certain classes of offences, and it hopes that the question of the use of the services of women in police forces will receive the fullest consideration of the Governments." League of Nations Publication, C. 293, 1925, IV.

This resolution was concurred in by 2 Conferences representing 27 voluntary organizations interested in the protection of immigrants, and by the Rome Conference on Emigration—May, 1924—where representatives were present from many nations, from the League of Nations, and from the International Bureau of Labor.[31]

While these last named resolutions carry no special mention of women police the general orientation of thought is the same as that which inspired the early appointments of police matrons—the forerunners of municipal and national women police.

As yet no definite program of work has been proposed for women police in connection with this Traffic. The Advisory Committee on the Traffic in Women and Children of the League of Nations appointed, at its second session, a Commission of Experts to study the problems which is their special responsibility. This commission is at present engaged in compiling information which may serve as a basis for the further consideration of the value of national and international women police.

Shoplifting: Besides the assignment of women officers to problems arising from prostitution, there is another assignment which is controversial—that of detection of shoplifters. In Washington, D. C. during the year 1924, two women officers were detailed "to store and market control." Both Major Pullman and Lieutenant Van Winkle preferred, in 1919, that the shopkeepers employ their own de-

[31] The Vigilance Record, December, 1924.

tectives.[32] The Department has adopted "the 'Flying Squadron' system in which . . . detectives visit all the stores." "No store," says Mrs. Van Winkle, "gets special protection; no worker is assigned to any special store." "It is," she continues, "to our advantage to get rid of these little shoplifters. They are a public nuisance and they are usually also pickpockets." The Detroit Department assigns no women officers to the detection of shoplifters, nor do the Departments of New York City, Chicago, or St. Louis.

The arguments for such assignments are that, since they are directly in touch with the shops the women officers have better opportunities for adjusting cases without a court trial which in many cases would be detrimental to the girl involved. The argument against the assignment is that the detection of shoplifters is a matter for the shopkeepers and that if proper relations are established between the police department and the merchants the women officers will be called in when doubt arises as to the advisability of making a definite court complaint. This method properly applied would, it is maintained, assure the presence of women officers when necessary, and would relieve her in other cases.

Résumé of the Patrol Service: The women police on patrol perform two types of service—that which is concerned with the searching out of individuals in need of corrective, directive or repressive treat-

[32] Hearings on Bill H. R. 7983, Part 2, 1919, Government Printing Office, Washington, D. C.

ment—and that which consists in the discovery and
investigation of community conditions which are
conducive to delinquency on the part of young
people. The former are referred to the social institution most fitted to meet their need—church, court,
protective agency. The second are referred to the
municipal department or civic agency where the
most effective action will be secured.

INVESTIGATION SERVICE

The Investigation Service makes a detailed study
of problems whether of individuals or of community
conditions. Its functions are: (1) to study, analyze,
and diagnose the case, be it that of an individual or
of a social condition; and (2) refer it for treatment
to the police service or other social agency, public or
private, best equipped to render the needed service.
Correct diagnosis and prognosis is the essential
quality of the Investigation Service. Every effort
is made to prevent mistakes and delays in the referring of individuals or conditions to other community
agencies.

In most larger communities there are well-estab-
lished courts for juveniles which receive numerous
complaints *each of which the city is legally held to
investigate.* Here it is possible to assign women
police officers to this duty.[33] Such procedure would
materially lessen the work required of semi-official
associations such as, for instance, Societies for the

[33] See Detroit and Chicago, Chapter VIII.

Prevention of Cruelty to Children. The women police officers, constantly on duty, would respond to all calls involving cruelty to minors and moral or physical neglect.

Case workers are pretty well agreed as to the moment when investigation, diagnosis, prognosis and treatment begin and end, but there is some difference of opinion as to how far the women police should go as "Treatment workers."

Numerous are the small communities where men police officers for years have filled the rôle of Big Brother to many small boys, counseling and warning them as to the ultimate consequences of anti-social acts.[34] The early women police officers carried a heavy load of follow-up personal work.[35] This has now become a specialized function of social agencies with a staff member as Case-Work Supervisor. It is increasingly recognized that the most successful case worker is a woman with a broad general culture and refinement supplemented by special study of the social sciences—sociology, psychology, social economy, criminology, and more recently, mental hygiene—together with technical case work and social service administration training.

---

[34] "In the evolution of civilization the policeman preceded the schoolmaster and I think we may say with perfect confidence that he has been one of the best schoolmasters." Sir Arthur Newsholme, *Proceedings, Imperial Social Hygiene Congress, Wembley,* May, 1924 (page 67), National Council for Combating Venereal Diseases, 120 Dean Street, Oxford, London, W. 1.

[35] *Proceedings of Conference of International Association of Police-women,* 1916.

Leaders in the women police movement agree that for effective diagnosis and prognosis in the Department there must be a number of such specialists. They differ as to the amount of treatment work which should be undertaken with the present limited number of women officers.[36] In the Detroit department, the individuals who need such personal help are referred to other community agencies and the time of the women officers is devoted to special police work which the other agencies cannot do. The Washington Women's Bureau carries a larger per cent of follow-up work. This difference in emphasis may be influenced by the facilities for such work in existing community agencies.

Lieutenant Van Winkle probably voices the general opinion on this matter as follows: "Common sense should rule in the selection of particular problems and only such cases should be treated by the police as can be adjusted by no other agency in the community. For the time being, women's bureaus must lean heavily on all relevant private social agencies, but some day there will be enough policewomen with educational background, training and experience for all-round case work performance." [37]

[36] Many earnest women officers, thinking only of the good of the individual, may hesitate to refer her to another agency for fear that the confidential relationship established may not be carried over. Experience shows this fear practically groundless. Further, the best relationships with an individual worker cannot ultimately give the strength found in relationships with institutions which have a continuous invigorating life—to whom new workers constantly bring increased energy.

[37] The Policewoman, Mina C. Van Winkle, *The Survey,* September 15, 1924.

Missing Persons: The tendency in police departments is toward a centralization of this work.
Whether there shall be a special service for women
and girls in the Women's Division, or whether
women officers shall be detailed to a special Departmental Service depends probably on the volume of
work and on local police administrators.

In New York City in 1924, 2,504 cases of women
and girls were referred to the Missing Persons
Bureau of which 1,905 were girls under twenty-one.
Two women officers were specially charged with the
search for 402 girls sixteen years of age. All other
cases of women and children were handled by men
officers. The Women's Division of the Detroit Division handled 1,360 requests for the location of
missing women and girls and satisfactorily disposed
of 1,273. In Washington, D. C., during this same
period, the search for 1,286 missing women and
girls became the duty of the Woman's Bureau. Of
this number 1,019 were from the city itself and 267
from other localities. Nine hundred and five of the
former and 154 of the latter were located.

COURT SERVICE

The amount of work devolving upon the Court
Service depends in part upon whether or not a departmental order requires that all or only certain
types of complaints, involving women and children,
should be referred immediately to the Women's Division for adjustment, and whether or not women
officers are detailed to enforce such laws as those

concerning prostitution. The volume of work is influenced also by the court procedure in regard to presentation of evidence.

If the arresting officer is required to present his own cases, this part of the court work of the department cannot be centralized. If the police officer acts, as in some cities, as an aid to the prosecuting attorney, in cases of sex offenses involving women and girls, one or more women officers may be delegated to this branch of the service and they can devote sufficient time to it to render valuable aid to the court and to the women and children involved.

Attendance in Court: All persons do not consider that it is necessary to have a woman police officer present in court at the hearing of all cases involving women and children. In the courts where the children's cases are not tried and where the women defendants are largely those brought in for common prostitution, drunkenness, disorderly conduct and similar charges, women probation or other officers are, as a rule, present. The practice of delegating to civilian employees—usually matrons—the escort of women prisoners between detention quarters and the court, obtains generally in the United States. This practice would seem to provide satisfactory supervision of the women prisoners, and at the same time free the trained women police for duties requiring more skill.

In most communities of any size in the United States there are Children's Courts and women are always present at the hearing in some capacity either as officers of the court or of private agencies.[38] The enforced presence of women police officers at all court hearings would not then seem to be at the present time the most urgent phase of activity for women police.

Relation of Court Service to Probation: In England the probation system is not yet definitely crystallized, and there has been some discussion of the assignment of women police to the courts to serve as probation officers. The Home Office (122) and the Scottish Office do not consider probation as a part of police work, an opinion not concurred in by Sir Leonard Dunning. Individual burghs in Scotland, do, at times, detail constables to probation duties. Glasgow, for instance, has 12 men and 5 women officers thus assigned.

Sir Nevil MacCready (236) favored probation assignments for women, but women who would be especially recruited for this duty because he could "not take them off the work we want them to do in the streets." The same opinion is expressed quite generally by other English people.

In the United States the use of probation has been

[38] In England, at a Conference of Government Heads, called by the Secretary of State at the Home Office, April, 1924, the opinion was strongly expressed "that an effort should be made to secure the attendance of a woman magistrate when child assault cases were down for hearing, and that suitable women officers of the court should be associated with the proceedings, e.g., women police or probation officers" . . . (*The Magistrate,* 83 Eccleston Square, London, W. S. 1, May, 1924.) In this country the general Federation of Women's Clubs in annual meeting in Los Angeles, 1924, moved "to encourage duly qualified women to seek office in the specialized courts created to deal with cases of women and children."

developed over a quarter of a century. There has been no suggestion that the special supervision of probationers should become a function of women police officers.[39] There is, however, a difference of opinion as to a possible division of labor between the woman police officer and the probation officer in those investigations which precede the disposition of the case by the court. There seems to be no question but that all investigations which have to do with the evidence, which the police woman must use in preparing the charge, should be made by her.

In many courts, both juvenile and adult, judges with a social outlook desire to have before them the results of a very complete investigation as to the family life, economic conditions and other possible causal factors before imposing sentences. Some, particularly in juvenile courts, wish a recommendation from the probation department.

Probation departments generally seem to question the wisdom of the police inquiry going further than to obtain information as to the evidence of guilt. It will be a valuable contribution to this discussion if accurate reports of results can be obtained from the courts using these two groups of public officials according to different plans over a considerable period of time. A comparison of such reports will lead in the future to greater harmony of opinion.

[39] The term ''Voluntary Probation'' has crept into discussions of this subject, but legally there is no such thing.

DETENTION SERVICE

After arrest and while awaiting the disposition of their cases, many women are held in custody. Programs of work for a woman's division in a police department sometimes include the maintenance and supervision of proper detention quarters for women. In those cities where the juvenile court does not have its own detention home, or where a private agency under public supervision does not maintain a satisfactory detention home for minors, the programs propose that the police department make proper provision also for the detention of children.

In Washington the Director of the Woman's Bureau is responsible for the detention home for women and children, and a civilian employee is in direct charge. In Detroit the Women's detention quarters is made a special service in the Women's Division and a woman police officer is detailed to its supervision. In this latter city the Juvenile Court—which is a County Court—has its own detention quarters for juveniles.

It may be said that a fundamental principle for whose application all civic groups are working is that there shall be in every community proper detention quarters for women and children under the direction of properly qualified women. In small communities where there are few women prisoners, and these of rather more than less decent character, a motherly upright dignified woman usually presides

as matron. In larger communities, where there are
always women prisoners, the facilities should provide for the proper segregation of different types of
women and their supervision by the Women's Division.

PAPER WORK

The amount of work in the police departments
which should be done by clerical employees and
police officers respectively, lends itself to serious
consideration. There can be no question certainly
that all police officers, men and women, should
have a thorough understanding of the place and
importance of this work in the department, and
further, that in so far as possible, this understanding should grow out of actual experience and should
not remain in the domain of theory.

Recently the Medical School of Yale University
opened a training school for nurses in which the
study of administrative machinery is reduced to a
minimum of intensive application. This is possible
because entrance requirements are high. If the
standard of requirements for women police can be
made commensurate with the importance of their
potential social contribution, it would seem possible
that an understanding of this essential part of
police machinery could be gained in a short period,
and that the responsibility for its continued execution could be placed in the hands of civilian employees, who in turn could be chosen with reference
to their special qualifications for this work.

There would always devolve upon the woman police a certain amount of paper work in the proper execution of her functions, but her time should be devoted largely to her special task, namely, the protection of women and children and the prevention of delinquency.

The Manual of the Metropolitan Police Department of Washington, D. C., 1923, says: "They shall make and file complete reports of every case assigned to them, submitting such reports to the officer in command, and shall in addition thereto make individual daily reports of their respective activities during the preceding twenty-four hours." Such duties as outlined in Chapter VIII D, Section 2: "They (privates detailed as station clerks) shall perform the clerical work of the station in recording arrests, preparing reports, requisitions, and property returns; receive, send and record telephone messages and perform such other duties as may be required of them," might well be left to clerical employees. As a matter of fact, in the Woman's Bureau in Washington, this work is assigned to two clerical employees, the record clerk and the telephone operator, and one woman police officer who is desk sergeant. In Detroit these general duties are made the responsibility of the Supervisor of the Service of Complaints and Records, who has stenographers and clerical assistance from civilian employees.

RÉSUMÉ

It would seem that a reasonable program of work for women police at the present day might read something as follows:

Women police should be primarily concerned with the execution of the accepted preventive functions of police departments. They should constantly be on the alert to uncover new and better methods with the direct object of preventing delinquency on the part of growing young people.

This end could be accomplished by definite activities through special services which are flexible in their make-up and which adapt themselves readily to differences of internal organizations and discipline of police departments of various communities.

These special services should embrace activities which could be indicated as follows:

1. Information.
2. Patrol.
3. Investigation.
   (a) Complaints involving individuals.
   (b) Complaints involving social conditions.
4. Court Work.
5. Detention.
6. Paper Work.

The information service would offer advice and assistance in cases involving women and children on matters within the scope of the police department.

The minimum Patrol Service would embrace the

general supervision—to the particular end of preventing juvenile delinquency—of places through which the public freely passes, or where people congregate in crowds.

The Investigation Service would analyze, diagnose, and refer complaints to the proper police division or other social agency.

Certain cases involving women and children should be carried to court by women officers. Proper care for women (and in some cases for children) detained by the police should devolve upon the women's division.

It has not, as yet, been demonstrated that there are definite administrative difficulties within police departments which would render such a program impracticable.

Opposition to such a program has come from three sources: (a) from those persons who are not convinced that the State should assume such functions, (b) from private organizations—negligible in number—who may conceivably believe the work of women police to be an encroachment on their own special functions and, (c) from policemen and officials, who may question the ability and willingness of women to work under police discipline and organization; the practicability of the program as a police program, its possible interference with departmental politics and its effect on the welfare of men officers.

This opposition is diminishing and time will play a large part in its complete dissipation. When only women enter this field of endeavor who are trained for the task and who are animated by the unique desire to serve the public good and with neither personal nor political ambitions, a great deal of the opposition will disappear quite naturally.

CHAPTER XIII

FORM OF ORGANIZATION—TYPE OF WOMAN—METHOD OF SELECTION

Forms of Organization already Tried—British Practice —United States Experiments: Present Sentiment—Type of Woman and Previous Experience Desirable: Great Britain, The United States, Poland, Résumé—Methods of Selection.

FORMS OF ORGANIZATION ALREADY TRIED

The last word has not yet been said on the form of organization for the work of women police. So far, both in Great Britain and in the United States three separate forms of organization have been tried —more or less consciously and, perhaps therefore, more or less successfully. These three forms of organization are:

(a) The creation in the police department—in large cities—of a definite Woman's Division whose work is supervised by one woman director, responsible to the head of the department. In some smaller cities where there are two or more women, one of them has, at times, been given the direction of the work.

(b) The placing of all women police in an already existing division, such as that of the detective or special service division, and where their work is supervised by a man officer.

(c) The assignment of women police by some directing officer of the department to the different precincts, districts or departmental bureaus, and where their work is directed by the officer in command.

Still two other plans have been followed at times: First, that in which the police department has paid in part or full, women working under private organizations and has given them limited police powers, and second, the granting of police powers to persons called policewomen, employed by private organizations, and who work in conjunction with the police.

BRITISH PRACTICE

London tried the first plan and later adopted the third. In the Provinces [1] and in Scotland, the second and third plans have been tried.

It is important in this matter to understand the causes which operate in any changes. In 1920 the Home Office Committee reported that: [2]

Though a contrary opinion has been expressed by some experienced witnesses, the great weight of the evidence favors the view that where women are employed in police

[1] See Liverpool, Chapter II.
[2] Report of 1920 Committee on the Employment of Women on Police Duties, 28 Abingdon Street, London, S. W. 1, Cmd. 877.

activities, they should form an integral part of the Police
Force, and be subject to the control of the Chief Constable
in exactly the same way as are the present male force.
(Par. 37.) Further:

With regard to the officering of police women (Par. 39)
we consider that where the number of police women is
sufficiently large, it would generally be better to place
them under the charge of a woman officer, as a separate
department to work on similar lines to the Criminal Investigation Department or the Detective Department; but
if only a few women are employed, this will obviously be
impracticable. The appointment of female officers should
be determined by the like considerations as in the case of
the male officers, and the rank conferred should be appropriate to their duties and responsibilities.

They also recommended (Par. 142) that a woman experienced in the routine of a government department and
in the organization of disciplined bodies of women be appointed as a subordinate to H. M. Inspectors of Constabulary at the Home Office to inspect and make recommendations with regard to the efficiency of policewomen.

In fact, in London, from December, 1918, to
February, 1922, the women police had thus been
working in one division under the direction of a
woman superintendent who was responsible to the
Commissioner alone. Their services had been of
such character that, as of January 1, 1921, the pay
of women police was standardized throughout the
British Isles. The Police Pension Act of 1921 had
established the position of women police on a firm
basis and allowed them pension benefits. The Commissioner and the Superintendent of Police of Lon-

don, in February, 1920, testified before the Home Office Committee that this form of organization, which they had followed for over a year, was completely satisfactory. It was therefore unexpected that in February, 1922, following the recommendation of the Geddes Committee, the Commissioner of Police was instructed by the Home Secretary to discontinue the yearly contracts of service with the women police. The number of women police was reduced from 114 to 20 and the third form of organization instituted. Unfortunately the conditions under which these changes were made were colored not only by financial considerations, but by the unfavorable attitude of some police officials in influential positions. It has never been officially proclaimed in Great Britain that this form of organization for women police was a failure. It has, however, been warmly contested, and it had and still has its partisans [3] and opponents.[4]

The fact remains that the Woman's Division did function satisfactorily for three years under a woman superintendent. The vote in the House of Commons which decreased its numbers and changed the form of organization of the work of women-police was influenced, to a large degree, by a charge of disloyalty on the part of some women police which was later disproved.[5] No other serious adverse

[3] See Minutes of Evidence: 266, 267, 200 to 204, 276-7, A, pages 60-65.
[4] See Minutes of Evidence: 158, 1798, 1866 and A 906.
[5] The History of the Official Policeman (to July, 1924), National Council of Women of Great Britain and Ireland.

criticism was made against the Woman's Division of the police force of London.

Australia and Canada follow largely the plan now in effect in Great Britain, and the women officers are generally directly responsible to chief constable.

Adelaide, Australia, has 11 women police, the largest number in any one constabulary in either of these two countries.[6]

UNITED STATES EXPERIMENTS

In the United States all three forms of organization obtain in one or more of the cities employing women in their police departments. In only a few of the larger cities is there a definitely organized woman's division directed by a woman officer.

In New York City 15 of the 100 women employed in the police department function in a Woman's Bureau under the supervision of a woman of equal rank.[7] The remaining 84 are assigned to other services or bureaus. In Chicago, women police are assigned from the office of the Superintendent of the Department to the various precincts and services, and there exists no uniform plan of work.[8] In St. Louis, the women officers are in a Women's Bureau directed by a man officer.[9] In Boston the women officers all work directly from the Chief Inspector's Office and are under his orders.[10]

[6] See Chapter III.
[7] See Chapter IX.
[8] See Chapter VIII.
[9] See Chapter IX.
[10] See Chapter VIII.

In Knoxville, Tennessee; Cleveland, Ohio;[11] Detroit,[12] Michigan; Washington, D.C.,[13] and in several other cities the women police function from a Women's Division of the Police Department, which is officered by a woman with rank.

In the United States there has been very little publicly organized opposition either to the creation of Women's Divisions or to the appointment of a woman director of women's work. This does not mean that such opposition is non-existent. The fact that, in the 92 of the 100 largest cities where women are employed in police departments, only in 6 do they work in a Woman's Division or under the direction of one woman may indicate either lack of conviction, indifference or active opposition.

PRESENT SENTIMENT

There is an ever increasing sentiment that in large cities where considerable numbers of women are employed, this is the form of organization under which women police can render the most effective service. The majority of those persons who have studied in detail the work either in Detroit or Washington, where women's divisions have, for several years, been actually functioning, under the direction of qualified women directors, respectively with the rank of deputy police commissioner and of lieutenant, who are responsible in the

[11] See Chapter VIII.
[12] See Chapter VIII.
[13] See Chapter IX.

one case to the superintendent and in the other to the commissioner of police, have been convinced that this plan of organization has produced good results.

The reasons given for successful work in cities like Detroit and Washington, are:

(1) The Directors are qualified for their positions by education, personality, and years of social service experience.

(2) They have been permitted and encouraged by the directing heads of their departments to select as members of their staff only qualified women showing not only special training, but aptitude for the work.

(3) They have been free to develop a method and a definite program of work where the preventive functions of the police can be effectually applied in the cases of women, girls and young children and in the prevention of delinquency.

It is certainly to be desired that experiments will continue in an impartial, open attitude of mind with the idea of discovering every possible means of executing successfully the preventive functions of the police. In the United States each community must decide for itself whether or not it desires to see its police department remain a purely punitive agency or develop into a social instrument for the prevention of delinquency. The tendency in municipal government seems toward the commission form with a City Manager. This officer can be selected entirely on his qualifications for the office regardless of age, residence, or political party. It is significant that the City Managers are more and more looking with favor on the work of women police, and, more recently on the idea of a woman's division in the police department. Police chiefs will do well to study this movement and to carefully consider the resolution, passed in their own association, that ''Policewomen attached to the department shall be under the direct supervision of the Chief of Police as a unit in the department, and where there is a sufficient number, at least one of them shall be a ranking officer in the department.[14]

TYPES OF WOMEN AND PREVIOUS EXPERIENCE DESIRABLE

The next questions which arise and on whose solution the work succeeds or fails are: What type of women shall be selected for women police; what educational and professional training shall be required of candidates; how shall women be selected; how shall their probationary training be effected? One can with difficulty divorce the type of woman from her previous social background. They must be considered together.

Where new public offices are created and, particularly where they offer opportunity for political patronage, care must be exercised if the offices are not to be filled with unqualified candidates. When the office can offer no other objective than the assur-

[14] Resolution passed at the 1922 Annual Meeting of the International Association of Chiefs of Police.

ance of a wage, however important in itself that may be, persons of proved social worth are not always attracted. Therefore, in considering the type of woman required, one must hold in mind the foregoing program of work, and there must be a readiness on the part of communities, and police departments, to encourage and permit of its development under the most effective form of organization.

An important point to be remembered is that a higher type of men police recruits, and of better training are being sought, required and secured at times, from other professions, in many police departments today both in Great Britain [15] and the United States. [16]

Further, as yet, very few women, who have had long police experience, and who are qualified to organize and direct the women's work and to integrate it into the work of the department as a whole, are available. This situation necessitates the appointment of women from other fields of endeavor. [17]

[15] 226 and 231.

[16] Proposed Senate Bill S. 4308, to establish a Woman's Bureau in the Metropolitan Police Department of the District of Columbia, 1925.

[17] Some members of the force hold it to be an injustice that a woman with little or no police experience should be given, almost immediately, rank and pay equal to that of men officers who have spent years in police work and who may actually command many times the number of subordinates as are directed by the women and, in addition, carry the full police responsibilities of a precinct or district. It may perhaps be helpful to recall that the woman has the responsibility of *creating* within the department a method for the organization and administration, if not of new principles and new functions, at least of a new conception of them, and that heads of police departments themselves are often men with little or no previous direct police experience, and that thus precedents for such action in relation to women's divisions exist within police organizations.

GREAT BRITAIN

The British people consider that their experience
has shown them that their women police should have
an undisputed high moral character, tact, discretion,
moral courage, initiative in emergency, and self-re-
liance. While not excluding women of elementary
school education, they would give the preference to
women graduates of a good secondary school and
consider that a proportion should have the cultured
background of higher education. Experience in social work, teaching, nursing, or in any type of work
which has taught self-discipline and which has developed initiative in emergencies and capacity to
understand human nature are distinct assets.[18]

The Committee of 1924 emphasized the contribution of women who possess "a sympathetic understanding of the daily life of those who are not well-
to-do" and held that as valuable recruits are to be
found among working women as elsewhere.[19]

The women police selected in 1918 and 1919 for
work in the women's division of the Metropolitan
Police Force of London, included women from all
ranks of life. The conditions of service which im-

[18] See Minutes of Evidence 156, 179, 627, 678, 1291, 1313, 1995,
2091, 2364, 2399, 2563, A. 141 to 143, 391, 473 to 477, 812 to 814,
935, 1029 to 1033, 1338, 1524, 1660, 1661 and 1920. Committee
Report 71 and 88 and 1924 Committee Report 20 and 35.
[19] From this statement one might infer that in England only women
of "well-to-do" parents have professional training. This reasoning could not of course be applied in the United States, or other
countries where many women University and Professional School
graduates know intimately and through personal experience "the
daily life of those who are not 'well-to-do.'"

posed a minimum age limit and offered small salaries, on the basis of yearly contracts, were held responsible for the fact that many of the better qualified applicants did not eventually accept appointment.

THE UNITED STATES

The first official woman police in the United States was a graduate of a recognized Theological School and an experienced social worker. Since that time varying types of women have served in this capacity. An effort was made in 1920 by the Association of Policewomen to learn the qualifications—educational and professional—of the women police then in active service. The returns on the questionnaire were too vague to be conclusive. The same association is compiling returns of a more recent questionnaire which is promised for early publication.[20]

Meantime, Detroit has submitted detailed information on its individual women police officers. In 1921, the Commissioner of Police of that city exercised his prerogative in the matter and waived the necessity for civil service examinations in the appointment of his officers. In the Women's Division of that department there are at present 30 officers who have been selected by the women directors on the basis of individual qualifications and aptitudes for the particular work in hand, applying the same general methods as obtain in any well-organized business corporation.

[20] For information communicate with the International Association of Policewomen, Evening Star Building, Washington, D. C.

The previous education and training of the 30 officers had been as follows:

Elementary School	1
Part time high school	2
High school graduates	6
High school and from one to two years university training	8
University graduates	5
Graduate nurses	6
Teachers' Training School graduates	1
Graduate law student	1

Two were, in addition, graduates of, and 1 had attended, the summer session of a training school for social workers.

Following the practice of the Department, the 14 women police appointed in 1924, were given intelligence tests. Their rating was considerably above the normal, a situation which augurs well for the future of the profession.

Before entering the Women's Division of the police department the professions of the 30 officers had been:

Teacher	2
Teacher and then social work	4
Teacher and then clerical work	1
Hospital nurse	1
Public health nurse	2
Hospital and later public health nurse	2
Social work	12
Office administration or clerical work	6

Those officers who had, after some few years in teaching, entered social work, did so as teachers in institutions for delinquents. Of the nurses, 2 had spent years as institutional nurses and both had seen overseas service and a third, after overseas service, had been follow-up nurse in the Veterans'

Bureau. Eleven of the 12 social workers had been engaged in work with delinquent girls either in institutions, as probation officers, or as officers in private protective associations. It is indeed gratifying that one of our largest cities has actually appointed women officers of such previous professional training. Six of the 7 officers who had previously been engaged in clerical work had been appointed before 1924. The one appointed during this past year is a high school graduate with a high mental age and intelligence quotient.

To deal with the police problems arising among the great number of negroes in that city, 2 of the 30 officers are colored women, one a graduate of a Teachers' Training School, and the other a University graduate. A Polish woman was appointed because of the large Polish population of the city. Observation of the results of the work of this division together with the perusal of its published reports, show an amazing volume of high grade work accomplished. While the same information is not available in relation to the women police of Washington, the standards for acceptance have been kept so high that the Director of the Woman's Bureau has experienced difficulty in obtaining a sufficient number of candidates for the positions to be filled.

POLAND

Poland quite recently selected 30 women for training in police work. The candidates were chosen among women whose names were submitted to the Minister of the Interior by women's organizations, particularly by the private protective associations, and who were experienced workers in this field. They were required to have a formal education comparable to that of the Junior High Schools in the United States or the *Ecole Primaire Supérieure* of France.

RÉSUMÉ

Educational Requirements: Based on the available evidence the preliminary requirements of candidates for the position of women police appearing in the proposed United States Senate Bill S.4308, are feasible. The minimum requirements proposed are: "Gradation from a standard high school or the completion of at least 14 college entrance units of study, and either not less than two years' responsible experience in systematic social service or educational work, or not less than two years' responsible commercial experience involving public contact and tending to qualify the applicant to perform the duties of the position."

Uniform: Whether or not women police shall wear a uniform has aroused little discussion in the United States. It has been almost tacitly accepted that they shall dress in quiet dark colors, but not in uniform when on ordinary duty.[21] On certain duties, such as special patrol of crowded public places a uniform might be useful.

[21] Proceedings of the 1916 Annual Meeting of the International Association of Policewomen.

In London and in some provincial forces, the
women police wear a uniform.

Age: The minimum age for women police has
been around twenty-five years. There is difference
of opinion as to the desirable maximum age both of
entry into and retirement from the service. The
general trend of opinion indicates a good maximum
age for entry as from thirty-five to forty years, and
for retirement from fifty to fifty-five.

METHODS OF SELECTION

The question of the methods of selection received
little attention until after the recent world war.
Until that time in those countries or cities where
women were employed on police duties, there was
really little conscious selection, as such. The heads
of departments employed those women who came to
their attention through divers channels of information. Now, however, that the work of women police
has taken on a more serious import, attention is
being given not only to the type of woman who shall
serve but to the manner of her selection.

In Great Britain three methods have been proposed: (a) Selection by Chief Constables;[22] (b)
Selection by Chief Constables assisted by a woman;[23]
(c) Selection by a Board.[24]

In the United States, in 1920, about one-half of
those cities employing women in their police de-

[22] 156, 509, 549, 550, 1314-7, 1622, 1644-8, 1653, 1824, 2085, A. 852,
923.

[23] 2073, 2166-7, 2518, 2692, A. 1735-6, 849.

[24] 194, 555, 623, 682, 1067-70, 1418, 2801-2. A. P. 37.

partments required civil service examinations.[25]
The tendency today in this country is distinctly
toward such a system of selection. The situation in
New York is a curious one. In that city there are
2 examinations for women police—1 that was used
for some years for police matrons and has no relation to the ability of the candidate to do other work
than that ordinarily required of such persons.
Seventy of the 100 women in the department have
been selected by this examination. The remaining
30—who are called patrolwomen—have passed a
different type of examination which has particular
reference to their ability to perform the preventive
functions of the police.[26]

Up to the present time it has been largely a matter
of chance if 2 cities use the same civil service examination questions. The Employment Service of the
United States Department of Labor has prepared
a set of civil service questions for women police
candidates, and which are coming to the attention
of many persons interested in this subject.[27] The
oral examination and personal interview are considered of prime importance in a field of work where
the proper temperament and personality are essential to effective results. In this country women are
playing an increasingly greater part in the selection
of women police.

There are two elements to be considered in the

[25] Tentative Digest of Questionnaire of the International Association of Policewomen.
[26] See Appendix II. 2.
[27] See Appendix II. 1.

selection of women police: the written examination
and the personal interview. The civil service examination questions should be of such type that to
properly answer them requires, not a superficial
knowledge of dissociated fragments of routine
information, but a well-grounded knowledge of conditions conducive to delinquency and the methods
which have proved most successful in controlling
them. The oral examination or personal interview
should be held before a selection board or commission composed both of men and women. There
would seem little doubt but that men experienced
in police service should pass upon the fitness of
women for actual police duty, and it is of equal importance that women should decide as to whether or
not they are temperamentally and emotionally fitted
for preventive work with young people and that they
actually know about the problems which form the
bulk of their work. In the United States this result
could be obtained through a carefully chosen Civil
Service Commission composed of men and women.
The Civil Service Commissions in this country have
generally welcomed suggestions for the examinations of women police candidates, and groups interested in the movement might find, at this point, their
best channel for effective work in raising the
standard of selection for their municipal women
police.

CHAPTER XIV

TRAINING AND TRAINING SCHOOLS

The United States: University of California, Boston School of Public Service, Police Department of New York City, New York School of Social Work, George Washington University—Great Britain: Peel House, Women Police Service School, Bristol School, Liverpool School, Scottish School—Résumé.

Different countries have approached the subject of the training of their men police from somewhat dissimilar points of view which have been influenced by their conception of police functions and of their relative importance in the social order.[1] In some countries the directing police officials are required to undergo training comparable to that of American Universities with added technical and field-work experience, while elementary school education is required of the patrolmen and petty officers.

In the United States prospective men recruits must pass a civil service examination and enter the ranks. Most frequently the officers who direct the actual police work in this country are men who have proved themselves "good officers" in the ranks.

[1] American Police Systems—European Police Systems. Raymond B. Fosdick.

Since the work of the women police is not of the same type as that entrusted to the men recruits, it would seem illogical to propose the same sort of training. In order to function properly under the program of work proposed, women police must have had special preparation.

In his book on police administration, Mr. Fuld says "that it is a well known principle of educational administration, that, whenever a need for any particular kind of training is felt in the community, the want is soon relieved by the establishment of an appropriate school."[2] This has been true with schools for civil service candidates, including men police recruits. These schools are created for the purpose of preparing candidates to pass a particular kind of examination by acquiring some new facts and refreshing the memory on various others. Until quite recently the training of women police received as little attention as did their selection. Indeed it would be both illogical and unintelligent to impose a period of training without knowing for what definite work the women police were being prepared. Now that it is generally accepted that women police shall carry on a program for the prevention of delinquency, methods of training for this work are being considered. It is evident that the present schools which prepare only for the ordinary civil service examinations would offer little of value in this field. The training within police departments themselves has emphasized those functions which

[2] Police Administration. Leonhard Felix Fuld, p. 85.

concern general law enforcement, public peace and order, detection of crime and regulation of traffic, and has given little attention to the purely preventive and protective functions. The only general programs of instruction at present tending to give the required preparation are found in colleges and universities or in a few special schools.

THE UNITED STATES

For years the colleges and universities of the United States have offered in their Departments of Economics, Sociology and Social Service, courses under various titles which supplied a theoretical background for the student who wishes to enter the field of social work. A quarter of a century ago, however, it began to be recognized that a technical instruction was needed for such workers.

Beginning with the New York School of Social Work, in 1898, specialized schools, providing such training in the social sciences and in social service administration, have developed. Those wishing to enter the fields allied to the work of women police—probation, parole, and the private protective agencies for children and for adolescents—have found in these schools the desired training. After twenty-five years of experimentation in independent schools, there is a tendency in universities to widen the range of their vocational courses. The pendulum is thus swinging back again and these schools are being absorbed into the universities under some such general titles as "Graduate School of Social Service" or of "Social Service Administration." The wisdom of this is still a moot question. Mrs. Anna Garlin Spencer, a pioneer in this field, questions whether the university will require ample field experience in actual contacts with individual, family and social problems—the laboratory of Social Service.[4] In some schools experiments have been or are being made with courses of instruction dealing with the work of women police.

University of California: The first school in the United States whose programs of instruction included definite courses on the work of women police, is the University of California, Southern Division, which in the summer session of 1918, offered in its Department of Criminology a course on Women Police and their work.[5]

The fact that this University is "by the terms of its charter an integral part of the educational system of the State" lent force and dignity to this course which was organized and directed by Mrs. Alice Stebbins Wells, then President of the International Association of Policewomen. In addition to Mrs. Wells, the lecturers included the Chief of Police of Los Angeles, a director of the Los Angeles Police School, City School Psychologist, Judges,

[3] The New York School of Social Work still remains an independent school.

[4] "Looking Toward the Future." Address before the Annual Meeting of the American Social Hygiene Association, January 17, 1925, New York City.

[5] University of California Bulletin, Third Series, Vol. II, No. 9, University of California Press, Berkeley, California.

Attorneys, Probation Officers, and other officers in public and private social agencies. The field work included observation visits to the various public and private social agencies in Los Angeles. Since that time the University has frequently had under consideration the question of offering special courses for women police and women probation officers. An effort was made to carry out this plan in connection with the 1925 summer session at Berkeley.[6]

Boston School of Public Service: A second effort to meet this need was begun in October, 1921, in the Boston School for Public Service, with a five months' course of instruction intended to prepare for definite public and civil service positions. Steadily this school has raised its requirements to include at least high school training and some experience in social service.

The course now consists of: first, academic work dealing with community organization, social case work methods, criminology and psychiatry, criminal law and procedure, history, organization and function of police work, preventive and protective measures applicable to such work, and second: field work, covering three full days weekly, dealing with the normal life and social resources of neighborhood groups, as with the adult and juvenile delinquency.[8]

[6] Communicated by Professor L. J. Richardson, Director, Extension Division, University of California, Berkeley, California, December 4, 1924.

[7] Under the auspices of the Women's Municipal League of Massachusetts Committee of the National Civic Federation. See Bulletin of League.

[8] Information received from Miss Helen Pigeon, Director of the School, 25 Huntington Avenue, Boston, Massachusetts.

Special extension courses—offered free to police officers—on "Presentation of Evidence in the Courts" have drawn unexpected numbers of men on active police service.

Police Department of New York City: New York City was the first city to offer to its women police officers instruction not given in the regular training school of the department. In May, 1922, Mrs. George E. Loft, then Honorary Deputy Commissioner in charge of the Welfare Division, arranged a series of lectures in Social Hygiene in connection with the New York Office of the United States Interdepartmental Hygiene Board. These lectures were designed for the women police who were assigned to work in the Welfare Division, and dealt with prostitution particularly in relation to a program of protective social measures.[9]

New York School of Social Work: Quite in harmony with the common procedure in all public service developments in the United States, volunteer organizations of private citizens concerned themselves with the question of women police. Particularly active in those efforts were the National Christian Temperance Union, the General Federation of Women's Clubs, the National League of Women Voters, the American Social Hygiene Association and various other national and local protective agencies.[10]

[9] "A course of eight lectures on Policewomen's Work and Social Hygiene."

[10] As was shown in the "War Period," the private protective agencies have been the chief channel of organized cooperation in this field. See Chapter VII.

Following a conference of such interested groups, arranged in February, 1923, by the American Social Hygiene Association, the New York School of Social Work secured the cooperation of that Association in offering a program of instruction on the work of women police.[11] The entrance requirements of the school demand a college training or its equivalent. The graduates are preparing themselves to serve as future executives in public service agencies. The courses were therefore designed more especially for potential directors of women's divisions in police departments who later would be capable of training their own staff.

Beginning in January, 1924, the school provided the general courses while the vocational lectures and special field work were under the direction of the American Social Hygiene Association, which also offered a number of scholarships for qualified students.

The New York City Department of Police, through the courtesy of Commissioner Richard E. Enright, sent members of its staff as special lecturers and provided facilities for field work within the department. Besides the police field work, attention was given to general social institutions with special

---

[11] After two days of deliberation the conference agreed that (a) there did exist a need for women police officers in the field of preventive and protective social measures; (b) that the best results would be obtained by women officers having at least secondary school education, and (c) that "carefully designed training courses would be of service in a gradual standardization of the work of this field of endeavor." (Digest of Conference.)

reference to their relation to the work of women police.

This venture was of sufficient value to cause the School and the American Social Hygiene Association to continue a second year of cooperation, slightly modified as to the details, but containing essentially the same elements.

George Washington University: Concurrently with the course in the New York School of Social Work, George Washington University, of Washington, D. C., with the cooperation of Lieutenant Mina C. Van Winkle, Director of the Woman's Bureau of the Metropolitan Police Department of the District of Columbia, offered a series of social service courses including police organization and administration.

These courses were placed between the hours of 5 and 7 P.M. in order to permit attendance of employed persons, a group which forms a majority of the students of this University. Fifty-five persons enrolled for the Social Service Courses. The majority of these students were actually engaged in professional social work and were not required to take the field work which was elected by only 11 of the 55. The field work consisted of practical service under supervision in case-working agencies. An interesting feature of this experiment was the number and type of social agencies contributing field work and lectures free. A similar program is being continued a second year.[12]

[12] Reports and Communications from Dr. Carl Roediger, Dean of Teachers College of the University.

GREAT BRITAIN

In Great Britain there is no uniformity either of opinion or of practice in the training of women police. Various schools under private auspices acted as emergency centers of training in the early days of the movement. Of the 123 women police in service in October, 1923, 17 were reported as having been trained in one or another of these schools; 59 were trained by the police themselves, and there is no information available for the remaining 47.[13]

The 1920 and the 1924 Committees recommend that the Chief Constable should be responsible for the training of women appointed to his force, but that as soon as qualified women instructors are available, it would be advisable that a certain amount of the training should be in the hands of women.

Peel House: The 114 women of the London Police were trained at the regular police school at Peel House, and received practically the same training as the men, (179) even to the physical drill and jiu-jitsu (217). Their instructors were men, but most of their training was received by themselves in squads of 20 (218-219).

Women Police Service School: The first special training school for women police in the British Empire was opened in London, in September, 1914, by

[13] Women Police, Questionnaire, October, 1923. National Council of Women of Great Britain and Ireland. Parliament Mansions, Victoria Street, London, S. W. 1.

the Women Police Service. This organization, as soon as the need for women police was precipitated by the war, formulated a definite program for training whole-time, uniformed women police and which was designed to eliminate the unfit and give all round training in discipline and general instructions to accepted candidates.[14]

The subjects of lectures included: special Acts of Parliament relating to women and children, social experiments, elementary principles of psychology, juvenile delinquency, and social problems dealing with the root of crime, disease and abnormalities. The practical work consisted of patrolling the streets in the earlier hours of the night, visiting places of amusement, attending police and children's courts, and instructions in the by-laws regarding places of amusement. Powers of observation were encouraged and a written weekly report of lectures, patrolling and of all occurrences was required. After four weeks of this intensive training the recruits were sent to the different centers where trained women police were actually in the field and under whose direction the recruit completed a period of probationary work.

Bristol School: [15] During the winter of 1914-1915, The National Council of Women, while engaged in organizing women patrols, saw the need of standardized training for patrol leaders. In August,

14 Women's Auxiliary Service Report of Work, 1918-1919.
15 Notes of the History of the Bristol Training School for Police Women and Patrols. National Council of Women, Miss M. H. Cowlin, January, 1925.

1915, they opened, in Bristol, a training school for patrol leaders and other women police.

The officials of the school recognized from the outset that such training as they supplied was of a preliminary nature, and in no sense replaced any further training in the Forces themselves. The school aimed at finding, testing, and preparing suitable women and then passing them on for appointment by Police Authorities or by Patrol Committees.

The earliest training courses provided by the Bristol School covered a period of two, soon extended to three months and, in 1918, to six months. This double period of training was rendered possible by cooperation with the Liverpool School, and also by the generosity of the Carnegie Trust, who made a grant from which maintenance could be provided for students in training.

The subjects included in the training courses provided by the Bristol School were: Physical Drill, Jiu-jitsu, First Aid, Discipline and Deportment, Street Duty, Handling of Cases, Rules of Evidence, Police Court Procedure, Report Writing, Elementary Criminal Law, Voluntary Organizations, Public Authorities and General Social Questions.

The first month was given over to theory, court visiting and physical training; the second month was largely devoted to family case work and in the third month the students did street patrol work (726-727).

After the Home Office in 1922 reduced the number of women police patrols in the Metropolis on the grounds of economy, there was a serious setback to the cause of women police throughout the country. Little demand was made by the provinces for trained women police and the Bristol Training School was closed.

Liverpool School: [16] In November, 1914, a Committee was appointed by the Liverpool Branch of the National Council of Women to consider the organization of Women Patrols in those parts of the city and district where soldiers and girls were brought into dangerous contact with each other especially in the evenings. The following January, Miss M. H. Cowlin was appointed to organize a band of voluntary workers to meet this situation.

These volunteer patrols were often asked to assist the police in special inquiries, and they cooperated whenever possible in their work on the streets. They attended the courts daily and were constantly appealed to to assist women and girls to prepare their evidence when applying for separation or affiliation orders, and to remain in court during the hearings.

This friendly cooperation with the police and the fact that the work had been stabilized by an annual grant from the city, made their center a specially valuable one for the training of women police in cooperation with the University School of Social Studies, and they federated with the Women Police Training schools already established in Bristol and Glasgow.

Scottish School: Early in 1918, the Standing

[16] History of the Liverpool Women Police Patrols and Training Schools for Women Police. Miss M. H. Cowlin, January 6, 1923.

Committee of the Branches of the National Council
of Women foresaw the need for trained, whole-time,
official women police to take over and develop the
work of patrols (1921). In June of that year, they
opened the Scottish Training School and the town
council gave the facilities for training. That autumn
the school trained 3 women, and in January, 1919,
it trained 12 patrols for the Women's Royal Air
Force (1923). The Committee soon decided that it
was futile to train women for posts which did not
exist. They, therefore, turned their efforts toward
creating a public demand for the appointment of
women police. In November, 1919, the Scottish
Office asked the Director of the Glasgow School,
Miss Edith Tancred, to prepare a draft scheme for
women police for Scotland, embodying conditions
of service that would provide a fair test of such
work (1924). Before any definite plan was per-
fected, the Home Office appointed a Committee of
Inquiry and special negotiations were discontinued.

Federated Training Schools: Sometime in the
course of events the three schools of the National
Council of Women formed a Central Committee of
Federated Training Schools for Women Patrols and
Police Women. They receive a grant from the
Carnegie Trust, providing scholarships in the form
of Maintenance—2 guineas per week—while in
attendance at school (705). A plan of cooperation
in training was evolved whereby the student received three months practical court and street
work (658).

At present, in Great Britain, outside of training schools within police departments, there is but one special school for the training of women police— that which is under the auspices of the Women's Auxiliary Service, and they have actually no students.

RÉSUMÉ

The training of women police has two distinct features: the one embracing training and experience before entry into public work, and the other definite instruction in actual police duties.

The present tendency everywhere seems to be that women police are to be graduates at least of secondary schools and are to have social service or other experience which will have prepared them to cope with the problems encountered in the execution of the preventive functions of the police. Once accepted as women police the trend in England is toward the completion of their training in police schools and perhaps in some one central school. Poland is now following this system.

Indications are that in the United States the schools of social service and universities departments of sociology, social and political economy, public health and social service administration, will, as the need arises, include courses for women police in their curricula as they have done in other allied fields.

It is quite in line with the trend of police organization that, one by one, the larger departments of police, public safety or public welfare will deem such instruction a necessary part of the training required for entrance into this and perhaps other branches of the service. The future surely holds out many interesting possibilities of development in this field of endeavor.

APPENDICES

Appendix I

Statistics of Cities in the United States [1]

A.—Present Number and Date of First Appointment of Police Matrons and Women Police

POLICE MATRONS

City	State	Present Number	Date of First Appointment
Attleboro	Massachusetts	1	Unknown
Chester	Pennsylvania	4	
Haverhill	Massachusetts	3	
Hoboken	New Jersey	4	
Indianapolis	Indiana	3	
Lynn	Massachusetts	1	
Newark	New Jersey	16	
Oklahoma City	Oklahoma	3	
Richmond	California	1	
Sacramento	California	1	
Portland	Maine	1	1876
Jersey City	New Jersey	2	1880
Chicago	Illinois	34	1881
Boston	Massachusetts	10	1883
Baltimore	Maryland	18	1884
Milwaukee	Wisconsin	(?)	1884
Philadelphia	Pennsylvania	26	1884
St. Louis	Missouri	11	1884
Denver	Colorado	1	1885
Detroit	Michigan	13	1885
Providence	Rhode Island	3	1885
San Francisco	California	4	1885
Cleveland	Ohio	4	1886
Lowell	Massachusetts	1	1886
Cincinnati	Ohio	4	1887

[1] It is earnestly requested that persons having corrections or new information communicate with the author.

283

POLICE MATRONS—*Continued*

City	State	Present Number	Date of First Appointment
Fall River	Massachusetts	2	1887
Rochester	New York	4	1887
Springfield	Massachusetts	4	1887
Lawrence	Massachusetts	1	1888
New York City	New York	39*	1888
Columbus	Ohio	5	1889
Kansas City	Missouri	4	1889
Los Angeles	California	8	1889
Buffalo	New York	5	1890
Lincoln	Nebraska	2	1890
Salt Lake City	Utah	1	1890
St. Paul	Minnesota	3	1890
Holyoke	Massachusetts	1	1891
Omaha	Nebraska	1	1891
Wilmington	Delaware	3	1891
Atlanta	Georgia	5	1892
New Haven	Connecticut	1	1892
Albany	New York	1	1893
Davenport	Iowa	1	1893
Hartford	Connecticut	1	1893
Pittsburgh	Pennsylvania	14	1894
Scranton	Pennsylvania	4	1894
Utica	New York	1	1895
Des Moines	Iowa	3	1897
Grand Rapids	Michigan	1	1897
Kansas City	Kansas		1897
Minneapolis	Minnesota	2	1899
Syracuse	New York	3	1899
Lansing	Michigan	(1 on call)	1900
Newark	New York	1	1900
Toledo	Ohio	4	1900
Wichita	Kansas	3	1900
Camden	New Jersey	1	1901
New Bedford	Massachusetts	1	1901
Peoria	Illinois	2	1902
Topeka	Kansas	1	1902
Dayton	Ohio	3	1904
Houston	Texas	3	1904
Oakland	California	4	1904
St. Joseph	Missouri	1	1904

*As of May 5, 1925. 36 policewomen and 3 patrolwomen were on matron duty.

POLICE MATRONS—WOMEN POLICE

POLICE MATRONS			WOMEN POLICE			Date of First Appointment
City	State	Present Number	City	State	Present Number	
			Baton Rouge	Louisiana	1	Unknown
			Memphis	Tennessee	5	Unknown
Charleston	So. Carolina	3	Portland	Oregon	6	1905
New Orleans	Louisiana	9				1905
Cambridge	Massachusetts	2				1906
Norfolk	Virginia	2	Burlington	Iowa	1*	1907
Seattle	Washington	5			6	1907
South Bend	Indiana	1				1907
Youngstown	Ohio	1				1907
Bloomington	Illinois	1				1908
Fort Worth	Texas	1				1908
Meriden	Connecticut	1				1908
San José	California	4			1	1908
Tacoma	Washington	2				1908
Gary	Indiana	1	Duluth	Minnesota	1*	1910
Jamestown	New York	1	Los Angeles	California	8	1910
Lackawanna	New York	1				1910
Waterloo	Iowa	1				1910
Bridgeport	Connecticut	1				1911
Geneva	New York	1				1911
Grand Forks	N. Dakota	1				1911
Little Rock	Arkansas	4				1911
Stamford	Connecticut	1				1911
Vallejo	California	1				1911
New Rochelle	New York	(1 on call)	Baltimore	Maryland	5	1912
Niagara Falls	New York	1	Birmingham	Alabama	2	1912
Peoria	Illinois	2	Decatur	Illinois	1*	1912
Portland	Oregon	3	Fargo	N. Dakota	1*	1912
San Diego	California	5	Galesburg	Illinois	1*	1912
Troy	New York	1	Omaha	Nebraska	1	1912
Worcester	Massachusetts	3				1912
Kingston	New York	1	Fort Wayne	Indiana	4	1913
Quincy	Illinois	1	Hannibal	Missouri	1*	1913
Tulsa	Oklahoma	2	Rochester	New York	1	1913
			Salem	Mass.	0	1913
			San Francisco	California	3	1913
			South Bend	Indiana	1	1913
			St. Paul	Minnesota	3	1913
			Wichita	Kansas	3	1913
			Winnetka	Illinois	1*	1913
Nashville	Tennessee	2	Chicago	Illinois	30	1914
Savannah	Georgia	1	Dayton	Ohio	3	1914
Somerville	Massachusetts	2	Denver	Colorado	3	1914
Springfield	Missouri	1	Des Moines	Iowa	1	1914
Watertown	New York	1	East Chicago	Indiana	1*	1914
Wilkes-Barre	Pennsylvania	1	Minneapolis	Minnesota	3	1914
Yonkers	New York	3	Pittsburgh	Pennsylvania	5	1914
			Racine	Wisconsin	0	1914
			Superior	Wisconsin	2	1914
			Syracuse	New York	1	1914
			Virginia	Minnesota	1*	1914
Croakston	Michigan	0	Flint	Michigan	2	1915
Flint	Michigan	1	Haverhill	Mass.	1	1915
Minot	N. Dakota	1	Minot	N. Dakota	1	1915
			Hornell	New York	1*	1915
			Madison	Wisconsin	2	1915

* Serving both as matron and woman police.

POLICE MATRONS—WOMEN POLICE—*Continued*

POLICE MATRONS			WOMEN POLICE			Date of First Appointment
City	State	Present Number	City	State	Present Number	
			Trenton	New Jersey	1	1915
			Washington	D. C.	21	1915
Binghamton	New York	1	Brookline	Mass.	1	1916
Mason City	Iowa	1	Buffalo	New York	5	1916
Richmond	Virginia	2	East Orange	New Jersey	1	1916
Schenectady	New York	1	Lafayette	Louisiana	1	1916
			New Orleans	Louisiana	1	1916
			Oskaloosa	Iowa	1	1916
			Santa Monica	California	1*	1916
			Salt Lake City	Utah	2	1916
			St. Louis	Missouri	18	1916
Atlantic City	New Jersey	3	Aurora	Illinois	1	1917
Billings	Montana	2	Erie	Pennsylvania	1	1917
Monroe	Virginia	3	Holyoke	Mass.	1	1917
			Houston	Texas	1	1917
			Jamestown	New York	1	1917
			Lexington	Kentucky	1	1917
			Muskegon	Michigan	1	1917
			Niagara Falls	New York	1	1917
			Provo	Utah	1	1917
			Spokane	Washington	1	1917
			Springfield	Mass.	2	1917
			Tacoma	Washington	2	1917
			Worcester	Mass.	2	1917
Gloversville	New York	1	Atlanta	Georgia	2	1918
Iowa City	Iowa	1	Bay City	Michigan	1*	1918
Lewiston	Maine	1	Burlington	Vermont	1	1918
Ogden City	Utah	1	Indianapolis	Indiana	19	1918
Pomona	California	1	Kalamazoo	Michigan	2	1918
Redondo	California	1	Lowell	Mass.	3	1918
Shreveport	Louisiana	1	Muskogee	Oklahoma	1	1918
			New Bedford	Mass.	1	1918
			Newark	New Jersey	3	1918
			New York City	New York	61†	1918
			Owosso	Michigan	1	1918
			Poughkeepsie	New York	1	1918
			Providence	Rhode Island	1	1918
			Rockford	Illinois	2	1918
			Utica	New York	2	1918
			Youngstown	New York	1	1918
Akron	Ohio	2			1	1919
Chisholm	Minnesota	1	Detroit	Michigan	31	1919
Rockford	Illinois	1	Everett	Washington	1*	1919
			Harrisburg	Pennsylvania	1*	1919
			Grand Rapids	Michigan	2	1919
			Gulfport	Mississippi	1	1919
Williamsport	Pennsylvania	1	Lynn	Mass.	2	1920
			New Castle	Pennsylvania	1	1920
			Oak Park	Illinois	1*	1920
			Passaic	New Jersey	2	1920
			Perth Amboy	New Jersey	1*	1920
			Reading	Pennsylvania	1	1920
			Riverside	California	1*	1920
Astoria	Oregon	1	Bloomington	Illinois	1	1921
			Boston	Mass.	5	1921

* Serving both as matron and woman police.
†As of May 5, 1925—34 policewomen and 27 patrolwomen were on other than matron duty.

POLICE MATRONS—WOMEN POLICE—*Continued*

POLICE MATRONS			WOMEN POLICE			Date of First Appointment
City	State	Present Number	City	State	Present Number	
			Cambridge	Mass.	1	1921
			Columbus	Ohio	2	1921
			Devils Lake	N. Dakota	1	1921
			Eau Claire	Wisconsin	0	1921
			Gary	Indiana	3	1921
			Hibbing	Minnesota	1	1921
			Jersey City	New Jersey	2	1921
			Lawrence	Mass.	1	1921
			Louisville	Kentucky	2	1921
			Michigan City	Indiana	0	1921
			Nashville	Tennessee	2	1921
			Norfolk	Virginia	0	1921
			Petersburg	Virginia	1	1921
			Portland	Maine	1	1921
			Rhinelander	Wisconsin	1*	1921
			Tampa	Florida	1*	1921
			Toledo	Ohio	4	1921
Dover	New Jersey	1	Appleton	Wisconsin	0	1922
Jamestown	N. Dakota	2	Atlantic City	New Jersey	5	1922
			Charleston	S. Carolina	2	1922
Richmond	Indiana	1	Cleveland	Ohio	5	1922
			Elizabeth	New Jersey	1	1922
			Fall River	Mass.	2	1922
			Herkimer	New York	1	1922
			Huntington	Indiana	1	1922
			Kenosha	Wisconsin	1	1922
Long Beach	California	2			3	1922
			Michigan City	Michigan	0	1922
			Milwaukee	Wisconsin	0	1922
			New Haven	Connecticut	1	1922
			Pontiac	Michigan	2	1922
			Richmond	Virginia	2	1922
			Saginaw	Michigan	1	1922
			(Director of Social Service)			
			Sault Ste. Marie	Michigan	1	1922
			(Social Worker, Health and Police)			
			Wausau	Wisconsin	1	1922
			York	Pennsylvania	1	1922
Monroe	Louisiana	0	Alliance	Ohio	0	1923
Sioux City	Iowa	1	East Cleveland	Ohio	1*	1923
			Gloucester	Mass.	1	1923
			Greensboro	N. Carolina	1	1923
			Lancaster	Pennsylvania	1	1923
			Oshkosh	Wisconsin	1	1923
			Savannah	Georgia	2	1923
			Topeka	Kansas	3	1923
			Trinidad	Colorado	1*	1923
Allentown	Pennsylvania	1	Belfast	Maine	1	1924
Hibbing	Minnesota	1	Benton Harbor	Michigan	1	1924
			Davenport	Iowa	1	1924
			Hamtramck	Michigan	2	1924
			Hattiesburg	Mississippi	1	1924
			Hutchinson	Kansas	1*	1924
			Ithaca	New York	1	1924
			Knoxville	Tennessee	4	1924
			New London	Connecticut	1	1924
			Port Arthur	Texas	1	1924
			Pueblo	Colorado	1	1924
			Wilmington	N. Carolina	2	1924
			Berkeley	California	1	1925

* Serving both as matron and women police.

B.—CITIES HAVING NEITHER POLICE MATRONS NOR WOMEN POLICE

Alliance, Ohio
Alton, New Hampshire
Ann Arbor, Michigan
Appleton, Wisconsin
Asbury Park,[1] New Jersey
Ashtabula, Ohio
Atkinson, Wisconsin
Austin, Texas
Beloit, Wisconsin
Blackwell, Oklahoma
Canton, Ohio
Cheltenham, Pennsylvania
Clarksdale, Missouri
Columbia, Pennsylvania
Croakston, Minnesota
Dallas, Texas
Englewood, New Jersey
Glacier,[2] Montana
Great Falls, Montana
Hamilton, Ohio
Helena, Montana
Hopewell, Virginia
Janesville, Wisconsin
Lafayette, Indiana
Lawton, Oklahoma
Madison, New Jersey
Manchester, New Hampshire
Meridian, Mississippi
Mexia, Texas

Miama, Florida
Michigan City, Michigan
Michigan City, Indiana
Monroe, Virginia
Monroe, Louisiana
Mora, Minnesota
Mount Vernon, New York
Muncie, Indiana
Niagara, Wisconsin
Oneonta, New York
Orlando, Florida
Prairie du Chien, Wisconsin
Provo, Utah
Racine, Wisconsin
Reno, Nevada
Rock Island, Illinois
Santa Anna, California
Santa Fe, New Mexico
Somerset, Kentucky
St. Johnsbury, Vermont
Traverse City, Michigan
Vincennes, Indiana
Waltham, Massachusetts
Warren, Pennsylvania
Washington, Pennsylvania
Waterbury, Connecticut
West Palm Beach, Florida
Weymouth, Massachusetts
Winona, Minnesota

C.—CITIES IN WHICH THE SAME PERSONS ACT AS MATRON AND WOMAN POLICE

Bay City, Michigan
Burlington, Iowa
Decatur, Illinois
Duluth, Minnesota
East Chicago, Illinois
East Cleveland, Ohio
Everett, Washington
Fargo, North Dakota
Galesburg, Illinois
Hannibal, Missouri
Harrisburg, Pennsylvania

Hornell, New York
Hutchinson, Kansas
Oak Park, Illinois
Perth Amboy, New Jersey
Rhinelander, Wisconsin
Riverside, California
Santa Monica, California
Tampa, Florida
Trinidad, Colorado
Virginia, Minnesota
Winnetka, Illinois

[1] During the summer months there are policewomen on call.

[2] It is reported that Glacier Park has an Indian woman police.   Information not officially confirmed.

D.—Cities having Police Matrons Only

Albany, New York
Allentown, Pennsylvania
Astoria, Oregon
Attleboro, Massachusetts
Billings, Montana
Binghamton, New York
Bridgeport, Connecticut
Camden, New Jersey
Chester, Pennsylvania
Chisholm, Minnesota
Cincinnati, Ohio
Dover, New Jersey
Fort Worth, Texas
Geneva, New York
Gloversville, New York
Grand Forks, North Dakota
Hartford, Connecticut
Hoboken, New Jersey
Iowa City, Iowa
Jacksonville, Florida
Jamestown, North Dakota
Kansas City, Missouri
Kingston, New York
Lackawanna, New York
Lansing, Michigan
Lewiston, Maine
Lincoln, Nebraska
Little Rock, Arkansas
Mason City, Iowa
Meriden, Connecticut
Milwaukee, Wisconsin
Newark, New York
New Rochelle, New York

Norfolk, Virginia
Oakland, California
Ogden City, Utah
Oklahoma City, Oklahoma
Paterson, New Jersey
Peoria, Illinois
Philadelphia, Pennsylvania
Pomona, California
Quincy, Illinois
Redondo, California
Richmond, California
Richmond, Indiana
Sacramento, California
Salem, Massachusetts
San Diego, California
Schenectady, New York
Scranton, Pennsylvania
Shreveport, Louisiana
Sioux City, Iowa
Somerville, Massachusetts
Springfield, Missouri
St. Joseph, Missouri
Stamford, Connecticut
Troy, New York
Tulsa, New York
Vallejo, California
Waterloo, Iowa
Watertown, New York
Wilkes-Barre, Pennsylvania
Williamsport, Pennsylvania
Wilmington, Delaware
Yonkers, New York

E.—Cities having Women Police Only

Aurora, Illinois
Baton Rouge, Louisiana
Belfast, Maine
Benton Harbor, Michigan
Berkeley, California
Birmingham, Alabama
Brookline, Massachusetts
Burlington, Vermont
Devils Lake, North Dakota
East Orange, New Jersey
Eau Claire, Wisconsin
Elizabeth, New Jersey
Erie, Pennsylvania
Fort Wayne, Indiana

Gloucester, Massachusetts
Greensboro, North Carolina
Gulfport, Mississippi
Hamtramck, Michigan
Hattiesburg, Mississippi
Herkimer, New York
Huntington, Indiana
Ithaca, New York
Kalamazoo, Michigan
Kenosha, Wisconsin
Knoxville, Tennessee
Lafayette, Louisiana
Lancaster, Pennsylvania
Lexington, Kentucky

Louisville, Kentucky
Madison, Wisconsin
Memphis, Tennessee
Muskogee, Michigan
Muskogee, Oklahoma
Oshkosh, Wisconsin
Oskaloosa, Iowa
Owosso, Michigan
Passaic, New Jersey
Petersburg, Virginia
Pontiac, Michigan

Port Arthur, Texas
Poughkeepsie, New York
Pueblo, Colorado
Reading, Pennsylvania
Saginaw, Michigan
Sault Ste. Marie, Michigan
Superior, Wisconsin
Trenton, New Jersey
Wausau, Wisconsin
Wilmington, North Carolina
York, Pennsylvania

F.—CITIES HAVING BOTH WOMEN POLICE AND POLICE MATRONS

Akron, Ohio
Atlanta, Georgia
Atlantic City, New Jersey
Baltimore, Maryland
Bloomington, Illinois
Boston, Massachusetts
Buffalo, New York
Cambridge, Massachusetts
Charleston, South Carolina
Cleveland, Ohio
Chicago, Illinois
Columbus, Ohio
Davenport, Iowa
Dayton, Ohio
Denver, Colorado
Des Moines, Iowa
Detroit, Michigan
Fall River, Massachusetts
Flint, Michigan
Grand Rapids, Michigan
Gary, Illinois
Haverhill, Massachusetts
Hibbing, Minnesota
Holyoke, Massachusetts
Houston, Texas
Indianapolis, Indiana
Jamestown, New York
Jersey City, New Jersey
Kansas City, Kansas
Lawrence, Massachusetts
Long Beach, California
Los Angeles, California
Lowell, Massachusetts
Lynn, Massachusetts
Minneapolis, Minnesota
Minot, North Dakota

Nashville, Tennessee
New Bedford, Massachusetts
New Haven, Connecticut
New Orleans, Louisiana
Newark, New Jersey
New York City, New York
Niagara Falls, New York
Omaha, Nebraska
Pittsburgh, Pennsylvania
Portland, Maine
Portland, Oregon
Providence, Rhode Island
Richmond, Virginia
Rochester, New York
Rockford, Illinois
San Antonio, Texas
San Francisco, California
San José, California
Salt Lake City, Utah
Savannah, Georgia
Seattle, Washington
South Bend, Indiana
Spokane, Washington
Springfield, Massachusetts
St. Louis, Missouri
St. Paul, Minnesota
Syracuse, New York
Tacoma, Washington
Toledo, Ohio
Topeka, Kansas
Utica, New York
Washington, District of Columbia
Wichita, Kansas
Worcester, Massachusetts
Youngstown, Ohio

Appendix II

Typical Civil Service Examinations for Women Police

1

United States Civil Service Commission
Series No. 2, June, 1921

POLICEWOMAN EXAMINATION

First Subject—Thesis

Directions to the Competitor—Read Carefully

Competitor must fill these blanks:

Time commenced......Date........Examination No.......

Time finished......Place of Examination..................
(City or Town)   (State)

N. B.—Do not write on this sheet. Blank sheets will be furnished. Write only on the ruled side of the blank sheets furnished.

Number consecutively the sheets of your thesis and write in the following space the total number of such attached sheets.

Number of sheets...........

Write a thesis of not less than 350 words on one (and only one) of the following subjects:

1. Give a comprehensive program for preventive and protective work by a police department in a large city.

2. Relations between police and health departments in cases where lawbreakers are suffering from venereal disease.

3. Give the value of a police department doing good preventive and protective work and of a private detective agency. Which is the more effective, and why?

291

Sheet 2.

UNITED STATES CIVIL SERVICE COMMISSION

POLICEWOMAN EXAMINATION

SECOND SUBJECT—PRACTICAL QUESTIONS

Directions to the Competitor—Read Carefully

Competitor must fill these blanks:

Time commenced......Date........Examination No.......

Time finished......Place of Examination..................
                                        (City or Town)   (State)

N. B.—Do not write on this sheet.   Blank sheets will be furnished
for the answers to the questions hereon.   Number answers to correspond
with numbers of questions.

Write only on the ruled side of the blank sheets furnished.

Number consecutively the sheets of answers to questions hereon,
and write in the following space the total number of such attached
sheets.

Number of sheets............

Answer any ten (and only ten) of the following questions:

Question 1. What is (a) a juvenile court, (b) a police court, (c) a
      criminal court?

Question 2. (a) What do you understand by "parole"?
      (b) What do you understand by "voluntary proba-
          tion"?

Question 3. (a) What is a policewoman?
      (b) What is a police precinct?

Question 4. Give the definitions of any five of the following terms:
(a) criminal; (b) misdemeanant; (c) venereal disease; (d) conviction;
(e) sentence; (f) hearsay evidence; (g) psychopathic; (h) truant;
(i) larceny; (j) warrant.

Question 5. Name the three general classes of persons usually
requiring attention by the police and social workers.

Question 6. State some of the qualities that any public servant should possess who is engaged in social work.

Question 7. Should offending children pending trial be separated from the general classes of criminals, and how?

Question 8. (a) What is a "fixed post duty"?
(b) What is "case work"?

Question 9. A girl of 19 years was arrested on suspicion and detained. She claims residence in another city. State method of making investigation, covering carefully all necessary work for identification.

Question 10. A man has been arrested for a sex offense with a girl 12 years old. Both man and girl are held by the police. Assume that this case goes to court the following day, and state the evidence necessary for conviction and sentence. Give the status of each of these persons before the law.

Question 11. (a) What do you understand by "day patrol"?
(b) What do you understand by "night patrol"?

Question 12. A girl 16 years of age, arrested for shoplifting, is feeble-minded, a truant; her father is dead; there are four younger children and the mother goes out to work. How would you handle this girl's case?

2

MUNICIPAL CIVIL SERVICE COMMISSION, NEW YORK

These questions are to be taken only for what they are. Questions actually set for the position named. For future examinations questions will be framed to suit the requirements of the position at the time of the examination.

PATROLWOMAN—POLICE DEPARTMENT

Date: May 13, 1921.

DUTIES—WEIGHT 4

PART I

To be finished by 12:30 P.M.

1. Discuss the so-called "commercial" dance hall as a sometime factor in the downfall of girls, and state fully the police attention these places should receive.

2. (a) Define "juvenile delinquency" according to the law.
   (b) Of what use are the so-called Big Brothers and Big Sisters in your opinion?
   (c) What is meant by "the age of consent"? What is the "age of consent" in this state?
   (d) Describe the manner in which children are linked up with the traffic in habit-forming drugs in New York City.

3. (a) State specifically the advice you, as a patrolwoman, would offer in a case where one member of a poor family is suspected of having contracted the most serious of venereal diseases.
   (b) In your opinion, what various specific acts or conditions could properly be prosecuted under the general charge of "impairing the morals of a minor"?

4. To what city departments or bureaus of other agencies should the following be referred?
   (a) Complaint alleging fraud on the part of a public employment agency.
   (b) Request for legal advice regarding the best means of protecting a poor family from an avaricious landlord.
   (c) Complaint about the inadequate heating of an apartment house during the winter months.

(d) Requests for aid in obtaining employment.
(e) Complaint alleging the giving of short weight by a retail dealer.
(f) Request for the commitment of children to some institution in a case where the parents are unable, though willing, to support them.
(g) Request for advice as to what should be done with the personal property of a man who died without leaving a will.

5. (a) In your opinion what constitutes "mashing" as an offense or practice of which the police of this city should take cognizance?
   (b) Where are "mashers" likely to be met with and what are the usual methods they employ?

DUTIES—PART II

To be finished at 3:30 P.M.

6. (a) Name and locate the passenger railroad terminals situated within the limits of New York City. State the more important cities or towns to which the railroad lines run from each of these terminals.
   (b) Name the various steamboat or excursion-boat lines that operate between New York City and nearby places throughout the year or during certain seasons of the year. Locate the terminus (landing place) of each line in New York City and state the places to which these boats run.
   (c) Name and locate the large public parks in New York City.
   (d) Name and locate the favorite outdoor commercial amusement places in New York City.

7. State the nature of the relief, if any, that can be afforded the persons named below and give, step by step, the procedure to be followed in order that the relief may be obtained.
   (a) An unmarried mother.
   (b) A dependent widow, who is a citizen of the United States and who has lived in New York City for the past five years. (Note: The husband of this woman died recently.)
   (c) A blind adult, supported by his brother and sister who are poor working people.

8. What types or classes of criminals or offenders against the law use minors as aides in the commission of crimes or the carrying on of nefarious practices and what classes or types of persons are accustomed to annoy children or prey upon them? Discuss fully.

9. (a) For what particular conditions or circumstances should a keen, observant patrolwoman be on the lookout in the following places?
   (1) A congested summer bungalow colony inhabited by the working class and containing many bungalows run by young men's social clubs.
   (2) A plain neighborhood, containing cheap furnished-room houses almost exclusively, and bordering on a busy thoroughfare where there are grouped several of the lower-class theaters, a passenger railroad terminal and two or three business schools.
   (3) A cheap motion-picture theater in a neighborhood inhabited largely by a foreign element.
   (b) (1) What places or neighborhoods in New York City should, in your opinion, be given special attention by patrolwomen after a large fleet of U. S. warships has returned to this city following a long cruise? Give your reasons.
   (2) What special precautions or measures should, in your opinion, be taken by the women's branch of the Police Department in connection with the observance of Mardi Gras week at Coney Island?

10. State fully what you, as a patrolwoman, would do
    (a) On seeing a man pick flowers from a decorative flower bed in Central Park.
    (b) On being assigned to investigate a complaint alleging immoral conditions in a certain commercial dance hall.
    (c) On being sent to find out what you can concerning the alleged use of narcotics by some children attending a certain public school.
    (d) If you saw a public taxicab driver drive his car unoccupied slowly along the curbstone and talking all the while to a nicely dressed young lady pedestrian who ignores the man entirely.

3

POLICEWOMAN EXAMINATION

KNOXVILLE, TENNESSEE, AUGUST 12, 1924

PART I

Write a thesis of not less than 350 words on the following subject: "What measures and remedies should be used for the prevention of delinquency and the suppression of prostitution?"

PART II

Answer *any ten* (and only ten) of the following questions. Choose those you can answer best. You may take the questions in any order you please, number them to correspond with the numbers given; but if you answer more than ten, only the first ten of your answers will be rated.

Question 1. What community agencies and institutions are essential for adequate care of all classes of dependents, delinquents, defectives, and criminals?

Question 2. Give the relative value of the institution versus private home for the child.

Question 3. Give definitions of (a) rape, (b) adultery, (c) seduction, (d) bigamy, (e) larceny.

Question 4. What qualities, personal habits, and ethics should a policewoman possess?

Question 5. What is meant by (a) evidence, (b) habeas corpus, (c) felony, (d) misdemeanor, (e) parole, (f) probation, (g) conviction?

Question 6. (a) What do you understand by "case work"? (b) Give a hypothetical case which fully illustrates your definition.

Question 7. What should be the relationship between a policewoman and a probation officer?

Question 8. (a) Why should a physical examination be given a delinquent before an adjustment of his case is attempted? (b) Why should a mental examination be given a delinquent before an adjustment of his case is attempted?

Question 9. (a) What kind of records should be kept by a woman's division in a police department? (b) What is the purpose of keeping these records?

Question 10. State how you would deal with a 19-year-old girl who is found stranded in a city to which she has come with a traveling carnival, having left the farm home of her aged father, who was unable to provide for her or to control her. There is no social agency in that community and the police department in the nearest town gives a bad report of the girl's behavior.

Question 11. State how you would deal with a 12-year-old boy who runs away from home repeatedly, often staying away until located by the police and who is usually found singing on the streets late at night and begging for money. The family do not object to the begging as long as the money is turned over to them.

Question 12. Write a letter to the Police Department in another city, giving them the necessary information for locating a 12-year-old girl who is believed to have run away to that city.

BIBLIOGRAPHY [1]

THE UNITED STATES

ADDITON, HENRIETTA S. 1. The Sphere of the Policewoman. National W. C. T. U. Publishing House, Evanston, Illinois. Per copy, 2 cents; per 50, 35 cents; per 100, 60 cents. 2. Functions of Policewomen. Reprinted from *Journal of Social Hygiene*, June, 1924. The American Social Hygiene Association, 370 Seventh Avenue, New York City. Single copies, 10 cents. 3. The Policewoman. *Proceedings of the National Probation Association, 1924.*

BEVERIDGE, EDNA A. Establishing Policewomen in Maryland in 1912. *Proceedings National Conference of Charities and Correction, 1915.*

BINFORD, JESSIE F. Community Protective Social Measures. *Proceedings National Conference of Social Work, 1924.*

BLIX, O. B. The Policewoman Movement (1921) Municipal Reference Library, Milwaukee, Wisconsin.

BOWEN, LOUISE DE KOVEN. 1. The Policewoman's Job. What it is and what it should be. *Bulletin Women's City Club of Chicago*, October, 1921. 2. Policewoman's Job. *Toledo City Journal*, February 11, 1922.

BRANDENBURGHER, JOHN A. Effective Work of Policewomen. *American City*, March, 1922.

BRUÉRE, H. Police as Welfare Workers. *American City*, March, 1914.

BURNSIDE, CLARA. International Association of Policewomen, Providence (R. I.) Meeting, 1922. *The Survey*, July 15, 1922.

CORNING, E. L. Women Police Service, 1714 Lane Street, Topeka, Kansas. Pamphlet, 25 cents.

DARWIN, MAUDE. Policewomen—Their Work in America. *Nineteenth Century*, June, 1914, page 1370.

DAVIS, KATHARINE BEMENT. 1. How the Public May Help. *Proceedings National Conference of Social Work, 1920.* 2. The Policewoman. *Woman Citizen*, May 30, 1924.

[1] This bibliography is designed to be a guide to those wishing to consult sources. Many short magazine and newspaper articles are not included.

DRISCOLL, MARY E. Women's Place in the Police Plan. *Policeman's News*, November–December, 1920.

FOSDICK, RAYMOND B. 1. American Police Systems, New York: Century Co., 1920. Bureau of Social Hygiene, 370 Seventh Avenue, New York City. $2.00. 2. European Police Systems, New York: Century Company, 1916. Bureau of Social Hygiene, 370 Seventh Avenue, New York City. $2.00.

FULD, LEONARD FELIX. Police Administration, New York. G. P. Putnam's Sons, 1909. (Edition exhausted. Consult Public Library.)

HALL, SOPHIA. Municipal Police Women. 1922 Information Report No. 22—Municipal Information Bureau, University of Wisconsin, Madison, Wisconsin.

HAMILTON, MARY E. 1. Women's Place in the Police Department. *The Independent Woman*, April 21, 276 Seventh Avenue, New York City. 10 cents. 2. Why We Need Policewomen. *National Police Bulletin*, October 31, 1921. 240 Centre Street, New York City. 3. Why Policewomen Are Needed. *Police Journal*, July, 1922. 4. Policewomen and Their Work. *Police Journal*, September, 1922. 5. The Policewoman: Her Service and Ideals. F. A. Stokes, New York City, 1924. Price, $1.50.

HARRIS, MARY B., PH.D. The Socialized Policewoman. *The Woman Citizen*, June 27, 1925.

HUTZEL, ELEONORE L. The Work of a Policewoman. *Proceedings, American Prison Association, 1922*.

KOELKER, E. S. Policewomen. *The Municipality* (League of Wisconsin Municipalities), Madison, Wisconsin, February, 1916.

LANE, W. D. Girls and Khaki. *The Survey*, December 1, 1917.

MADDEN, LILLIAN. The Modern Policewoman's Work. *Police Journal*, April, 1924.

MARSHALL, SABINA. Development of the Policewoman's Movement in Cleveland, Ohio. *Journal of Social Hygiene*, April, 1925.

MASON, BLANCHE H. Women's Protective Division, Seattle Police Department. *Civil Service Age*, May, 1918. 449 New York Building, Seattle, Washington. Price, 10 cents.

MINER, MAUDE E. 1. The Girl Problem in War Time. *Proceedings, National Conference of Social Work, 1918*. 2. Policewomen and the Girl Problem. *Proceedings National Conference of Social Work, 1919*. 3. A Community Program for Protective Work. *Proceedings National Conference of Social Work, 1920*.

MINER, STELLA A. Protecting Girls in War Time. *Proceedings New York City Conference of Charities and Corrections, 1918*.

MITCHELL, HANNAH. The Lady Cop—She Fills a Need and is Here to Stay. *Woman Citizen*, May 21, 1921.

MURRAY, VIRGINIA N. Policewomen in Detroit. *American City*, 1921.

NICHOLS, MARIAN C. Policewoman Movement in Massachusetts, *Bulletin Massachusetts Society for Social Hygiene*, April, 1920.

NILES, ALFRED S. The Police Department and the Social Problem. *Proceedings National Conference of Charities and Corrections, 1915.*

O'GRADY, ELLEN S. Policewomen and Their Work. *American Citizen*, 1919.

OWINGS, CHLOE. Women Police. *Journal of Social Hygiene*, 370 Seventh Avenue, New York City, January, 1925. Reprint, 10 cents per copy.

PARKER, VALERIA H. A Policewoman's Life. *Woman Citizen*, June 28, 1924.

PULLMAN, R. W. Police and Public Health. *Journal of Social Hygiene*, July, 1919.

RIPPIN, JANE DEETER. 1. Specific Problems in Camp Communities. *Proceedings National Conference of Social Work, 1918.* 2. Outline of Organization and Methods. Section on Women and Girls —War Department Commission on Training-camp Activities.

ROGERS, H. B. Policewomen Here to Stay. *Police Journal*, October, 1923.

ROOD, HENRY. Policewomen and Their Work. *The Delineator*, March, 1916.

SAWYER, R. Policewomen for University Towns. *Woman Citizen*, March 22, 1924.

SMITH, A. W. Colored Policewomen of Washington. *Southern Workmen*, March, 1922.

SMITH, CLARENCE B., JR. The True Sphere of Policewomen. *Police Journal*, April, 1922.

SMITH, J. W. Enter the Lady Cop of Gotham. *Boston Evening Transcript*, May 18, 1918.

TAUSSIG, EDITH. The Attack on the Women's Bureau. *The Voice of the People*, April 22, 1922.

VANDYKE, IRENE. No Man's Land in Police Work. What Women's Precincts Are Doing to Solve the Runaway-girl Problem. *The Forecast*, August, 1921.

VAN WINKLE, MINA C. 1. What is a Policewoman? National W. C. T. U. Publishing House, Evanston, Illinois. Per copy, 2 cents; per 50, 35 cents; per 100, 60 cents. 2. Work of the Woman's Bureau of the Metropolitan Police Department, Washington, D. C. *Proceedings American Prison Association, 1919.* 3. Standardization of the Aims and Methods of the Work of Police women. *Proceedings National Conference of Social Work, 1920.* 4. Municipal Policewomen: Their Duties and Opportunities, *American City*, 1921. 5. Policewomen Do Not Find Themselves in Ruts. *The Globe*, New York City, April 15, 1921. 6. Women Police Officers and General Social Work. *Policeman's News*, July, 1921. 7. Purpose and Scope of a Woman's Bureau. *Police Journal*, November, 1922. 8. The Policewoman. *Proceedings National*

Conference of Social Work, 1924.   9. The Policewoman.   *The Survey,* September 15, 1924.   10. Socializing the Police.   *Woman Citizen,* June 13, 1925.

WELLS, MRS. A. S.   1. Need for Policewomen in City Work.   *Chicago City Club Bulletin,* October 31, 1912.   2. Women on the Police Force.   *American City,* April, 1913.   3. Women Police Officers. *The Vigilance Record,* June, 1913.   4. Need for Policewomen. *Proceedings National Conference of Charities and Corrections, 1915.*   5. The Policewoman Movement, Present Status and Future Needs.   *Proceedings National Conference of Charities and Corrections, 1916.*

WALBROOK, H. M.   Women Police and Their Work.   *Nineteenth Century,* February, 1919.

WHITE, I. PARLEY.   The Work of Policewomen in Salt Lake City. *American Citizen,* June, 1917.

WOODS, ARTHUR W.   1. Crime Prevention.   Princeton University Press, 1918.   Price, $1.00.   Princeton, New Jersey.   2. Policeman and Public.   New Haven, Connecticut.   Yale University Press, 1919.   Price, $1.50.

REPORTS, PUBLICATIONS AND SOME UNSIGNED ARTICLES APPEARING IN PERIODICALS AND NOT LISTED ABOVE

American City (The), 443 Fourth Avenue, New York City.   1. Municipal Policewomen—Their Duties and Appointments, April, 1917. 2. The Duties of a City Mother, Los Angeles, California, March, 1922.

Dayton Municipal Review.   Efficiency and Effectiveness of Policewomen, March, 1921.

Detroit Community Fund News, 316 Jefferson Avenue, S., Detroit, Michigan, August 16, 1925.—Police women as Social Workers.

International Association of Policewomen, Evening Star Building, Washington, D. C.   1. The Policewoman Movement.   Present Status and Future Needs.   Alice Stebbins Wells.   2. President's Letter—June 22, 1916.   3. President's Letter—Year 1918–1919. 4. Proceedings, 1916, Annual Meeting.   5. Tentative Digest of the Work of Policewoman, 1920.   6. Bulletins 1 to 10, 1924 and 1925.

Journal of Social Hygiene, 370 Seventh Avenue, New York City, February, 1924.   Program of vocational training for directors of policewomen's units.

Literary Digest.   1. Policewomen in Chicago, August 23, 1913.   2. What Police Read, June 13, 1914.   3. Indianapolis and Their New Methods, April 23, 1921.   4. Mothers of Disillusioned Girls in New York City, March 15, 1924.

Manual for the various agents of the Interdepartment Social Hygiene Bureau, Washington, Government Printing Office, 1920.

Municipal Journal, 243 West 39th Street, New York City, February 1, 1919. Capital to Have Thirty Policewomen.

National Police Magazine. 1. Work of Lola Baldwin, Portland, Oregon, April, 1913.

New York Police Department, 240 Centre Street, New York City. 1. Annual Reports, 1918, 1919, 1920, 1921, 1922, 1923. 2. Duties of Police Matrons. Municipal Year Book of the City of New York, 1916.

New York State Bureau of Municipal Information. Women on the Police Force of Cities, 1916. Information Report No. 88.

Outlook. Police as Social Workers, December 16, 1914.

Police Journal. 1. International Association of Policewomen Meets in Milwaukee, June, 1921. 2. In the Policewomen's Sphere, April 25, 1921. 3. Women's Protective Division of Portland, Oregon, February, 1920.

Policeman's News. 1. Wants Policewomen in Every Large City, April, 1917. 2. The Question of the Policewoman, December, 1918. 3. Organizing a Bureau of Policewomen, October,. 1920.

Report on the Work in Military Camps in the United States. War Department—Commission on Training Camp Activities, Washington, D. C.

Survey (The). 1. To Make Social Workers of Policemen, June, 1914. 2. Policewoman of the Future, January 17, 1914. 3. Women Police in England, September 1, 1917. 4. A Policewoman on Trial, April 15, 1922. 5. To Make Social Workers of Policemen, June 13, 1924.

Toledo City Journal (The). The Indianapolis Policewomen, November 27, 1920.

U. S. Bureau of Census, Washington, Government Printing Office. General Statistics of Cities, 1915. Policewomen. Page 18.

U. S. War Department. Annual Report, 1918. Page 13. Training-camp Activities.

Washington, D. C. 1. Police Department Manual, 1923. 2. Annual Reports Since 1915. 3. Investigation of Salaries of Metropolitan Police Members. Hearings—H. R. 7983. Part 1, Part 2, Part 3, 1919. Washington, Government Printing Office. 4. Women's Bureau, Police Department, District of Columbia. Joint Hearing on S. 4308, February 20, 1925. Washington, Government Printing Office, 1925.

Women Citizen (The). 1. Women Police, December 29, 1917. 2. When Mothers Are Policewomen, March 9, 1918. 3. Woman's Police Bureau, September 6, 1919. 4. North Carolina Policewoman, May 5, 1923.

COUNTRIES OUTSIDE OF THE UNITED STATES

ALLEN, MARY S.   1. Women Police. Pamphlet, September 30, 1924,
7 Rochester Row, London, S. W.   2. Personalities and Powers
(Commandant Mary Allen, O. B. E.).   *Time and Tide*, June 20,
1924.

BEAUJON, CORNELIA.   Die Mitarbeit der Frau bei der Polizei—Haag:
Nighoff, 1912.   (Can be secured from Dr. Beaujon, 95 Johan Van
Olden Carnaveltlaan, The Hague, Holland.)

BECKER, MARY LAMBERTA.   London's Latest Bobbies Are Policewomen. *The Evening Post*, New York, April 13, 1918.

CARDEN, W. G.   Women Police in Great Britain, September, 1924.
Published by the International Bureau for the Suppression of
Traffic in Women and Children, 2 Grosvenor Mansions, 76 Vic-
toria Street, London—S. W. 1.

CREIGHTON, L.   Women Police. *Fortnightly Review*, v. 114, p. 109–117,
July, 1920.

CROWDY, DAME R.   The League of Nations: International position
with regard to prostitution and the suppression of the traffic in
women and children.   *Proceedings of the Imperial Social Hygiene
Congress*, Wembley, 1924, and *Journal of Social Hygiene*, December, 1924, 370 Seventh Avenue, New York City.

LYTTLETON, DAME EDITH.   *League of Nations Official Journal Special
Supplement*, No. 13, Geneva, 1923, pp. 51 and 52.

MOULDER, PRISCILLA E.   1. The Work of Women Police and Patrols.
World's Work (London), January, 1919.   2. England's Girls and
the Women Police. *Life and Labor*, May, 1919, 311 South Ashland
Boulevard, Chicago, Illinois.

PAPPRITZ, ANNA.   Handbuch der amtlichen gefahrdeten Fürsorge.
Berlin, Steglitz, Mommsenstrasse 23, Germany.

PETO, D. O. G.   1. The Training of Women Police and Women Patrols.
Englishwoman, October, 1916.   2. Police Work as a Profession for
Women. *Contemporary Review*, May, 1918, 18 Adelphi Terrace,
London, W. C. 2.   3. Policewomen's Conditions of Service.
Englishwoman, December, 1919.   4. Status of the Policewoman.
Spectator, 123:805–6, December, 13, 1919.   (Spectator Ltd., 1 Well-
ington Street, Strand, London, England), 7d.   5. Policewomen.
The Making of a Type. *Englishwoman*, September, 1920.   6. Po-
licewomen of the Future. *Spectator*, September 11, 1920.

TITE, C.   Policewomen: Their Work in Germany. *Nineteenth Century*, June, 1914, v. 75:1378–1383.

REPORTS AND PUBLICATIONS

Central Council for Rescue and Preventive Work in London. Report on the work of the Voluntary Rescue and Preventive Homes in the Metropolitan Area. 117 Piccadilly, London, W., December, 1923.

Committee Minutes of Evidence and Reports. 1. Committee on the Employment of Women on Police Duties (Major Sir John Lawrence Baird, Chairman). *Minutes of Evidence*. H. M. Stationery Office, 28 Abingdon Street, London, S. W. 1, 1921. (Cmd. 1133) 2/. 2. Report of the Committee on the Employment of Women on Police Duties. H. M. Stationery Office, 28 Abingdon Street, London, S. W. 1 (Cmd. 879) 3d, 1920. 3. Committee on the Employment of Policewomen. *Minutes of Evidence* (1924) 9/. 4. Report of Departmental Committee on the Employment of Policewomen. (Cmd. 2224) 6d. 5. Committee on the Police Service (Geddes Committee). *Minutes of Evidence,*(Cmd. 874) February, 1922. 6/.

Handy Guide to the Police Forces of the British Empire. The Police Review Publishing Company, 8 Red Lion Square, London, W. C. 1, March, 1924. Price, 7d.

Health and Empire. Journal of the National Council for Combating Venereal Diseases (now the British Social Hygiene Association) 102 Dean Street. Oxford Street, London, W. 1. Annual subscription, 7/. (Consult files.)

International Bureau for the Suppression of Traffic in Women and Children. 2 Grosvenor Mansions, 76 Victoria Street, London, S. W. 1. 1. Report of Preparator Conference, October, 1923. Price, 2/. 2. *Proceedings Sixth International Congress*, 1924. Price, 7/6.

International Women Suffrage News. The Monthly Organ of the International Woman Suffrage Alliance, 11 Adam Street, Adelphi, London, W. C. Annual subscription, 6/. (Consult files.)

Liverpool Women Police Patrols and Training Center for Women Police. Annual Reports, particularly 1920, 1921 and 1923. 5 Cases Street, Clayton Square, Liverpool.

League of Nations Publications. 1. International Conference on Traffic in Women and Children. c. 227. M. 166. 1921. IV. 2. Advisory Committee on the Traffic in Women and Children. c. 225. M. 129. 1923. IV. 3. Advisory Committee on the Traffic in Women and Children. C. T. F. E. 195. (Preparatory Documents) 1924. 4. Advisory Committee on the Traffic in Women and Protection of Children. c. 293. 1925. IV.

Magistrate (The), 84 Eccleston Square, London, S. W. 1. Bulletin of the *Magistrate's* Association. (See files since 1916.)

The National Council of Women of Great Britain and Ireland. 1. Annual Reports, particularly since 1916. Parliament Mansions, Victoria Street, London, S. W. 1. 2. Women Police. A Ques-

tionnaire. October, 1923. Price, 2/6. 3. The History of the
Official Policewomen. Price, 6d. National Council of Great
Britain and Ireland. Parliament Mansions, Westminster, S. W. 1,
1924.

National Union of Societies for Equal Citizenship. Annual Reports
since 1918. 15 Dean's Yard, Westminster, London, S. W. 1.

Penal Reform League. Quarterly Record. 68A Park Hill Road,
London, N. W., July, 1914. (Reprinted in *Journal of Criminal
Law and Criminology*. U. S. A. November, 1914.)

Police (Counties and Boroughs, England and Wales). Reports of
H. M. Inspectors of Constabulary, 1924, H. M. Stationery Office,
28 Abingdon Street, London, S. W. 1. Price, 9/.

Police Review (The), March 17, 1916, 8 Red Lion Square, London, W. C.

Vigilance Record (The). The Organ of the National Vigilance Association, 2 Grosvenor Mansions, 76 Victoria Street, London, S. W. 1.
Single copy, 2d. (Consult files.)

Vote (The). High Holborn, 144 W. C. 1. (See files since 1916).
Price, 1d.

Woman's Leader (The), 15 Dean's Yard, Westminster, S. W. 1. Annual
subscription, 6/6. (See files since 1916.)

Women's Auxiliary Service (The), 7 Rochester Row, Westminster,
London, S. W. 1. 1. The Women Police Service. Annual Report,
1918–1919. 2. The Women's Auxiliary Service (late Women
Police Service), Annual Report, 1920–1921. 3. Work and Ideals.
Undated 4-page pamphlet. 4. Benevolent Department. Un-
dated 4-page pamphlet.

Women Police—Women's Freedom League, 144 High Holborn, London, V. C. T. Undated 4-page pamphlet. Price, 1d.

INDEX

Abandonment, women police deal with cases, 171

Aberdeen, deputation from, requesting that appointment of women police be legalized, 50; favored appointment of women police, 52

Abortive practitioners, investigation of, 132, suppression of activities of, 163

Act, amending New York City charter, 160

Adelaide, principal woman police constable supervises 10 women police, 57

Advertisements, watched, 57, 78, 132, 171

Age, limits for women police, 265; in New York, 155

Aged, sick and disabled, care of, duty of women police in Finland, 69

Aged, supervision of homes for, 88

Alexandria, women police meet boats, 91

Aliens, inquiries regarding, 55

Allen, Mary S., 11, 18, 49, 75

American Female Reform Society secured appointment of matrons in 1845, 98

American Social Hygiene Association, sponsored movement for women police, 97; pre-war control of venereal disease, 108; Miss Murray to Cleveland, 141; Departments of Protective and Legal Measures, 199; give help to International Association of Policewomen, 198; concerned themselves with the question of women police, 273; conference arranged, 274

Amsterdam, 80, 81; children's police, 80

Amusement places, supervision of, 55, 60, 61, 62, 81, 221, 224, 227; near training camps, 110; instruction in by-laws regarding, at Women Police Service School, 277

Annual Conference of Social Work, Association of Policewomen an integral part of, 200

Anti-social conduct defined, 204

Anti-social diseases of crime and delinquency, 204

Antwerp, one woman police, 66

Appointment of policewomen easy to secure where there is progressive leadership, xii

Apprehend women, 61

Argentine, unfavorable to idea of women police, 90

Arrest, woman's bureau in Washington, 184; women police make arrests, 170; power of, 33, 38; without power of, 53, 58; women used to limited extent in making, 67. *See also under* Police Power

Ashby, Mrs. Corbett, 74

Assaults, 63, 153

Associated Charities, agents of, given police powers, 105; Portland, Oregon, 167

Astor, Lady, asked if government had decided to abolish women police, 32; President of Association of Police Women invited to assist English women, 196

Atlantic City, first annual meeting of International Association of Police Women, 194

Attendance in court, when women

307

Boston section of the Council of
Jewish Women, 126
Boston Society for the Care of
Girls, 126
Boyle, Nina, 9, 10, 13
Brandenburger, John A., super-
visor of Police Woman's Bureau, St. Louis, 169
Brazil, women not employed on
police duties, but have held positions in police departments,
90
Bremen, Germany, women official
police officers, 71
Brisbane-Greensland, Australia,
has no women police, 56
Bristol, England, women police
in, 43; Federated Training
School, 41, 280
Bristol Training School, 41, 43,
277–279
British General Headquarters,
official headquarters for women
police in Cologne, 76
British Isles, women police in, 1–
55; Women Police Service, 13–
21; Women Police Volunteers,
9–13; Women Patrols, 21–23;
Women Patrols in London, 23–
38; present status, 38, 39;
early efforts to secure women
for preventive work, 2–6; reports and acts, 6–8; women
organize for police duty, 8;
provincial women, 40–48;
Northern Ireland, 48–50; Scotland, 50–55
British Military Police, 75
Brothels, observation of, 17, 55;
supervision of, 73
Brownlow, Louis, found method
of employing women on police
salaries and as members of
regular force, 175
Buenos Aires, women patrols advocated but not accepted, 90
Bureau of Social Hygiene, history of women police movement
and working of women police,
xix, President of Association

of Police Women has sought
help from, 198; sponsored
women police movement, 97
Bureau of Social Welfare, of the
State University of Iowa, 106
Burglary, women police handle
cases of in Lancashire, 46
Burma, no women police, 92
Burnside, Clara, 146
Busson, Netherlands, women po-
lice in, 81

Cabarets, investigation of, 81,
128, 132;
Cafes and cafeterias, inspection
of, 34, 88, 151, 188
Camp Custer, 145
Camps, conducted by objectionable persons who harbor young
girls, 184; scouting around,
157
Carnegie Trust, grant to Federated Training Schools, 280
Case work, most successful type
of worker, 239; women peculiarly fitted for and experienced in, 218
Cases cited, R vs. Briggs, 2
Catholic Associations, preventive
and protective social agency,
210
Catholic Social Agencies engaged
actively to secure women police, 130
Central Association for Supervising Conviction on License,
supervision of women convicts,
2
Central Committee of Police Federation, recommended removal
of all women police, 32
Central Council of the Scotland
Police Federation, opposition
to women police, 37
Central Council of the Scottish
Cooperative Women's Guild,
backed movement of women police, 54
Ceylon, no women police, 92

George Washington University, xix, 275
Girl Scouts, 213
Girl's Friendly Society, 5
Girls, personal work with, near training camps, 110; to prevent young girls being registered as prostitutes, 72; protective bureaus, 110; protective work for, 110
Girls' Protective League, Detroit, 144, 145, 155, 156, 157, 210
Girls' Service Club of New York, 97
Girls' Service League of America, 210
Glasgow, 50, 52, 53, 54; corporation, 50; town council, 51; officers assigned to probation duties, 243; school, 280
Gloucestershire, women police in, 46
Government police commission of inquiry, 90
Grand Forks, police matron with duties of women police, 101
Grantham, England, work of women police in, 12, 13, 14, 41
"Graduate School of Social Service," 271
Graz, Austria, 84
Great Britain, forms of work tried, 252–255; methods of selection, 265; program of work for women police, 220, 221, 222; public social conduct, 227; qualifications for women police, 260; training schools, only one at present outside of police department, 281
Greece, has no women police, but Sir Frederick Haliday is planning to appoint women, 77
Guarding women witnesses, 33

Hadden, Maud Miner (Mrs. Alexander) 146. See also Maud Miner.
Hague, The, 77, 78, 79

Haliday, Frederick, Sir, 77
Hall, Mrs. Kepple, 140
Hamburg, 71, 74
Hamilton, Mary E., 158, 161, 164
Handling of cases, taught in Bristol School, 278
Harburn, Miss, 12, 75
Harrison, Mayor, 131
Hartford, 186
Harvey, Miss, 105
Haverhill, first women police officer in Massachusetts, appointed in, 125
Hebrew Association, 210
Helsingfors, Finland, women police in, 68
Henry, Dorothy D., 143
Henry, Sir Edward, 10, 11, 14, 15, 22, 23, 24
Hobart, women police in, 60
Hodder-Egger, Mme., 84
Holland, women police in, 77
Holten Heath Cordite factory, 24
Holyoke, 125
Home Office, probation not police work, 243; circulated report to police authorities, 7; home office circular, 7
Home Office Committee, report of, 252; testimony before, 254
Home Secretary, urged to appoint women police, 4; met committee of police federation, they adopted recommendation for the removal of women police, 8; gave official recognition to women patrols, 22; approved payment of a subsidy, 23; negotiations for women patrols, 25; appointed committee on the appointment of women on police duties, 29; circular regarding pay of women officers, 31; removal of women police recommended, 32; gave power of arrest to women police, 33; received resolutions regarding women police, 35; urged to institute women po-

men police should be, 248;
program of work where can be
effectually applied, 257; women police employed in, 121,
122, 123
Preventive work, will have lasting effect on those with whom
the women police come in contact, 58; in Toronto, 60
Principal Woman Police constable, controls and supervises
women police, 57
Private agencies, agents of, given
police power, 105; difference
in private and public, 211,
214; preventive and protective
work, 212-213
Private organizations, 33, 34, 35;
opposition to program of work,
249
Probation, in Home Office and
Scottish office, probation not
considered police duty, but
some burgs assign constables
to probation duties, 243; relation of court service to, 243,
244; special supervision of
probationers, not function of
women police in United States,
244
Probation Departments, question
wisdom of police inquiry going further than to obtain evidence of guilt, 244
Probation Officers, function of,
208; near training camps, 110;
woman to deal with women and
girls who are first offenders,
136; should be responsible for
follow up work in probation
cases after court action, 196;
working under vice bureau,
138; men not women investigate cases of girls in Chicago,
but there is an independent
social investigation made by a
woman probationer of the
court, 138; in Vienna one woman officer acts as probation
and parole officer, 66

Probation, Voluntary, 106
Procedure in Court Cases, in Detroit, 153
Procurers, in sections around
military camps, 113; motor vehicle drivers serve as, 184;
special charge on women officers on patrol, 232
Program of work, 219-250; British opinion, 220; control social
conduct, 225-227; court service, 242-244; court service,
relation to probation, 243-244;
detention service, 245; fundamental principle in formulation of duties of women police,
222; general considerations,
219; information service, 223;
investigation service, 238-241;
opinion in the United States,
221-223; opposition to, 249-
250; paper work, 246-247;
patrol work, 223-238; present
tendencies, 223; procurers, special charge on women officers
on patrol, 232; prostitution
commercialized, 228-232; shoplifting, 236, 237; social control
over public conduct, 220; subway mashers, 227; supervision
of public conduct, 225-227;
traffic in women and girls,
232-237; resumé, 248-250;
universal program, not possible, 220
Prostitutes, apprehension of,
133; cabarets abetting, 128;
clandestine, 113; created need
for recreational facilities, 186;
enforcement of laws concerning, 187; investigation of cases
concerning, 83; ''patriotic,''
113, 115; to prevent young
girls being registered as, 72;
supervision of, 84; under supervision, 73; warning and apprehending, 132; watching out
for, 224; women police in
Cologne do not deal with, 75;
women police track and search